The Sustainability and Spread of Organizational Change

This important new addition to the *Understanding Organizational Change* series examines issues affecting the sustainability and spread of new working practices. The question of why good ideas do not spread, 'the best practices puzzle', has been widely recognized. But the 'improvement evaporation effect', where successful changes are discontinued, has attracted less attention. Keeping things the way they are has been seen as an organizational problem to be resolved, not a condition to be achieved. This is one of the first major studies of the sustainability of change focusing on the example of the NHS, by a unique team of health service and academic researchers. The findings may apply to a variety of other settings.

The agenda set out in 2000 in *The NIIS Plan* is perhaps the largest organization development programme ever undertaken, in any sector, anywhere. The NHS thus offers a valuable 'living laboratory' for the study of change. This text shows that sustainability and spread are influenced by a range of issues—contextual, managerial, political, individual, temporal. Developing a processual perspective, this fresh analysis considers policy implications, and strategies for managing sustainability and spread. This book will be essential reading for students, managers, and researchers concerned with the effective implementation of organizational change.

David A. Buchanan is Professor of Organizational Behaviour at Cranfield University.

Louise Fitzgerald is Professor of Organization Development at De Montfort University.

Diane Ketley is Head of Research and Evaluation, at the NHS Institute for Innovation and Improvement.

Understanding Organizational Change

Series editor:
Dr Bernard Burnes

The management of change is now acknowledged as being one of the most important issues facing management today. By focusing on particular perspectives and approaches to change, particular change situations, and particular types of organization, this series provides a comprehensive overview and an in-depth understanding of the field of organizational change.

Titles in this series include:

Organizational Change for Corporate Sustainability
A guide for leaders and change agents of the future
Dexter Dunphy, Andrew Griffiths and Suzanne Benn

Reshaping Change
A processual perspective
Patrick Dawson

Agency and Change
Rethinking change agency in organizations
Raymond Caldwell

The Sustainability and Spread of Organizational Change
Modernizing healthcare
Edited by David A. Buchanan, Louise Fitzgerald and Diane Ketley

The Sustainability and Spread of Organizational Change

Modernizing healthcare

Edited by
David A. Buchanan, Louise Fitzgerald
and Diane Ketley

Routledge
Taylor & Francis Group

LONDON AND NEW YORK

First published 2007
by Routledge
2 Park Square, Milton Park, Abingdon, Oxon OX14 4RN

Simultaneously published in the USA and Canada
by Routledge
270 Madison Ave, New York, NY 10016

Routledge is an imprint of the Taylor & Francis Group, an informa business

Typeset in Times New Roman
by Keystroke, 28 High Street, Tettenhall, Wolverhampton
Printed and bound in Great Britain
by Antony Rowe Ltd, Chippenham, Wilts.

British Library Cataloguing in Publication Data
A catalogue record for this book is available from the British Library

Library of Congress Cataloging in Publication Data
The sustainability and spread of organizational change : modernizing healthcare /
edited by David A. Buchanan, Louise Fitzgerald, and Diane Ketley.
p. ; cm.
Includes bibliographical references and index.
1. Health services administration–Great Britain. 2. Organizational change–Great
Britain. 3. Health promotion–Great Britain. 4. Medical informatics–Great Britain.
I. Buchanan,David A. II. Fitzgerald, Louise, 1945– III. Ketley, Diane.
[DNLM: 1. Great Britain. National Health Service. 2. Organizational Innovation–
Great Britain. 3. State Medicine–Great Britain. 4. Diffusion of Innovation–Great
Britain. 5. Program Evaluation–Great Britain. W 225 FA1 S964 2006]
R858.S87 2006
362.10941–dc22
2006014688

ISBN10: 0–415–37094–9 (hbk)
ISBN10: 0–415–37095–7 (pbk)

ISBN13: 978–0–415–37094–3 (hbk)
ISBN13: 978–0–415–37095–0 (pbk)

Contents

Illustrations

Figures

Tables

Notes on contributors

Helen Bevan is Director of Service Transformation, NHS Institute for Innovation and Improvement. She is a leader of the healthcare improvement movement at a national and international level. Her role is to help keep NHS improvement practice fresh, effective and in line with leading edge thinking. She is the architect of the groundbreaking Ten High Impact Changes. Previously, she led the establishment of a number of major national improvement programmes including the National Booking Programme, the Cancer Services Collaborative and Pursuing Perfection.

David A. Buchanan is Professor of Organizational Behaviour at Cranfield University School of Management, and has worked previously at the University of Glasgow, Loughborough University, and De Montfort University, Leicester. His research interests include change management and organization politics. He is author of over 20 books, including *Organizational Behaviour* and *Power, Politics, and Organizational Change*.

Louise Fitzgerald is Professor of Organization Development at De Montfort University and has previously worked at City, Warwick, and Salford Universities. She has been involved in research related to organizational change in healthcare for 20 years. Her current work explores the effective management of networks in healthcare. She has written for journals such as *Human Relations*, and is co-editor of the book *Knowledge to Action? Evidence-Based Health Care in Context*.

Rose Gollop is an Assessment Manager at the Healthcare Commission. She was previously a Research Associate with the NHS Institute for Innovation and Improvement and the NHS Modernisation Agency. She started her career as an occupational therapist, specializing in burns rehabilitation, and has also worked in clinical audit and public health.

Jane Louise Jones is a Clinical Systems Engineer in Hereford Hospitals NHS Trust and West Midlands South Strategic Health Authority. She worked as a Research Associate with the NHS Modernisation Agency for three years. Prior to this, she worked in a variety of roles within the NHS, focusing on staff and service development, and as a Senior Lecturer in health studies and evidence-based service improvement. Her PhD focused on understanding and improving patient experiences of daycase surgery.

Diane Ketley is Head, Research and Evaluation, at the NHS Institute for Innovation and Improvement. She was previously with the NHS Modernisation Agency as Head of the Research into Practice team, and before that at Leicester Royal Infirmary where she worked on re-engineering programmes, completing a PhD on translation of evidence into practice. Diane started her career as a clinical pharmacist working, for 15 years, in Britain and the United States, gaining experience and insight into the challenges of implementing change in the NHS. She is an Honorary Lecturer at the School of Medicine, University of Leicester.

Sharon Saint Lamont is General Manager with the North East of England Strategic Health Authority, leading on the management of long-term conditions. She was previously employed as a Research Associate with the NHS Modernisation Agency and was involved in research into the spread and sustainability of health service improvement, working with accident and emergency departments and cancer services. Prior to that, she worked as a Qualitative Researcher with Newcastle University and her research topics included dementia and diabetes. Her doctorate was based on an exploration of community health development programmes.

Annette Neath is an Associate for Innovation Practice at the NHS Institute for Innovation and Improvement. She was previously employed by the NHS Modernisation Agency as a Research Associate investigating spread and sustainability of health service improvement and as an Associate for the Futures and Innovation Team. Annette has a background in occupational psychology, with particular interests in organizational change and stress management. She has over 10 years' research and consultancy experience in organizational change with both private and public sector organizations.

Elaine Whitby is Associate Director for Greater Manchester Screening Programmes. She is also Project Director of the Liverpool Education Pilot at the Marie Curie Palliative Care Institute Liverpool, a collaboration between Marie Curie, the Royal Liverpool and Broadgreen University Hospital Trust, and the University of Liverpool. She began her career as a nurse, and has held posts in senior management, consultancy, education, and research. Developing leaders, and managing change to improve patient-centred services, have been primary interests throughout her career.

Series editor's preface

It is an accepted tenet of modern life that change is constant, of greater magnitude and far less predictable than ever before. For this reason, managing change is acknowledged as being one of the most important and difficult issues facing organizations today. This is why both practitioners and academics, in ever growing numbers, are seeking to understand organizational change. This is why the range of competing theories and advice has never been greater and never more puzzling.

Over the past hundred years or so, there have been many theories and prescriptions put forward for understanding and managing change. Arguably, the first person to attempt to offer a systematic approach to changing organizations was the originator of Scientific Management, Frederick Taylor. From the 1930s onwards, the Human Relations school attacked Taylor's one-dimensional view of human nature and his over-emphasis on individuals. In a parallel and connected development, in the 1940s, Kurt Lewin created perhaps the most influential approach to managing change. His planned approach to change, encapsulated in his three-step model, became the inspiration for a generation of researchers and practitioners, mainly – though not exclusively – in the USA. Throughout the 1950s, Lewin's work was expanded beyond his focus on small groups and conflict resolution to create the Organization Development (OD) movement. From the 1960s to the early 1980s, OD established itself as the dominant Western approach to organizational change.

However, by the early 1980s, more and more Western organizations found themselves having to change rapidly and dramatically, and sometimes brutally, in the face of the might of corporate Japan. In such circumstances, many judged the consensus-based and incrementally focused OD approach as having little to offer. Instead, a plethora of approaches began to emerge which, whilst not easy to classify, could best be described as anti-OD. These newer approaches to change were less wary than OD in embracing issues of power and politics in organizations; they did not necessarily see organizational change as clean, linear and finite. Instead, they viewed change as messy, contentious, context-dependent and open-ended. In addition, unlike OD which drew its inspiration and insights mainly from psychology, the newer approaches drew on an eclectic mix of sociology, anthropology, economics, psychotherapy and the natural sciences, not to mention the ubiquitous postmodernism. This has produced a range of approaches to change with suffixes and appellations such as emergent, processual, political, institutional, cultural, contingency, complexity, chaos and many more.

It is impossible to conceive of an approach which is suitable for all types of change, all types of situations and all types of organizations. Some may be too narrow in applicability whilst others may be too general. Some may be complementary to each other whilst others are clearly incompatible. The range of approaches to change, and the confusion over their strengths, weaknesses and suitability, is such that the field of organizational change resembles more an overgrown weed patch than a well-tended garden.

The aim of this series is to provide both a comprehensive overview of the main perspectives on organizational change, and an in-depth guide to key issues and controversies. The series will investigate the main approaches to change, and the various contexts in which change is applied. The underlying rationale for the series is that we cannot understand organizational change sufficiently or implement it effectively unless we can map the range of approaches, and evaluate what they seek to achieve, how and where they can be applied, and, crucially, the evidence which underpins them.

Series editor
Bernard Burnes
Manchester School of Management,
UMIST

Foreword

The NHS Plan (Department of Health, 2000a) established an ambitious organization development programme, providing unparalleled opportunities radically to rethink, redesign and thereby to improve patient care. The NHS Modernisation Agency was created in 2001 as a national body to support this change process across the service. The size and challenge of the change agenda were unparalleled anywhere in the private or public sector. It is important to recognize that most service improvements were not straightforward one- or two-dimensional changes, but involved complex combinations of changes to organization structures, roles, systems and procedures, clinical practice, inter-organizational collaborations, and in some cases to physical facilities as well.

As NHS Modernisation Agency staff around the country shared experience on developments and progress, two problems quickly became evident. These concerned the sustainability and spread of new working practices. Some clinical services would find a way to achieve, for example, dramatic reductions in patient waiting times, but would then struggle to maintain that performance level, more or less gradually regressing to their previous position. This was described in one Agency report as 'the improvement evaporation effect'. Similarly, while one clinical service had developed an effective way to reduce waiting times, other services did not then apply those methods. In organization theory, this is called 'the best practices puzzle'. While experience varied from one location to another, these sustainability and spread problems were frustrating both for local project leads and for national Agency staff, particularly as the questions that they faced over those issues were disarmingly simple: 'You've solved that problem; why have you gone back to how things were before?' 'If unit *x* can make those changes and meet those targets, why can't unit *y* do the same?'

Consequently, the Research into Practice team was established to shed light on those two broad sets of questions. The team worked initially with the National Booking and Cancer Services Collaborative Programmes, and subsequently with a number of other initiatives. Three attributes of the team and its work were significant. First, the researchers were recruited from within the health service, and most had clinical backgrounds. An external team could have taken much longer to become familiar with the specialized programmes and their issues, and thus to establish presence and credibility, and to generate useful findings. Second, the team worked in close collaboration with local and national staff responsible for those service improvement programmes, ensuring that the research was conducted 'close to the customer', with a good understanding of end-user interests and needs. Third, research methods were not based on biomedical practice, with the apparatus of randomized controlled trials, but involved instead a range of qualitative methods appropriate to the study of dynamic processes in different and rapidly evolving organizational contexts.

The team's work has generated a number of significant lessons. First, sustainability and spread are closely linked. Sustainability problems can inhibit spread, and the manner in which new practices are spread can either enhance or jeopardize sustainability. Second, the terms sustainability and spread defy precise definition; they are better seen as categories of problems sharing common properties. Third, these are complex processes that unfold over time, influenced by numerous related factors at different levels of analysis. Fourth, there are no simple tick-box checklists for managing these issues effectively. We know what kinds of factors, issues and processes are important influences on sustainability and spread, but timing and context determine which issues are likely to be significant. So, rather than a mechanical factor-based approach, this suggests instead a diagnostic perspective, involving management attentiveness and vigilance, sensitive to the combinations of issues that respectively support or jeopardize these processes in a given context. Paying attention to those issues may not always guarantee sustainability and spread, but can certainly improve the odds.

The NHS Modernisation Agency was disbanded in June 2005. How should its successor organization, the NHS Institute for Innovation and Improvement, build on this work? Three issues in particular stand out. First, with regard to the spread of 'best practice', it is clear that, in almost every case, significant adaptation or customization is required to make new methods, approaches, systems and arrangements work effectively in another context. Very few innovations in service delivery can be 'copied' as they stand, without some tailoring to fit. The staff involved need to learn the issues, and develop adaptations that are relevant to their particular setting. That development process takes time, particularly where the changes are multi-faceted. Second, with regard to sustainability, while it is important that some changes are sustained and developed, it is also clear that some changes should be allowed, if not encouraged, to decay. Circumstances evolve, and rigid methods that are not adaptable prevent staff from implementing further relevant changes and improvements.

Finally the significance of timing, sequencing and pacing runs through all of this work. Some less complex changes can spread with surprising speed, if other conditions are also in place. However, that seems to be uncommon. Indeed, attempts to implement and spread changes too rapidly can damage the impact and sustainability of those improvements, and also jeopardize further spread if the appropriate conditions are not in place. Efforts to sustain changes beyond their useful life are also damaging. The role of the NHS Institute for Innovation and Improvement involves supporting the rapid adoption and spread of new ideas, facilitating the swift implementation of changes that will benefit both staff and patients. The evidence presented here demonstrates the importance of having a number of factors in place: that local teams have access to sources of good practice and generalizable evidence; that they are able to develop systems for local learning and discovery to enable them to experiment and adopt new practice; that performance management and incentive systems support improvement; that local leaders manage the appropriate timing, sequencing and pace of change to increase the probability of effective and sustained improvements in patient care. There are no 'magic bullets' or shortcuts, but many ways to increase the likelihood of effective, sustainable, wholesale change. These are important lessons as we move into the next stage of NHS system reform.

Helen Bevan
Director of Service Transformation
NHS Institute for Innovation and Improvement

 **Preface**

Sustainability and decay, spread and containment

In 2004, the National Health Service (NHS) employed 1.3 million people in England, making it the third largest organization on the planet. Only the Chinese Army (2.3 million) and the Indian State Railways (1.5 million) had more staff. The NHS had an annual budget of £85 billion (expected to rise to over £100 billion by 2008), exceeding the combined sales of Microsoft and Tesco. It employed around 397,000 nurses and midwives, 117,000 doctors, and 38,000 managers and senior managers (Department of Health, 2005a). *The NHS Plan* (Department of Health, 2000a) launched a 10-year, government-inspired 'modernization' initiative, with numerous performance targets and deadlines. This was the largest and most systematic organization development initiative ever undertaken, in any sector, anywhere. One of the 'core principles' (p.5) was that 'The health and social care system must be shaped around the needs of the patient, not the other way round', reflecting the view that the service was run primarily in the interests of the organization and its staff. The central themes of the change agenda were thus customer orientation, patient choice, and cost-effectiveness. The aim was to make patient focus a defining feature of the service; the phrase 'patient-centred' appears 10 times in the 140 pages of *The NHS Plan*. To achieve changes in organization culture, and to meet those targets on time, many changes in working practices were required.

The research reported here was conduced by a team working in the NHS Modernisation Agency (hereafter 'the Agency'), a body established in 2001, initially responsible for stimulating and leading national service improvement programmes. The way in which the role of the Agency evolved is explored in Chapter 1. From studies of parts of the modernization agenda, this book aims to contribute to understanding, debate, and practice in the field of organizational change in general, and with particular reference to healthcare. This aim extends to organization theory, knowledge management, practice, and policy concerning strategies for organizational change and service improvement across the public sector.

How many targets?

The exact number of performance targets in *The NHS Plan* (Department of Health, 2000a) was unclear. No explicit number was given, and the word 'target' appeared only 57 times in the document. However, one Agency manager told us that she had counted over 320. The subsequent 'NHS Plan Implementation Programme' (an internal Department of Health planning document) identified 98 targets for 2001–2002 alone, covering most aspects of the service: access, waiting times, cancer services, capacity and IT infrastructure, coronary heart disease, children's services, mental health, quality improvement and patient focus, care of the elderly, public health, workforce and skill mix, communications across the service, and the implementation of performance management. *The NHS Cancer Plan* (Department of Health, 2000b; 2005d) identified 82 targets for cancer services. The National Service Frameworks for other clinical services similarly identified their own targets. From *The NHS Plan* and *The NHS Cancer Plan*, the Agency produced in 2001 a summary identifying 31 waiting times targets for inpatients, outpatients, and booked admissions, to be achieved in a phased manner between December 2000 ('all urgent cancer referrals to be seen within two weeks') and 2008 ('maximum wait for inpatient treatment reduced to three months'). In shifting the language from 'modernisation' to 'improvement' (Department of Health, 2004a), targets became 'key commitments', and at the time of writing the performance of acute hospitals was being monitored on around 40 measures. Whatever the number, the health service since 2000 became a 'target-rich environment'.

This book focuses on two issues that the Agency encountered at an early stage. One concerned *sustainability*. Priorities were established, resources were committed, staff were recruited, changes were implemented, performance improvements were achieved. In many cases, those gains continued. However, experience varied. In some cases, performance levels fell back to where they began. Why this should happen was unclear.
A second issue concerned *spread*. A hospital, say, or a specialty, a clinic, or a doctor, developed a better way to carry out a particular process, deliver a service, or meet a target. Once again, while some new practices were quickly adopted by others, other approaches were not more widely used, despite the demonstrable benefits. These variations in experience, with regard to sustainability and spread, represented threats to the modernization agenda, prompting research into the causes, in order to find ways to overcome the 'decay' of improvements, and the 'containment' of good ideas, and to increase the spread of new ideas and working practices more widely. Our working definitions of these terms are:

Sustainability The process through which new working methods, performance enhancements, and continuous improvements are maintained for a period appropriate to a given context. The opposite of sustainability, where change is not maintained and benefits are lost, is *decay*.

Spread   The process through which new working methods developed in one setting are adopted, perhaps with appropriate modifications, in other organizational contexts. The opposite of spread, where changes at one site are not adapted and adopted by others, is *containment*.

The central argument of this book is that the sustainability, decay, spread, and containment of new working practices are processes influenced by a combination of contextual, processual, organizational, political, and temporal factors, affected also by attributes of the substance of the changes under consideration. These intertwined processes are fragile and vulnerable, and can take significant periods of time to unfold. In particular, attempts to accelerate the process of spread can be damaging. Relevant theoretical constructs (explored later) for understanding these processes include theoretical narratives and probabilistic explanations, involving cumulative effects, conjunctural causation, and path dependency. Consequently, there is no simple policy directive or effortless management strategy to guarantee either the durability of new working practices or their wide and rapid spread. Political and media commentaries often imply that injections of public funds for healthcare must have instantaneous and demonstrable results. However, it seems that national policy and local management must operate instead with a more realistic framework of expectations concerning the pace of adoption of 'best practice', and also the period over which gains can be maintained.

This is not an argument that change in healthcare is doomed to be glacial, incremental, and transient. On the contrary. Significant improvements in service delivery have been achieved and, while not instantaneous, some have been implemented with impressive speed, especially where a favourable conjunction of factors has been in place. Public sector healthcare is conventionally regarded as cumbersome, bureaucratic, slow, and outmoded in comparison with commercial practice. That stereotype is oversimplified and inaccurate. For those employed in the NHS, the pace of recent change has been breathless. The focus on customer care and performance improvement has been pervasive.

Neither is this an argument that modernization has been without problems and is now complete. It is a safe prediction that any organization attempting change on such a scale will combine successes with mistakes, meet difficulties, and find that the project consumes more time and resources than anticipated. The pace of change and the rate of performance improvement will rarely meet either political or public expectations. A systematic evaluation will require an evidence base wider than that which underpins this book. However, this study of the processes of sustainability and spread offers a useful lens through which to consider the wider dimensions of organizational change. Commercial enterprises have much to learn from the culture of creativity, innovation, and strategic change in healthcare, from the techniques and outcomes of process redesign, and from the new models of working practice and inter-organizational network relationships that have been developed.

Objectives

This book draws on the work of a unique research team, working in the Agency from 2001 to 2005. Team members included healthcare leaders, managers, and researchers, most of whom had clinical qualifications and experience. Considering the potential threats to modernization with regard to sustainability and spread, the objectives of this book concern:

1   The *sustainability* or *improvement evaporation problem*: we explore the processes through which new working practices are maintained and developed in some settings, while they regress and decay in others.
2   The *spread* or *best practices puzzle*: we explore the processes through which new working practices in healthcare are either contained where they were first implemented, or are adapted, adopted, and subsequently transferred to other units.
3   *Implications*: we identify the theoretical, practical, and national policy implications of this experience of major organizational transformation in healthcare.

The book has three parts, concerning context, experience, and implications.

The **context** part introduces the modernization agenda, and explains the role of the Agency, as a national organization development body, in facilitating change. Several of the chapters in the following part are based on studies of two of the Agency's main programmes: the National Booking Programme and the Cancer Services Collaborative Programme. As these initiatives recur throughout the volume, *Chapter 1* explains the background to *The NHS Plan*, and describes the roles of the Agency and the Research into Practice team. *Chapters 2 and 3* respectively summarize the literature relating to the sustainability and spread (or diffusion) of change. While diffusion of innovation is a well-established research tradition (concentrating more on product innovations than on working practices), several commentators note that the sustainability problem has attracted less attention (Ham *et al.*, 2003; Greenhalgh *et al.*, 2004). These chapters argue for a perspective that views sustainability and spread as ongoing processes to be understood in relation to the contexts in which they unfold.

The **experience** part reports studies of different initiatives in the modernization agenda.

Chapter 4 explores the views of staff in national lead roles in the booking and cancer collaborative programmes, with regard to influences on the sustainability and spread of the new working practices associated with those initiatives. Staff experience demonstrates that these processes are closely linked, and are affected by a complex set of factors, including the substance of the changes, key roles and relationships, and modes of individual engagement. Staff views also highlight the significance of collective leadership, the protracted timescales required for effective change, and the role of the organizational context.

Chapter 5 considers the nature and causes of scepticism and resistance to modernization among healthcare staff who might be expected to welcome ways to improve patient care. This study showed that the roots of scepticism and resistance lie not exclusively with the individual, but also with the history and culture of a professional organization, elements of the change substance, and aspects of timing and context. Overcoming resistance depends on understanding the benefits, and on the tailored interventions of skilled change leaders.

Chapter 6 examines the nature and achievements of the National Booking Programme. The aim was simple: let patients choose appointment dates. However, defining a 'booked appointment' was problematic and controversial, but critical as the proportion of patients 'booked' was a performance target. To achieve this simple aim, complex process redesign was necessary, involving changes to roles (clinical and administrative), procedures, computing systems, physical facilities, and inter-organizational collaborations. The spread of booking was inhibited by confusion over the concept and by medical scepticism, as there was little evidence to show that booking improved quality of care. Sustainability, however, was reinforced by the benefits to staff and patients.

Chapter 7 continues the focus on booking, shifting from a national perspective to the experience of an acute hospital, Parkside NHS Trust. This again shows how sustainability and spread are affected by organizational context, and by aspects of the change substance, process, and timing. Issues influencing receptiveness to booking included key people in lead roles, good relations between management and medical staff, a history of successful change, and the presence of a dedicated process redesign team. Good preplanning and timing were also critical to sustainability and spread; booking was first piloted in a small number of receptive areas, where evidence was accumulated, before the underlying principles were shared more widely. Booking was not compatible, however, with some clinical specialties.

Chapter 8 takes a fresh look at the role of change leadership, arguing that change can be driven effectively by staff at all levels of the organization, in positions not normally identified as leadership roles, operating quietly 'below the radar'. Those staff often have a number of advantages: length of service, depth of local knowledge, established relationships with powerful colleagues, credibility, and political sensitivity. Their role is in sharp contrast with the fashionable stereotype of the visionary, transformational, charismatic senior executive. While such dispersed change leadership may be vital to achieve the scope of change required in healthcare, their role is not always recognized, supported, or rewarded.

Chapter 9 also explores the experience of an acute hospital, Walkerville NHS Trust, with sustaining and spreading cancer collaborative programme methods. The context for these changes was complex, involving the development of new inter-organizational processes and relationships between individuals, teams, hospitals, and networks. Sustainability and spread were supported by continuity of strategic goals, and by good relationships between managers and medical staff. Managers played a covert role in transferring ideas across organizational and professional boundaries, but there was little evidence of senior medical staff sharing new working practices and information with each other. Teamwork, and the collection of service-specific performance data, were instrumental in maintaining the focus on this initiative.

Chapter 10 examines the implementation of 'rapid access' prostate cancer assessment, one of the 'high-impact' changes in cancer care. Driven by national targets for waiting times, the spread of this initiative was dependent on consultant urologists, whose autonomous decisions led to differences in practice, between hospitals, and also in the same urology department. Rapid assessment does not necessarily lead to better treatment for this disease. Consequently, some clinicians did not adopt the approach, prioritizing clinical evidence above the preferences of patients for quick test results which significantly reduced their anxiety. The cancer collaborative staff, working with clinical teams, had little impact on medical staff.

Chapter 11 considers the change from traditional triage methods in hospital accident and emergency departments to 'see and treat'. This new approach spread rapidly to most emergency departments in England, apparently triggered by two factors: the visibility of the problem (lengthy queues) in emergency departments, and national waiting times targets. However, those factors were not sufficient to explain the diffusion process, and numerous other issues were also significant, including the straightforward substance of the changes, the absence of a complex decision process to implement, the nature of the accompanying communications, the wider support infrastructure for this initiative, and the visibility of the benefits (no queues).

This is an example of 'conjunctural causation', where the outcomes of interest are generated by a particular configuration or cluster of events and factors.

The **implications** part considers the contribution to theory and practice with regard to organizational change in general, and the sustainability and spread of new working practices in particular. *Chapter 12* develops a processual perspective, drawing on the concepts of theoretical narrative, cumulative effects, conjunctural causation, and path dependency, to explain the sustainability and spread of operational innovations. *Chapter 13* also argues for new ways of conceptualizing change processes, involving modes of thinking that are more circular and less linear, regarding traditional 'cause and effect' as less relevant than conjunctural forms of causation, where outcomes follow from the shifting configurations of a range of factors operating in particular contexts over time. Relatively intangible, this mode of thinking encourages new ways of approaching the practical management of change, sustainability, and spread processes. Three policy implications are explored: the role of a central 'organization development' unit, the implications of performance targets, and expectations with regard to time lags between legislating outcomes and the demonstration of tangible progress towards those goals. *Chapter 14* considers the methodological issues raised by this research, conducted during a period of rapid change, by a team employed by the organization under analysis, funded by the internal customers for the findings.

We hope that this book will be of interest to four sets of readers. First, our primary readership concerns participants on leadership and management development programmes focusing on change, organizational behaviour, and public sector management, and candidates on Masters degree programmes. Second, the book will be relevant to healthcare practitioners in project lead, process redesign, and change implementation positions. Many such roles at national and local levels combine managerial duties with service improvement and (occasionally) research responsibilities. The combination of theory, empirical evidence, practice, and policy will therefore appeal to this group. Third, the content will also be of interest to academic researchers and instructors working in the fields of organization development and change. While the content will be of generic relevance, this work will appeal in particular to healthcare management and public sector specialists. Fourth, the argument of the book will be relevant to health service staff in senior change leadership, policy formulation, and performance management roles. Many such staff have moved from 'front line' healthcare positions, and are familiar with the issues and change initiatives covered in this book, if not with the underpinning theoretical perspective and the implications of our findings.

These readership groups are not as discrete as they appear. Many healthcare managers are responsible for, or are engaged with, internal research and service improvement projects, and many are also enrolled in postgraduate degree programmes, working on their own projects related to healthcare management issues. Many academic researchers in this field (including the editors) are engaged in practice with the service through advisory positions on committees, boards, steering groups, and project teams. These apparently diverse populations share a number of overlapping concerns with research and practice relating to change and modernization in the public services in general, and healthcare in particular.

Terminology

Attentive readers will note inconsistencies in the spelling of 'ise' and 'ize' words. The use of 'z' is widely regarded as American. That is typically not the case. For most such words, the 'z' is correct English, for historical, etymological, and phonetic reasons. Our editorial policy is thus to follow correct English spelling, with reference to *The Oxford Dictionary for Writers and Editors*. The NHS Modernisation Agency is an exception, as it was given this title by *The NHS Plan*.

Some readers may also feel uncomfortable with the use of the term 'modernization', which is associated with national political rhetoric and agendas, applied across the public sector, as well as with substantive efforts to improve the health service. The term is often used indiscriminately, suggesting that the benefits must be clear and unquestionable, which is a suspicious presumption; staff, patients, and carers may not always benefit from, or agree with, ideologically inspired initiatives. The symbolism, implying that the health service is not modern, but old-fashioned and out of date, is yet another false generalization. However, the term is retained here for two reasons. First, this was the label given to the NHS Modernisation Agency which was initially responsible for driving service improvement initiatives in pursuit of *The NHS Plan*'s objective to develop a more patient-centred healthcare organization, and to meet the plan's many targets. The Agency also supported the research reported here. Second, the term was in widespread use at the time of this research, and offers a convenient shorthand for the broad, systemic, and ambitious organizational change and service improvement agenda that the health service has sought to develop. It is interesting to observe, however, that by 2005, most staff had stopped using this once fashionable term altogether, referring more often instead to transformation and reform.

The terms 'sustainability' and 'spread' have been chosen deliberately. These terms were used by the Agency to articulate recurring concerns. The term 'spread' also distinguishes these issues, in part, from commentary on diffusion of innovation (Chapter 3), which tends to focus more on new products than on multi-dimensional organizational changes. Before research in these areas began, Agency staff, including our research team, phrased the sequence 'spread and sustainability' in a taken-for-granted manner. But what is the temporal logic here? Does change or innovation first need to spread, across more than one area, before attention turns to sustaining new practices? Or is it necessary for those advocating new methods first to demonstrate that these can indeed be sustained, before others will adopt the approach? The temporal logic can thus run in either direction, depending on context. The terms sustainability and spread are reversed throughout the book to reflect these possibilities.

Other terms that can cause confusion are 'medical' and 'clinical'. Following dictionary usage, 'medical' refers to doctors (who practise medicine). In Britain, the most senior doctors and surgeons are known as consultants. 'Clinical' refers to everyone (i.e. clinicians) involved in treating patients, including nurses, pharmacists, radiographers, physiotherapists, dieticians, occupational therapists, phlebotomists, and other clinical professions. Note that a reference to clinical staff can thus also include doctors and hospital consultants.

Another potentially confusing term is 'trust'. Terms now used to describe healthcare providers in Britain include, for example, primary care trust, acute hospital trust, ambulance trust, mental health trust, or just plain 'trust' where the context indicates which organization is being discussed. The first NHS trusts were created in 1991, as a result of government policy giving providers a degree of freedom (or 'earned autonomy'; Department of Health, 2002b) from central control if they demonstrated satisfactory performance levels and a commitment to patient-centred care, and devolved greater responsibility to clinical teams. Trusts were funded not by the Department of Health directly, but through service-level agreements with their local strategic health authorities (previously regional offices of the Department). For example, most hospitals (primary care trusts were a later development) adopted a form of clinical directorate structure, in which consultants became part-time managers for their specialties, often becoming responsible for large numbers of staff and significant budgets (the clinical directorate for surgery in a medium-size district general hospital might have an annual budget of over £10 million, for example). In the 1990s, applying for, and being granted, trust status was thus a key objective for most providers. From 2004, following another policy initiative, trusts meeting specified performance criteria (concerning patient care, financial performance, and corporate governance) could apply for Foundation Trust status. This was a controversial policy, which granted trusts considerably more financial freedom, while significantly increasing local involvement in trust management which would become accountable to an independent regulator.

While the terminology of trust status should not detain us here, these policy shifts have implications for sustainability and spread, for two sets of reasons. First, the time and effort required to prepare a successful bid to upgrade the status of your organization, over what is often a lengthy period of time (several months to several years), cannot be overestimated. This burden does not fall only on management, as clinical (including medical) staff are also involved in helping to meet the performance criteria and then to prepare the details of the application. Involvement in a corporate exercise of this kind often means that less attention is paid to other items on the agenda, which for that period may be regarded as less important, such as sustaining and spreading organizational changes. Second, these bids invariably rely on the organization's ability to demonstrate satisfactory performance on a number of predefined measures. Activities, areas, services, and processes not linked to those measures are thus also given lower priority, and attract less attention, than those which will generate a stronger assessment profile. One reason why new working practices are more likely to remain contained, and why improvements are more likely to decay, is because they have simply ceased to be important in a context that gives other issues and measures a higher priority.

Acknowledgements

Many people, at all levels across the National Health Service, involved with a number of modernization initiatives, have contributed to this work in various ways, through interviews, informal discussions, workshop participation, and by providing critical and constructive feedback at different stages on the findings reported here. Without their willing collaboration and contributions, this work would not have been possible, and we wish to extend our gratitude to them all for their support. In addition, this work would not have been possible without the support of the NHS Modernisation Agency (succeeded in 2005 by the NHS Institute for Innovation and Improvement), which triggered and funded the lines of enquiry explored in this book. The Agency provided unique facilities for the research team, particularly with respect to access to key national and local healthcare staff. In expressing our deep and sincere thanks to all those who have assisted in this endeavour, the editors and authors remain wholly responsible for the gaps and flaws in this work.

Part I
Context

1 Changing by numbers

Diane Ketley and Helen Bevan

Chapter aims

1 To explain the background to the large-scale, systematic healthcare modernization agenda for radical change in healthcare launched in 2000 by *The NHS Plan*.
2 To describe the role and context of the NHS Modernisation Agency, a national body established to support service improvement and the adoption of best practice.
3 To describe the role and context of the Agency's Research into Practice team, formed to capture learning concerning the sustainability and spread of effective new practices, and responsible for the research reported in this book.

Key point summary

- *The NHS Plan* launched in 2000 was probably the most ambitious and wide-ranging organization development and change agenda ever attempted by any organization, in any sector.
- *The NHS Plan* linked additional investment in healthcare with reform, introducing national targets to encourage the provision of equitable high-quality care.
- In 2001, the government created the NHS Modernisation Agency, a central body, to spread best practice. The Agency supported the implementation of major national service improvement programmes, including those aimed at decreasing waiting times and improving standards in cancer care and patient booking.
- Through initial successes, the Agency grew in size and influence; as local capabilities increased, resources and responsibility were devolved to local NHS organizations, and the Agency focus shifted from leading and implementing to facilitation and support.
- The Research into Practice team was established by the Agency in 2001 to address two problems encountered from the early days of the modernization

process: explaining why some successes in service improvement were not being sustained, and understanding why 'best practices' were not always being more widely adopted.

● The Research into Practice team worked inside the health service, collaborating with the sponsors and users of the research, rather than as a conventional external academic research team. The team was able through this approach to develop fresh insights that influenced practice at national and local levels in a rapidly evolving context.

● The Agency was succeeded in 2005 by a new NHS Institute for Innovation and Improvement, responsible not for implementing change, but for the design and dissemination of innovations in healthcare service improvement.

The NHS Plan, 2000

In part, the NHS is failing to deliver because over the years it has been underfunded. In particular, there have been too few doctors and nurses and other key staff to carry out all the treatments required. But there have been other underlying problems as well. The NHS is a 1940s system operating in a 21st century world. It has:

- a lack of national standards
- old-fashioned demarcations between staff and barriers between services
- a lack of clear incentives and levers to improve performance
- over-centralization and disempowered patients

More money will fund extra investment in:

- 7,000 extra beds in hospitals and intermediate care
- over 100 new hospitals by 2010 and 500 new one-stop primary care centres
- over 3,000 general practice premises modernized and 250 new scanners
- clean wards, overseen by 'modern matrons', and better hospital food
- modern IT systems in every hospital and general practice surgery
- 7,500 more consultants and 2,000 more general practitioners
- 20,000 extra nurses and 6,500 extra therapists
- 1,000 more medical school places
- childcare support for NHS staff with 100 on-site nurseries

But investment has to be accompanied by reform. The NHS has to be redesigned around the needs of the patient. Local hospitals cannot be run from Whitehall.

Source: *The NHS Plan, A Summary* (Department of Health, 2000a)

The big plan

> It will be important not to let change overwhelm us. The philosophy will be to take it one step at a time; plan the pace of change and prioritize and understand that the aim is evolution not revolution.
>
> *Source*: *A First Class Service: Quality in the New NHS*
> (Department of Health, 1998, p.76)

The NHS Plan (Department of Health, 2000a) was launched in July 2000 as a 10-year programme of radical reform. It argued that, despite many achievements, the health service had failed to keep pace with social changes. Particular areas for improvement concerned the times that patients had to wait for diagnosis and treatment, and unacceptable variations in healthcare standards across the country. The purpose and vision of *The NHS Plan* was to create a health service designed around the needs of patients. It was produced following extensive consultation with service users and staff, and was publicly endorsed by 25 leading public, patient, and professional stakeholders.

The strategy built on two documents, *The New NHS, Modern, Dependable* (Department of Health, 1997) and *A First Class Service: Quality in the New NHS* (Department of Health, 1998). *The New NHS* confirmed that healthcare modernization was a key government objective, and announced the 10-year plan. The aim was to encourage evolutionary change rather than organizational upheaval, to increase quality, and to decrease variations in access to care. *A First Class Service* emphasized that the objective was to change thinking and behaviour, and that this was not about 'ticking checklists'; this document focused on improving quality of care, through a strategy for delivering the government's 'third way', setting national standards and expectations, with local responsibility for meeting those standards, supported by consistent monitoring. In other words, this 10-year programme of investment was to be accompanied by reform, with the Department of Health setting national performance standards which would be monitored by the Commission for Healthcare Improvement (evolved as the Commission for Healthcare Audit and Inspection in 2004). *The NHS Plan* also announced the formation of a national agency to spread best practice.

The priority and resources allocated to this agenda were unprecedented. *The NHS Plan* has been described as 'the most ambitious, comprehensive and intentionally funded national initiative to improve health care quality in the world' (Leatherman and Sutherland, 2003), and Don Berwick of the

American Institute for Healthcare Improvement described it as 'the largest concerted systematic improvement effort ever undertaken, anywhere, in any industry'. To give patients equitable access to high-quality care, the Department of Health, with the assistance of leading clinicians, managers, and other staff, set national standards which would take three forms:

- national standards for key clinical conditions and diseases through National Service Frameworks, including the first ever comprehensive National Cancer Plan (Department of Health, 2000b);
- guidance on best treatments and interventions from the National Institute for Clinical Excellence (popularly known as NICE);
- a number of ambitious (but considered achievable) national targets, including those relating to waiting times which, in 2000, were long, and were considered unacceptable and unnecessary (evidence suggested that waiting times were the aspect of healthcare of which the public were most critical; Ham, 2004, p.211).

These targets were controversial. Were there too many, and were these the 'right' targets? Among the details, two of the priorities in *The NHS Plan* were decreasing waiting times and increasing the standard of care in cancer services. Consequently, these were the areas in which much of the Agency's work on sustainability and spread was to focus.

Decreasing waiting times

The aim was to reduce waiting times at all stages of acute care. Two major national programmes were identified, concerning the booking of hospital appointments and the reduction of waiting times in accident and emergency departments. *The NHS Plan* argued that a booked appointment system, where patients would be given a choice for the date and time of their hospital appointments, would encourage reform at several levels, as well as making this process more convenient for patients and doctors. *The NHS Plan* identified three main targets that hospitals should meet by the end of 2005:

- waiting lists for hospital appointments and admissions were to be abolished, and replaced with booking systems giving all patients a choice of convenient time within a guaranteed maximum waiting time;
- the maximum waiting time for a routine outpatient appointment was to be halved, from over six months to three months;
- the maximum waiting time for inpatient treatment was to be cut from 18 months to six months by the end of 2005, and to three months by the end of 2008.

This represented a staged reduction in waiting times, linking the pace to building the capacity and capability to provide care without delay. The target for accident and emergency departments was that, by the end of 2004, no patient would wait more than four hours from arrival to admission, transfer to another unit, or discharge. The Agency's role was to help to decrease waiting times by 'rolling out' the booked admissions programme across England, and by helping to spread best practice in emergency services (see Chapters 6, 7, and 11).

Improving cancer services

An earlier review of cancer services (Calman and Hine, 1995) had produced a framework for commissioning higher-quality care for cancer patients. The recommended new structure was based on networks of care with three levels:

1 primary care, seen as the focus of care, where referral and follow-up would take place;
2 cancer units, established in main district general hospitals, to manage patients with the most common cancers;
3 cancer centres, treating all patients with cancer in the local geographical area, and less common cancers by referral from cancer units, as well as providing specialist diagnostic and therapeutic techniques.

Based on this framework, *The NHS Cancer Plan* set out how improvements in the speed, convenience, and quality of care offered to cancer patients would be introduced. Acknowledging previous underfunding, the plan announced an additional £280 million for cancer services in 2001–2002, an additional £407 million in 2002–2003, and £570 million in 2003–2004. This increased investment in cancer services was to take place alongside reform through new ways of working around the needs of patients, by extending roles and through guidance to ensure high standards of treatment and care. New targets for reducing the waiting times for diagnosis and treatment were announced, so that by the end of 2005 there would be:

1 a maximum one-month wait from diagnosis to treatment for all cancers;
2 a maximum two-month wait from urgent referral by a general practitioner to the commencement of treatment for all cancers.

The ultimate goal was that, by 2008, for all suspected cancers, patients would wait for a maximum of one month from an urgent referral to the beginning of treatment, except where there was sound clinical reason or through patient choice. This target was broadly consistent with the best that patients could experience in Europe and North America. In 2000, this was already being achieved in England for some uncommon cancers, such as acute leukaemia. Also by 2000, a national improvement programme, the Cancer Services Collaborative, was working with nine cancer networks across England to pilot approaches to streamline and more effectively co-ordinate all stages of the patient pathway through primary, secondary, and tertiary care. The role of the Agency in improving cancer services was to extend this collaborative approach to all cancer networks by 2003 (see Chapter 9).

What is a collaborative programme?

A collaborative programme is a comprehensive way of creating specific improvements for patients based on evidence-based principles for spreading best practice. It has proven improvement techniques developed from the learning of thousands of improvement projects. A collaborative programme will give you all the components you will need to make a difference, and is designed to succeed. The collaborative programme methodology originates from the work of the Institute for Healthcare Improvement (IHI) in the United States. In 1996 the IHI launched the 'breakthrough series' of collaborative programmes to support local teams to make significant improvements for patients (Kilo, 1998).

A collaborative programme is a time-limited programme, which focuses on a specific topic. The programme supports participating improvement teams in implementing changes by creating the time and opportunity for teams to reflect and discuss. Improvement teams then use a continuous method of improvement in which ideas for change are tested on a small scale. Results are analysed and either implemented or further refinements made to make the changes more effective. What initially was thought to be a solution may not be and after small-scale testing the team may decide to look for a different idea. Changes are of an incremental nature, but the increments are very fast and expected to progress rapidly to wider and bigger change.

Source: NHS Modernisation Agency (2002c, p.10)

The Agency role

The launch of the Agency was announced in *The NHS Plan*, to help local clinicians and managers to redesign their services around the needs and convenience of patients. The Agency was to work with all NHS organizations to support continuous service improvement. Some of the ideas that led to the Agency's formation came from outside the NHS. The discipline of improvement (Langley *et al.*, 1996) had a long track record in the private sector, and methods such as process redesign, systems thinking, statistical process control, and project management were widely used. Healthcare systems in other parts of the world were known to be using these approaches, but prior to 1998, there was minimal evidence of the NHS building capability for improvement in a systematic way outside a few pioneering hospitals and primary care practices. However, it became apparent that the methods of process re-engineering, total quality management, continuous quality improvement, and 'lean thinking' were directly relevant to healthcare (Locock, 2001).

From 1998, the Department of Health established a series of national teams to support the health service in addressing key priorities. The National Patients' Access Team was established to help reduce waiting times for hospital care. The National Primary Care Development Team focused on improving access to primary care and chronic disease management. The National Clinical Governance Support Team supported improvement in clinical quality. Critically, these teams were led at a national level by people who had a strong track record of delivering change in local NHS organizations. All were skilled in the discipline of improvement and were able to transfer their expertise to a national level.

The Department of Health provided these 'entrepreneurs' with the support and resources to innovate and experiment with new approaches. Previously, at a national level, the focus had been on the 'what' (or the substance) of change: for example, what target had to be met in what timescale. For the first time, these teams also concentrated on the 'how' of change: how to equip healthcare teams with the skills to improve their services, and how to support them through the change process. The Agency was formally established in April 2001, as part of the Department of Health, and the Agency's director was accountable to the NHS chief executive for achieving the Agency's component of the Department's overall business plan. The Agency's creation thus represented a move from a series of project teams, each with a limited life, to a continuing national commitment to service improvement.

Early days: 2001–2003

The Agency's first publication in 2001 identified the core purpose as to help the health service to make both radical and sustainable changes. Key to these aims were:

- supporting clinical and management leaders to transform services;
- building service improvement capabilities across the health service;
- supporting the redesign of care to achieve significant improvements for patients;
- leading national service improvement initiatives, including clinical governance and learning;
- designing programmes to spread best practice across the health service;
- identifying and evaluating innovation;
- transferring new learning into the health service.

Agency priorities for 2001–2002

The Agency's work programme is based on explicit goals and targets.
Some of its constituent programmes include quantified measures of improved
patient experience. Some use process measures such as targets for increased
participation in improvement activity amongst front line staff and leaders.
Some will add to the growing portfolio of good practice guidance and training
support. Some cover all three dimensions: clinical improvement, participation,
and good practice. All pick up the importance of leadership development and
the links with organizational development.

Source: NHS Modernisation Agency (2001a, p.3)

The Agency aimed to produce innovative reactions to big challenges, linking
with other improvement specialists in the public and private sectors, in
Britain and globally, to learn about new ideas. It developed new approaches
through pilot and prototype schemes and helped to spread new ways of
working across the health service. The Agency's style was to be supportive
and developmental, echoing the evolution of 'the new public management'
based on networked organizations, managerialism, formal procedures,
control through policy frameworks, with 'the centre' exercising strategic
control while service providers are responsible for designing and
delivering services (Walshe, 1995). It was believed, therefore, that
change would be achieved most effectively by supporting staff, allowing
them to use their creativity, and harnessing the talents of all staff. The
Agency's role was therefore catalytic, as an enabler of change, and
accountability for achieving modernization targets lay primarily with
staff themselves. The Agency brought together individuals and teams
with established reputations for modernizing services and developing
leadership. It was unique in combining service modernization with the
development of current and future leaders and managers for the health
service.

In the early stages, the Agency focused on *The NHS Plan* targets, improving
organizational performance, and the drive to improve quality. Much of this
effort reflected *The NHS Plan* priorities, and particular pressure points in the
service. Programmes were thus established to improve delivery of mental
health, cancer, and cardiac services. Initiatives focused on the areas with the
biggest delays for patients, including orthopaedics, plastic surgery, cataracts,
and general surgery. Established work was extended, including programmes
to enhance the clinical governance skills of healthcare staff, and to improve
patient access to primary care. New areas of work included workforce
reform and organization development for primary care organizations. There
was a major expansion of leadership development through the establishment

of the Leadership Centre as part of the Agency. Explicit targets and priorities for supporting delivery were (NHS Modernisation Agency, 2001a):

- to highlight and record the growing number of examples of improvements seen through the eyes of patients and front line staff;
- to support the service to make improvements necessary to meet national targets;
- to help to create long-term capacity, capability, and networks for continuous improvement beyond *The NHS Plan*'s lifespan.

The initial work programme thus included:

- extend the booked appointments system to every service in every hospital (see Chapters 6 and 7);
- extend the Cancer Services Collaborative initiative to every cancer service in the country (see Chapter 9);
- establish a similar collaborative programme to reduce waiting in accident and emergency departments (see Chapter 11).

The Agency used a variety of approaches. Some had a local focus, including for example tailored programmes to help primary care trusts to develop local services. Others had a national focus, such as helping to develop 'implementation-ready' policies for workforce and pay reform. The outcomes of the early work programme demonstrated the different roles the Agency would take, ranging on a continuum from direct intervention (supporting organizations with significant performance challenges), through to the provision of expert advice and knowledge management.

In its first year, the Agency's staff of 200 clinicians and managers, drawn mainly from the health service, led more than 50 projects and programmes, worked with more than 1,000 local project teams across a range of trusts, and supported more than 30,000 leaders and managers. The Agency worked across the health service, including primary and secondary care, mental health and ambulance trusts, and across the whole performance spectrum. The Agency was able to demonstrate achievements (NHS Modernisation Agency, 2001a). The local teams that took part in the first programme to improve patient access to primary care achieved a more than 60 per cent reduction in the time patients waited to see a general practitioner, and a 50 per cent reduction in waiting times to see a nurse. Hospitals with long waiting times, and which received support and guidance from the Agency, were able to demonstrate tangible improvements at a quicker rate than hospitals receiving no support.

It was explicit in the early days of the Agency that the aim was to embed transformation across the whole of the health service in order to create a 'modernization movement'. The plan was that the Agency would continue to co-ordinate national initiatives, but that over time the focus would

Agency programme comparisons, 2001

The Agency's portfolio contained a broad spectrum of different kinds of activity. Two of the initiatives explored in this book concern booked admissions and the Cancer Services Collaborative. Some of the main contrasts between these two programmes, viewed at the time the research began (the position may now be quite different), were as follows:

Booked admissions	*Cancer Services Collaborative*
The National Booking Programme, launched in 1998 in 24 pilot sites, was the longest running of the Agency's initiatives. The objectives were to make the NHS more convenient for patients to use, and to make better use of resources, by allowing patients to choose and pre-book the dates of their healthcare appointments	The Cancer Services Collaborative programme began in 1999 in nine network pilot sites, focusing on five main types of cancer. Phase 2, in 2001, extended to 34 networks, and to a wider range of cancers. The objectives were to improve the provision of cancer services, and meet national targets, by redesigning care processes in networks
The programme was implemented in waves, each lasting for 18 months; the fourth and final wave was called 'moving to mainstream'	The programme was implemented in three phases, and by 2003 it also covered radiology and chemotherapy services, and was extended to all cancers

Other comparisons

Service focus	Disease focus
Insufficient clinical input in early stages	Strong clinical involvement throughout
More managerially driven	More clinically driven
Right across healthcare	Largely secondary care focus
Stand-alone site improvements	Based on collaboration and shared learning
No specific underpinning redesign model	Driven by 'plan–do–study–act' approach
Difficulty in sustaining changes (research)	Difficulty in sustaining changes (anecdotal)

increasingly be on providing customized support for local NHS organizations which would develop their own change processes, using the systematic and evidence-based tools that the Agency championed. This was consistent with the Agency's core role of supporting the development of local capacity and capability for modernization. The goal was that, by 2006, capability for ongoing improvement would be embedded at every level in the health service. It was estimated in 2001 that less than 15 per cent of NHS staff were actively involved in modernization work (Bate *et al.*, 2004), and the aim was to increase this to 100 per cent. This represented a desire to make modernization a 'mainstream' activity.

Traditional NHS performance improvement strategy

- Design the system to prevent performance failure.
- Create awareness of targets and performance requirements, and raise leadership intent to deliver them.
- Seek to improve the performance of specific departments, specialties, practices or parts of the system.
- Work harder.
- Implement measurement systems to monitor compliance with the required performance.

Potential NHS performance improvement strategy

- Design the system to continuously improve.
- Take a process view of patient flows across departmental and organizational boundaries.
- Work smarter by:
  focussing on the bottlenecks that prevent smooth patient flow;
  managing and reducing causes of variation in patient flow;
  segmenting patients according to their specific needs.
- Implement measurement systems for improvement that reveal the true performance of the system and the impact of any changes made in real time.

Source: NHS Modernisation Agency (2004b, p.11)

An evolving role: 2003–2005

By June 2003, the Agency had completed two years' work as a catalyst for change. It had grown to over 800 staff, and developed many more programmes. However, this was not a remote central body. The Agency had offices in Leeds, Leicester, and London. Many staff worked from home, which meant that the Agency's reach covered the country. It had grown rapidly, and was striving to meet growing expectations while trying not to spread resources too thinly. In addition, it had developed a style of working that encompassed explicit principles of modernization, such as 'the three Rs' and 'the five rules' (see box on p.14). This approach aimed to build trust in those with whom they worked, and to engage them in the change process. The style was not to give orders, issue directives, or enforce compliance, but to give staff the knowledge, tools, and confidence to bring about local change themselves.

Principles of modernization

The three Rs:

1 *Renewal*: more modern buildings and facilities, new equipment and information technology, more and better-trained staff.
2 *Redesign*: services delivered in radically different ways with a much greater use of clinical networks to co-ordinate services around the patient.
3 *Respect*: a culture of mutual respect between politicians and the NHS, between different groups of staff in the service, and, crucially, between the NHS and those who are served by it.

The five rules:

1 See things through the patients' eyes.
2 Find a better way of doing things.
3 Look at the whole picture.
4 Give front line staff the time and the tools to tackle the problems.
5 Take small steps as well as big leaps.

Significant achievements were reported by the Agency in the 2003 Annual Review, including:

● over 9 million patients had benefited from continued growth in the number of appointment bookings at a date and time of their own choice;
● 3,000 patients a month had benefited from collaborative action on cancer;
● there were dramatic reductions in the length of time patients waited to be treated in accident and emergency departments.

Agency staff began to work with manufacturing systems engineering concepts, and to adopt expert industrial improvement techniques in healthcare. One example of how manufacturing techniques can be adapted to improve care was in improving patient access. The traditional response to waiting list problems had been to invest in additional staff and equipment. However, analysis showed that the problem in many cases lay not with insufficient resources to meet demand, but with variations in the system caused by the organization and use of existing resources. Healthcare teams were trained to use basic manufacturing principles to improve the flow of patients through the healthcare system, to increase patient throughput, and to match patient demand with service capacity more effectively.

During this phase, the Agency faced several challenges. It had to continue the early entrepreneurial work, but within a framework of defined objectives and growing local improvement capability. It had to build on the successes of the separate programmes, while integrating them into a more coherent and 'joined up' approach. In addition, the government's aim to shift the balance of power in the health service, by devolving resources and decisions closer to the 'front line', significantly affected the Agency's role.

Although the Agency would continue to act as a catalyst for change, with a plan to maintain and expand programmes, there was clearly a need to respond to this shift of power. Partnership agreements with strategic health authorities (the local headquarter teams of the health service) were developed to support individual objectives for modernization, and specific funding, resources, and expertise were committed to each authority. The strategic health authorities were increasingly acting as champions of local change; by 2003, 80 per cent of provider organizations had a director of modernization (or equivalent) compared with only a minority 18 months previously. Local NHS organizations saw modernization as an intrinsic part of what they did. The role of the Agency was shifting from leadership to support.

The PDSA improvement technique: plan–do–study–act

One technique used with consistent success was the PDSA model, which had two components (Langley et al., 1996). The first established the starting point by:

1 setting precise *aims* (what are we trying to accomplish?);
2 defining *measures* that would show whether or not those aims were being met (how will we know that a change is an improvement?);
3 identifying *change concepts* (what can we do to make an improvement?).

The second component adapted Walter Shewart's 'plan, do, check, act' quality improvement technique from the 1970s, now termed 'plan–do–study–act', or PDSA:

Plan   plan the change to be tested or implemented.
Do   carry out the test or change.
Study   study data before and after the change and reflect on what was learned.
Act   plan the next change cycle or plan implementation.

Improvement teams were trained to implement rapid PDSA cycles, testing changes with a small number of clinicians and patients (e.g. one consultant, one clinic), gathering evidence before implementing changes permanently and more widely. If a change was not successful, this was discovered quickly, with no risk, and for little or no cost. If a change was successful, however, there was systematic evidence to demonstrate the gains, thus encouraging widespread local application, and providing data with which to persuade others. Measurement was critical to this approach, to identify progress, to demonstrate improvements, and to establish the sustainability of the gains achieved. Teams were thus asked to identify a small number of measures reflecting their overall aims, where possible relating to patient access, flows, and satisfaction, and to clinical effectiveness, capacity, and demand.

Looking to the future, there was consensus that work should embrace whole systems, including local government and social services. The Agency also had to work closely with the new independent bodies established to regulate healthcare standards, such as the Healthcare Commission (initially the Commission for Healthcare Improvement). The focus of the Agency's activities shifted to reflect this new environment. The Improvement Partnership for Hospitals was established in 2002, and aimed to support every hospital in England to provide 'better care without delay'. Rather than focus on a single specialty, patient, or disease group, as with previous Agency programmes, the improvement partnership initiative sought to capture the lessons from a range of programmes. It developed a macro-level change package that organizations could use to create systemic improvements.

Similarly, in 2004, the Agency published the 'ten high impact changes' which generated the most significant tangible gains, or 'improvement dividend'. This highly influential initiative analysed the 'best practice' advice that all of the Agency teams were providing (NHS Modernisation Agency, 2004b). Through expert panels, literature reviews, and knowledge gleaned from local projects, 10 changes were identified which, if systematically applied by every healthcare organization, would create a step change in performance in terms of patient and staff experience, clinical quality, and value for money. Again, this represented a move from specific local projects to an organization-wide approach to service improvement, with two key aspects. First, it responded to the feedback that the Agency was providing so much advice that it was difficult to identify those changes that would make the biggest corporate difference. Second, it reflected the growing maturity of the NHS as a system with capability for continuous improvement.

The aim of the Agency had always been to 'make modernization mainstream', and to build capacity for improvement on the front line. In early 2004, it was announced that an external review of the Agency would develop recommendations for a successor organization. By the middle of 2004 it was planned that, by April 2005, most existing work would be devolved to local organizations, and that the Agency would be succeeded by a new national centre that would concentrate on innovation and development in healthcare improvement. However, this decision was brought into a wider review process, and in late 2004 it was decided that the Agency, the developing NHS university, and the Leadership Centre would be abolished at the end of June 2005, and would be succeeded in July by a new national organization, the NHS Institute for Innovation and Improvement, which would also incorporate the planned new National Innovation Centre.

Ten high impact changes for service improvement

We know these changes work and we have the evidence to prove it.

1. Treating day surgery (rather than inpatient surgery) as the norm for elective surgery could release nearly half a million inpatient bed days each year.
2. Improving patient flow across the whole NHS by improving access to key diagnostic tests could save 25 million weeks of unnecessary patient waiting time.
3. Managing variation in patient discharge, thereby reducing length of stay, could release 10 per cent of total bed days for other activity.
4. Managing variation in the patient admission process could cut the 70,000 operations cancelled each year for non-clinical reasons by 40 per cent.
5. Avoiding unnecessary follow-ups for patients and providing necessary follow-ups in the right care setting could save half a million appointments in just orthopaedics, ENT, ophthalmology and dermatology.
6. Increasing the reliability of performing therapeutic interventions through a care bundle approach in critical care alone could release approximately 14,000 bed days by reducing length of stay.
7. Applying a systematic approach to care for people with long-term conditions could prevent a quarter of a million emergency admissions to hospital.
8. Improving patient access by reducing the number of queues could reduce the number of additional finished consultant episodes required to hit elective access targets by 165,000.
9. Optimizing patient flow through service bottlenecks using process templates could free up to 15–20 per cent of current capacity to address waiting times.
10. Redesigning and extending roles in line with efficient patient pathways to attract and retain an effective workforce could free up more than 1,500 general practitioners and consultants (whole time equivalents), creating 80,000 extra patient interactions a week.

Source: NHS Modernisation Agency (2004b)

NHS Institute for Innovation and Improvement Mission (December 2005)

To improve health outcomes and raise the quality of delivery in the NHS by accelerating the uptake of proven innovation and improvements in healthcare delivery models and processes, medical products and devices, and healthcare leadership.

We will accomplish this by deploying innovation and improvement that has direct impact on:

● improving health outcomes across the NHS;
● improving the operating performance of the health service, both quality and cost;
● building capability and change capacity in the health service.

The NHS Institute was formed, as a special health authority with trading company capability, with a first-year budget of £80 million, and a quota of around 150 staff (including some who were previously with the Agency, the NHS university, and the Leadership Centre). This was seen as heralding a new era of improvement and change for the health service in England. The Institute's mission was to support the health service and its workforce in accelerating the provision of world-class healthcare for patients and the public by encouraging innovation and developing front line capability. In particular, the Institute was to:

- work closely with clinicians, healthcare organizations, patients, the public, academics, and industry, in Britain and worldwide, to identify best practice;
- develop the capability of the health service for transformation, technology and product innovation, leadership development, and learning;
- support the rapid adoption and spread of new ideas by providing guidance on practical change ideas and ways to facilitate local, safe implementation;
- promote a culture of innovation and lifelong learning for all staff.

This small national body was to source, field-test, and share innovative practices and improvement techniques that had been refined to ensure ease of application in healthcare organizations. The core purpose was 'innovation for improvement'.

The story of the birth and demise of the Agency and the creation of the NHS Institute demonstrate the dynamic and emergent nature of the contemporary backdrop to healthcare improvement. National bodies such as these must clearly both influence and evolve with the wider system so that they are perceived to be constantly at the leading edge, relevant, and adding value to the provision of care locally. Commissioning and championing the kind of effective 'real-time' research that was the hallmark of the Research into Practice team were important levers in this mission.

Research into Practice

Why was the Research into Practice team formed? Influencing healthcare staff to use ideas and knowledge generated by others was fundamental to meeting the aims of *The NHS Plan*. However, the local uptake of good ideas developed elsewhere in the service was at best varied and at worst poor. The spread of improved practices from the early stages of the first two major national improvement programmes, the National Booking Programme and the Cancer Services Collaborative, was patchy. In addition, an evaluation of the first wave of the booking programme demonstrated that a third of the participating organizations were not able to sustain their improvements, 'slipping back' to previous performance levels once the pilot phase of the initiative was over (Ham *et al.*, 2002). There was a need to understand the factors influencing both the sustainability and the spread of service improvements, in order to develop strategies to increase the speed and extent of this spread, and to hold on to the gains achieved. The aims of the research conducted by the team, therefore, were:

- to inform national improvement programmes;
- to contribute to the growing body of theory on sustainability and spread;
- to provide practitioners with useful models and tools.

The Research into Practice team was thus established within the Agency in 2001, to explore the issues of sustainability and spread in depth. The name 'Research into Practice' reflects the team's rationale and purpose: to conduct research and to produce findings that could be used by the leaders of the national programmes studied and healthcare staff at local levels throughout the service. In other words:

- researching healthcare practice to identify factors influencing how change is sustained and spread;
- working in partnership with sponsors so that the research was meaningful and useful to healthcare practitioners.

In contrast with a traditional research unit, the team worked in close partnership with sponsors, to ensure that the research findings would be relevant. In addition, the aim was to be 'quick and clean', to conduct research and share findings within short timescales, maintaining high research standards, assisted by academic partnership with a local university. Researchers recruited to the team combined qualitative research skills with clinical experience. It is also important to note that this research was carried out in an organizational context characterized by significant ongoing changes in working practices, and that this had major implications for research aims and methods (see Chapter 14).

Being positioned in the Agency, and part-funded but not directly employed by the programmes participating in the research, the team was able to develop partnerships with sponsors while maintaining objectivity. This enabled the work to be planned, conducted, and fed back with minimum delay, and in the context of a rapidly changing environment. Findings were also available to influence the development of other national initiatives. This unique 'socially distributed' model allowed relationships between researchers, and research sponsors and users, to develop in a manner not possible with traditional academic research (Ferlie and Wood, 2003). In contrast, as the team worked with those service improvement programmes, as well as studying them, dissemination was an integral component of the research plan. Dash *et al.* (2003) argue that opportunities to generate research that can feed into service planning and improvement have not been fully exploited. The Research into Practice experience demonstrates the benefits, and challenges, in this regard (see Chapter 14).

The research approach was primarily qualitative, as process issues (why does this happen? how can this be increased?) are not best understood using conventional quantitative variance-based approaches (Murphy *et al.*, 1998). The team findings were thus rich, descriptive, and explanatory, often confirming and reinforcing the anecdotal experience of those involved in service improvement programmes, as well as available quantitative data. Although the team's initial focus concerned the booking and cancer collaborative initiatives, other Agency programmes commissioned research and evaluation projects from the team, including:

- Improvement Partnership for Hospitals
- Emergency Services Collaborative 'see and treat' initiative
- Health and Social Care Awards Programme
- Federation of Older People's Collaborative Programme
- Osprey Programme
- Orthopaedics Collaborative.

These additional, and unanticipated, commissions expanded the scope of the team's work, and team membership grew in 2003 from four (3.2 whole-time equivalents) to six (5.4) core researchers, with funding from the Agency programmes requesting the team's services.

The team's work identified that a significant number of factors can influence the sustainability and spread of service improvements. These factors interact, are specific to each local context, and can change over time; sustainability and spread are complex interacting processes. The findings were shared through meetings, workshops, and events, in addition to publications and national and international conference presentations. Topics of particular interest to the programmes studied included understanding and dealing with scepticism (Gollop *et al.*, 2004), the significance of teamworking (Gollop, 2003), the importance of leadership at all levels (Neath, 2004a), and engaging staff in service improvement (Research into Practice, 2004).

As a result, the team's work, disseminated through over 20 reports, influenced the implementation strategies of the various service improvement programmes through:

- providing robust evidence of issues about which programme leaders were already informally aware through their own communication channels;
- explaining variations in practice in terms of the sustainability and spread of service improvements;
- raising the awareness of programme leaders to new issues influencing sustainability and spread;
- making recommendations for action based on the findings.

Conclusions

As the health service went through radical changes in organization structure and culture from 2000 to 2005, the scale, focus, and scope of national efforts to support service improvement reflected these changes. The Agency was created to meet the needs of the service, particularly with respect to achieving targets and learning how to improve services, and grew to become a significant driver of national improvement programmes. As the service moved resources and responsibility to a local level, the Agency changed accordingly, downsizing significantly, and ultimately closing in mid-2005. The creation of the NHS Institute for Innovation and Improvement, to design but not to implement innovations and improvements, saw the beginning of a new phase in the development of the wider healthcare improvement system. The implementation strategies of several national improvement initiatives were positively influenced by outputs from the team's collaborative research approach. The model of working developed by the Research into Practice team was thus an effective method for informing and for influencing the rapidly changing service improvement agenda. The advantages and limitations of this approach are explored in Chapter 14.

Critical debates

1 The NHS Modernisation Agency was a pivotal component in the change strategy for implementing *The NHS Plan*. For a large public sector organization, like the health service, what are likely to be the main benefits of, and challenges facing, a central organization development agency responsible for promoting, supporting, and implementing major changes at national and local levels?

2 The research team studying change from inside the organization has several advantages compared with an externally based team. What are these advantages, and what difficulties might such a team face? In what ways would those advantages and challenges be influenced by the scale (national or local), pace (rapid or evolutionary), and mix (similar or varied) of the organizational changes involved?

3 From the perspective of those working in the health service 'front line', how might views differ between a national body responsible only for identifying, developing, and *disseminating* innovative methods for service improvements, on the one hand, and one responsible for developing, leading, supporting, and *implementing* those changes, on the other? Which approach, in the medium to long term, would you expect to be more likely to succeed in effectively sustaining and more rapidly spreading best practice, and why?

2 Improvement evaporation: why do successful changes decay?

David A. Buchanan and Louise Fitzgerald

Chapter aims

1 To introduce the problems of sustaining organizational change, managing decay, preventing the evaporation of improvements.
2 To explore research evidence concerning the sustainability of organizational change.
3 To consider the theoretical and practical implications for sustaining changes in the professional organization.

Key point summary

- Keeping things as they are is traditionally seen as an organizational problem to be resolved, not a condition to be achieved. As a result, sustainability has attracted less research attention.
- The ability to sustain new working methods and associated performance improvements has now become a strategic imperative for many organizations concerned with improvement evaporation and initiative decay.
- Sustainability can be defined in different ways in relation to work methods, goals, or continuous improvement, over differing timescales. The definition and timing that matter are those applicable to a given organizational setting.
- In some circumstances, shifts in context can make work methods and goals obsolete, and sustaining one approach may inhibit staff development and the implementation of other new ideas. It can be appropriate to allow or to encourage some change to decay.
- The sustainability or decay of organizational change is influenced by several factors at different levels of analysis: individual, managerial, leadership, organizational, financial, cultural, political, processual, contextual, temporal, and the change substance. The influence of these factors, and their interactions, depend on context.
- Organizational processes dependent on the continuing presence of such a range of factors are potentially fragile and vulnerable to decay.

- A focus on the process of sustainability in context is useful in capturing the range of issues which over time affect the sustainability and spread of new working practices.
- The processes of sustainability and spread are interlinked, and narrative explanations exploring path dependency may be helpful in understanding mutual interactions.
- There are no simple prescriptions for managing sustainability. This requires a vigilant diagnostic approach to monitoring the factors which either support or threaten sustainability, and monitoring the timescale over which sustainability should be encouraged.

Improvement evaporation

> Sustainability is when new ways of working and improved outcomes become the norm. Not only have the process and outcome changed, but the thinking and attitudes behind them are fundamentally altered and the systems surrounding them are transformed in support. In other words it has become an integrated or mainstream way of working rather than something 'added on'. As a result, when you look at the process or outcome one year from now or longer, you can see that at a minimum it has not reverted to the old way or old level of performance. Further, it has been able to withstand challenge and variation; it has evolved alongside other changes in the context, and perhaps has actually continued to improve over time.
>
> *Source*: NHS Modernisation Agency (2002b, p.12)

Why do some changes to working practices appear to be irreversible, while others are abandoned? From its inception in 2001, the NHS Modernisation Agency encountered the 'improvement evaporation effect', as new working practices and increased performance levels were not maintained. One of the national initiatives affected was the booking programme (Chapters 6 and 7) where many of the gains of 1999 to 2000 had been 'eroded' by 2001 (Ham *et al.*, 2003). But sustainability is not a new problem, having been famously described by Lewin (1951) as the need to 'refreeze' behaviour once change has taken place.

Sustainability implies that changes are maintained for an appropriate period, or routinized until they reach obsolescence (Greenhalgh *et al.*, 2004). While the evidence suggests that initiative decay is widespread, and not confined to healthcare (Buchanan *et al.*, 1999), the sustainability problem has attracted little attention in healthcare. Most accounts of change focus on implementation at a single site, do not explore diffusion, and do not consider how and why changes are either maintained or decay. There are at least four reasons for this. The first concerns the nature and focus of change theories. Episodic change models describe phases of equilibrium, or relative stability, punctuated by periods of adaptation (Tushman and Romanelli, 1985). Stability is explained either in terms of 'fit' with environment (which is not a problem), or as 'inertia', an absence of activity, a lack of capability, a failure to pay attention to signals. Attention thus focuses on the next punctuation mark. The 'ideal organization' is capable of ongoing adaptation, where 'tendencies to normalization' are undesirable signs of inertia, and change agency is defined in terms of moving and redirecting, rather than stabilizing (Weick and Quinn, 1999). Identifying the mechanisms or 'motors' driving change, Van de Ven and Poole (1995) do not consider how to switch those motors off.

A change toward a higher level of group performance is frequently short lived; after a 'shot in the arm', group life soon returns to the previous level. This indicates that it does not suffice to define the objective of a planned change in group performance as the reaching of a different level. Permanency of the new level, or permanency for a desired period, should be included in the objective. A successful change therefore includes three aspects: unfreezing (if necessary) the present level L^1, moving to the new level L^2, and freezing group life on the new level. Since any level is determined by a force field, permanency implies that the new force field is made relatively secure against change.

Source: Lewin (1951, pp.228–229)

Second, researching change is more interesting than studying stability, and for most managers, the next initiative promises more career value than continuing with routine operations. Third, while implementation is studied over relatively brief periods, sustainability requires longitudinal methods and resources to which many researchers do not have access. Finally, in a turbulent environment, organization structures, cultures, and practices that remain static are regarded as legitimate targets for change. Sustainability has traditionally been regarded, not as a condition to be achieved, but as a problem to be solved.

Sustainability can be defined in various ways (Figure 2.1). This may involve the stability of work methods, or the consistent achievement of goals independent of the methods used. It may also be defined in terms of the pursuit of a trajectory of changes generating performance improvements beyond initial expectations. At one end of this spectrum, maintaining methods and goals suggests a static view. A focus on ongoing development implies a dynamic perspective. Consequently, it is more helpful to regard the term 'sustainability', not as a concept with one precise meaning, but as a label for a broad category of problems.

stable work methods   consistent goal achievement   ongoing development

Figure 2.1 *The sustainability continuum*

Sustainability may not always be desirable. Efforts to sustain changes, even where they have been successful, may be counter-productive, in at least three ways. First, working practices, procedures, outcomes, and lines of development can be rendered obsolete by changes in the wider organizational or social context. Second, a focus on sustaining current practices, however effective they may appear, may block further and more significant development. Third, a desire to sustain existing practices may prevent staff from acquiring valuable new skills and experience, perhaps reducing morale, and inhibiting further improvements in performance. These observations suggest a dynamic perspective, involving continuous improvement. However, that is what many organizations sought to achieve during the 1990s, generating what some commentators labelled 'initiative fatigue' (Morgan, 2001). Continuous change may only be effective where the timing and pace are carefully phased (Abrahamson, 2000; Meyerson, 2001). The central question may thus concern the sustainability of particular methods for periods appropriate in a given context.

This chapter summarizes seven approaches to understanding sustainability (Buchanan *et al.*, 2005). While these accounts each approach the problem from a different perspective, based on evidence from sectors other than healthcare, they share a view of sustainability as an ongoing process linked with the process of spread. The contributions outlined are:

1 the dance of change;
2 anchoring change;
3 institutionalizing change;
4 sustaining best practice;
5 sustaining total quality management;
6 momentum busters;
7 the process of sustainability in context.

For each contribution, factors influencing sustainability are identified. Then, drawing on a processual perspective, these factors are used to develop a provisional process model of sustainability, to inform the interpretation of research evidence.

The dance of change

Concern with the problem of sustainability first arose in Lewin's (1951) work on unfreezing, moving, and refreezing behaviour change. For Lewin, the main freezing mechanism was group decision. His examples include changing the habits of housewives to using fresh instead of evaporated milk, changing baby feeding practices to using more orange juice and cod liver oil, and changing the styles of recreational leaders from autocratic to democratic. Other freezing methods concern the commitment of individuals to decisions in which they have taken part, and the desire to follow group norms, which 'stabilize the individual conduct on the new group level'. Lewin emphasized that group decision alone would not guarantee the permanence of change, and that other factors could be important in many cases.

Lewin's thinking is reflected in the work of Senge *et al.* (1999, p.10; Senge and Kaeufer, 2000) who argue that in order to sustain change, it is necessary to understand 'growth processes' and 'the forces and challenges that impede progress'. The interplay between growth and limiting forces is described as 'the dance of change', which echoes Lewin's (1951, p.204) concept of the 'force field'. Sustainability in this perspective is regarded, not as a discrete phase, but as one element in an extended process involving implementation, diffusion, and continuous improvement.

This perspective argues that sustainability is dependent on the following factors:

individual   those involved are committed to group decisions and norms, and accept that fear is a natural response and a learning opportunity

managerial   managers tackle the 'difficult' and 'high-risk' problems, they accept changes to their own behaviour, and they address the underlying causes of problems

cultural   change has 'mainstream' or 'cult' status, and there is a perceived need to go beyond measures and assess how the needs of multiple stakeholders are met

processual   sustainability is regarded as one stage in an extended process of implementation, spread, and development

Anchoring change

Kotter (1995) asks why corporate transformations fail, and suggests why change is not sustained. Step 7 in his model involves 'consolidating improvements', and error 7 is 'declaring victory too soon', which can kill momentum. Changes must become part of the corporate culture, which he argues can take up to 10 years: 'new approaches are fragile and subject to regression'. Momentum is thus lost when 'the urgency level is not intense enough, the guiding coalition is not powerful enough, and the vision is not clear enough' (p.66).

Step 8 involves 'institutionalizing new approaches', and error 8 concerns the failure to anchor change: 'Until new behaviours are rooted in social norms and shared values, they are subject to degradation as soon as the pressure for change is removed' (p.67). Anchoring has two dimensions. The first concerns demonstrating the links between changes in behaviour and improvements in performance. The second concerns ensuring that 'the next generation of management really does personify the new approach' (p.67). Successors must continue to champion the changes of their predecessors, or the change effort degrades.

This perspective argues that sustainability is dependent on the following factors:

managerial   new managers champion the initiatives of their predecessors

leadership   the vision is clear

cultural   there is a sense of urgency about change, new behaviours are rooted in social norms and values, and the links to performance are clear

political   the guiding coalition is powerful enough to maintain momentum

temporal   time has been allowed for change to become part of the culture

Institutionalizing change

Jacobs (2002) observes that most change efforts do not persist, and should ideally last until goals have been achieved. Institutionalization, as one element in a complex causal chain, is defined as change that has 'relative endurance' and 'staying power over a length of time' (p.178). His model first identifies two sets of factors, concerning characteristics of the organization and of the intervention. The former include compatibility of change with the organization, stability of the social context, and trade union agreement. Intervention properties include goal specificity, control mechanisms, the organizational level targeted by the change, internal support, and change champions. These sets of factors in turn affect institutionalization processes, which include training, meeting reward expectations, the further spread of new ideas, and monitoring and control processes. Where institutionalization is effective, the desired outcomes are likely to be achieved.

This model suggests that decay is caused by inadequate attention to any combination of the organization or intervention characteristics, or institutionalization processes. To ensure long-term success, institutionalization processes require as much attention as the other parts of the framework, if not more so.

This perspective argues that sustainability is dependent on the following factors:

substantial changes are consistent with and 'fit' the organization

individual competence, commitment to change, and rewards are adequate

leadership goals are clear, consistent, stable, and challenging

processual the change has champions, internal support, and monitoring and control mechanisms, and diffusion beyond first implementation

contextual there is social stability and trade union agreement

Sustaining best practice

Rimmer *et al.* (1996) studied 42 Australian firms to establish why some organizations adopt and sustain 'best practice', while others do not (making this also a study of spread or diffusion). Best practice concerned the integration of strategy, team-based structures, new technology, process improvement, measurement and control, people management, external linkages, change leadership, and empowerment. Arguing that change is a complex and pluralistic political process, they conclude that sustainability depends on social convention:

> Given the importance of its cultural ingredients, we have to rate the chances of success for any particular experiment largely in terms of whether it is swimming with or against the tide of popular opinion within corporate elites and society more generally.
>
> (Rimmer *et al.*, 1996, p.216)

Interestingly, Shortell *et al.* (1998) also found that late adopters of quality improvement in healthcare were concerned with their external image and credibility, because it was 'the right thing to do'. From a study of American banks, Fox-Wolfgramm and Boal (1998) conclude that organizational image and identity are stronger forces for change than success.

Rimmer's model identifies four environmental forces influencing sustainability.

1 *Capital markets*: investments in human resources tend to be undervalued, relative to initiatives with visible impact on profitability, and management is unlikely to sustain investment not affecting share prices.
2 *Corporate governance*: dominant stakeholders can exclude management and employees from decision making, and take the organization culture in other directions.
3 *Government policy*: labour relations and legislation can influence management–employee partnerships.
4 *Institutional infrastructure*: where provision for public goods such as training is weak, 'free-riding' by competitors is encouraged, and investment is discouraged.

The balance of costs and benefits is also significant. Best practice is difficult to value, but costs arise in several areas: consultants, benchmarking travel, equipment, installation downtime, training, customer and competitor surveys, redundancies, management time. There are 'twin peaks' in the typical revenue curve. The first comes with cost reductions from obvious economies and the 'novelty effect'. However, after those 'easy gains', the improvement rate can slow down, and does not recover unless the best practice core elements are implemented. Rimmer *et al.* (1996, p.219) conclude that the problem here is 'winning the time, especially during periods when it is perceived that costs exceed benefits – a period of uncertain duration, when best practice may be discontinued as not cost-effective'.

This perspective argues that sustainability is dependent on the following factors:

substantial   change is consistent with competitive strategy

managerial   a focus on long-term goals considers a range of benefits

cultural   the climate is receptive, changes are consistent with management values, and perceived benefits outweigh perceived costs

financial   change contributes to key performance measures, and the perceived benefits over time are greater than the perceived costs

political   change has the support of dominant stakeholders who involve others in decisions, and powerful coalitions are supported by external networks

contextual   change is consistent with social norms and popular opinion, legislation encourages management–employee partnership, there is good public training provision

temporal   time has been allowed to demonstrate benefits beyond
                    initial easy gains

Sustaining total quality management

Dale and colleagues studied the sustainability of total quality management
in manufacturing (Dale *et al.*, 1997a; 1997b; 1999; Kemp *et al.*, 1997).
They define sustainability as 'maintaining a process of quality
improvement', combining: commitment and leadership, planning and
organization, improvement techniques, education and training, employee
involvement, teamwork, performance measurement and feedback, and
culture change (Dale *et al.*, 1999, p.370). They studied 12 manufacturing
sites in six organizations, and developed a sustainability audit based on five
sets of factors.

External and internal environment

External factors include the behaviour of competitors and issues in
recruiting, developing, and retaining skilled employees. Problems there can
destabilize change initiatives. Three internal factors are also significant,
including meeting customer requirements; willingness to invest in new
equipment, education, and training; and addressing 'the fear factor', or
uncertainty about the future, which leads to reactive, short-term decision
making.

Management style

The first factor in this category is industrial relations. Managers and staff
must share the same objectives, but the transition to shared goals can be
problematic where there is adversarial collective bargaining. A second
factor is management–worker relationships. Quality management should
develop high-trust, high-discretion relationships through empowerment
and teamwork. A traditional autocratic management style tends to reinforce
a low-trust, low-discretion climate which is damaging to sustainability.

Policies

An organization's policies should support quality goals. Human resource
policies, for example, can undermine teamwork through a rewards system
focusing on individual contributions. The complexity and transparency

of salary structures can contribute to perceived discrimination in relation to effort and reward, stifling initiative and commitment. Inconsistent appraisal schemes can have a similar effect, as can discrimination between staff levels on sickness and leave benefits. Finance policies that encourage short-term decision making inhibit the pursuit of longer-term goals. Maintenance policies focusing on cost reduction, rather than planned maintenance, affect equipment performance. Manufacturing policies which focus on output, rather than on quality and customer satisfaction, can also damage sustainability, having a detrimental effect on training, which comes to be seen as a waste of time, as are improvement team meetings in similar circumstances.

Organization structure

There are five factors in this category. First, the roles of those responsible for change should be clear. Second, barriers between departments, functions and shifts can be obstacles to cross-functional co-operation. These barriers are often a legacy of established hierarchies, which lead to empire building and a lack of understanding of other sections. Third, communications are significant, particularly methods by which achievements are recognized. Fourth, high dependence on key people in specialized roles can put changes at risk if they leave, so job flexibility and staff cover are significant. In addition, flexibility regarding staff numbers and task allocation is important in responding to changing circumstances. Without that flexibility, a system under strain may abandon recent initiatives. Fifth, quality initiatives rely on a team leader style of supervision, and not on a traditional autocratic supervisory role.

Process of change

This category includes seven dimensions. First, adequacy of the infrastructure in terms of steering committee, facilitators, and problem-solving procedures. Second, training to meet individual and organizational needs. Third, effective teamwork and support mechanisms. Fourth, procedures 'to counteract problems and abnormalities'; ability of staff to understand procedures; willingness of management to respond to suggestions for improvement. Fifth, effectiveness of the quality management system and the need to ensure that quality manual and procedure owners seek continuous improvements. Sixth, a planned approach to applying tools and techniques, and to integrate them with routine operations. Finally, the degree of confidence in top management. Confidence is damaged by lack of success, by an inability to complete projects, by inconsistency between promises and actions, by management changes, and by conflicting priorities which suggest that improvement is no longer important. Dale *et al.* (1999, p.369) conclude that 8 to 10 years may be required to embed quality principles, practices, systems, attitudes, values, and culture, reinforcing the view that sustaining change of this complexity can be as difficult as initial implementation, if not more so.

This perspective argues that sustainability is dependent on the following factors:

individual
fear and uncertainty about the future are absent, attitudes towards innovation and change are welcoming

managerial
management style encourages high-trust relationships, managers are open to suggestions, improvement tools and techniques are used in a planned and integrated way

leadership
senior figures enjoy staff confidence due to their success, consistency, and durable priorities

organizational
reward and appraisal systems are transparent and consistent; staff are skilled, flexible, and responsive to pressure; training meets individual and organizational needs; personnel, finance, maintenance, and operational policies encourage change; structural barriers to cross-functional collaboration are absent; there are mechanisms for recognizing achievement and procedures for monitoring problems

cultural
employees have shared goals, continuous improvement is a priority, teamworking is encouraged

processual
responsibilities for change implementation are clear, strong improvement infrastructure with steering committee, facilitators, and problem solving

contextual
change is an appropriate competitive response, meeting customer requirements; market allows recruitment and retention of skilled staff

Momentum busters

Reisner (2002) analyses the experience of the United States Postal Service (a large public sector bureaucracy) which, during the 1990s, 'transformed itself from the butt of sitcom jokes into a profitable and efficient enterprise' (p.45). By 2001, however, morale and performance were low, and losses were predicted. Why was the transformation not sustained? Reisner (Vice-President for Strategic Planning) blames three 'momentum busters': the indifference of senior managers who regarded aspects of the strategy as a 'distraction'; resistance from trade unions whose role had been marginalized; and a budget process which favoured traditional initiatives over innovations. Innovation was also stifled by governance constraints. The Postal Service could not have initiated what a competitor (UPS) achieved without a prior hearing before the Postal Rate Commission, and structural changes would have required Congressional approval. The situation was exacerbated by a weak economy, problems with e-commerce, and terrorist assaults on the US Postal Service.

This perspective argues that sustainability is dependent on the following factors:

leadership   there is top management commitment and support for change

organizational   budget approval processes welcome innovation, and decision processes are rapid and flexible

contextual   there is trade union support and no external threats or distractions

The process of sustainability in context

While defining and approaching the concept of sustainability in different ways, these commentators share a view of sustainability as a component or phase in a sequence of events. This event sequence is subject to influence from a range of factors within the organization, and by social, economic, commercial, legislative, and political pressures arising in the wider external context. These observations imply a processual–contextual view of change and sustainability, although none of the contributions reviewed explicitly adopts this perspective.

Processual–contextual perspectives have been influenced by the work of Pettigrew (1985; Pettigrew *et al.*, 2001) who cautions against looking for single causes and simple explanations, pointing to the many factors, individual, group, social, organizational, and political, which influence the nature, process, and outcomes of change. Change is an 'untidy cocktail' of rational decisions, mixed with competing perceptions, stimulated by visionary leadership, spiced with 'power plays' and attempts to build coalitions behind ideas. Pettigrew argues that the focus of analysis should lie with *the process of change in context*. This involves paying attention to the flow of events, and not considering change as static or time-bounded. This also involves considering both the local and the wider context of change, and not thinking narrowly in terms of one particular location.

For our purposes, *the process of sustainability in context* is a useful unit of analysis. Context has three dimensions. The internal context includes the organization structure and culture, patterns of behaviour, and attitudes which may be more or less receptive to change (Pettigrew *et al.*, 1992). The *external context* includes customer demands, competitor behaviour, and economic conditions, which create opportunities and threats to be exploited or addressed. *Past and current events* also condition current and future thinking. It is easy to forget how previous events have shaped current perceptions and responses. It is also easy to forget continuities, to ignore aspects of the past which have not changed and which are still with us, and which again condition current thinking.

In his seminal study of the chemicals company ICI, Pettigrew (1985) proposes a four-stage model of strategic change. The first two stages involve problem-sensing and developing concern with the status quo, followed by acknowledgement of the problems to be tackled. The two final stages concern planning and acting, and 'stabilization'. These stages can be lengthy and iterative and do not always follow that sequence. The evidence suggests that the triggers of strategic change include external events and trends, 'insubordinate minorities' who mobilize an energetic 'caucus of concern', and senior managerial leadership.

This approach is based on the concept of legitimacy, for 'dominating ideas', 'frameworks of thought', 'definitions of core issues', 'concepts of reality', 'new rationalities and ideas', and 'strategic frames'. The management task, therefore, concerns 'the way you tell it' or, more accurately, 'the way you *sell* it' to organization members, to legitimize change proposals in the face of competing ideas, and to gain consent and compliance. Management must establish legitimacy for courses of action, while delegitimizing opponents' views. It is the persistence of those dominating ideas which guarantees sustainability. Pettigrew argues that the management of change is thus equated with 'the management of meaning', with symbolic attempts to establish the credibility of particular definitions of problems and solutions.

Pettigrew (1985) found that, in ICI, continuity was more evident than change, with episodes of change activity from 1960 to 1964, from 1970 to 1972, and from 1980 to 1984. The intervening periods are described as 'occasions for implementing and stabilizing changes' (p.447). There were two main threats to sustainability. The first concerned external events prompting another 'insubordinate minority' (often senior management) to challenge existing thinking. The second concerned loss of continuity of leadership. Pettigrew describes how change in the Agricultural and Petrochemicals Divisions regressed with the departure of senior managers. These cases, Pettigrew concludes, 'indicate the importance of strong, persistent, and continuing leadership' (p.454). As such threats to the sustainability of change are potentially unavoidable, a more realistic goal is 'periodic stabilization'.

The processual perspective has been developed by Dawson (1994; 1996; 2003a). His approach 'is based on the assumption that companies continuously move in and out of many different states, often concurrently, during the history of one or a number of organizational change initiatives' (Dawson, 2003b, p.41). He also argues that, to understand this process, we need to consider the organization's context, the substance of change, the tasks, activities, decisions, timing, and sequencing of the transition process, political activity within and external to the organization, and the interactions between these sets of issues. A processual perspective thus appears to offer a useful lens through which to examine sustainability, by focusing on the flow of events in a wider spatial, temporal, and political context. This perspective thus identifies seven categories of influence on sustainability:

substantial   the scale of change will not consolidate opposition, and the change is perceived as central to performance and survival

managerial   management plans and ideas are seen as credible and legitimate

leadership   leadership is strong and persistent

political   challenges to management have been defeated as lacking credibility

processual   a period of relative calm has allowed management to stabilize change

contextual   external stability raises no challenges to the status quo

temporal   do the timing, sequencing, and history of the change process contribute to sustainability?

Implications: theory and practice

The process of sustaining organizational change thus depends on a range of factors, at different levels of analysis. In this section, we explore primarily the theoretical implications of this observation. The practical implications for managing sustainability are considered briefly, and we return to these issues in Chapter 13, in the light of empirical evidence.

Implications for theory

Explanations for the sustainability, or decay, of change thus turn on the presence or absence of the factors summarized in Table 2.1. Is change consistent with organizational goals, or not? Are people committed and competent or not? Are management ideas and style credible and open or not ? Has leadership established a clear and consistent vision or not? A high 'yes' count predicts sustainability, and a 'no' count predicts decay. A process dependent on the presence of such a wide range of issues is clearly vulnerable, leading to the conclusion that sustainability is fragile, and that decay is more probable (as Kotter, 1995, p.66, argues). In their evaluation of the national booking programme, Ham et al. (2003, p.433) emphasize the interplay of the numerous factors affecting implementation, concluding that: 'To achieve substantial change that can be sustained over time requires as many of the conditions favourable to quality improvement as possible.'

This line of reasoning has limitations. First, it says nothing about the relative factor weightings. Do policies, procedures, systems, and structures have more influence than individual commitment and competencies? Do the shared beliefs, perceptions, norms, and values of the organization culture outweigh stakeholder and coalition power? Or do the visions, goals, and

Table 2.1 *Factors affecting sustainability*

Factor	Sustainability influences
substantial	scale of change, fit with organization
individual	commitment, competencies, emotions, expectations
managerial	style, approach, preferences, behaviours
leadership	vision, values, purpose, goals, challenges
organizational	policies, mechanisms, procedures, systems, structures
financial	contribution, balance of costs and benefits
cultural	shared beliefs, perceptions, norms, values, priorities
political	stakeholder and coalition power and influence
processual	implementation methods, project management structures
contextual	external conditions, stability, threats, wider social norms
temporal	timing, pacing, flow of events

challenges set by leadership sweep other obstacles aside? Second, this approach does not reveal interactions between those sets of factors; the change substance, for example, can threaten to upset the existing balance of power among stakeholders, triggering political behaviour to shift that balance, to gain the commitment of particular individuals. Third, 'context' is seen here as another cluster of factors to consider. However, in a processual perspective, answers to questions about factor weights and interactive effects invariably begin with 'it depends on the context', which can influence, and in turn be shaped by, aspects of the organizational change process. While a rapid and politically acrimonious series of top team changes may be critical in one setting, a combination of contextual, structural, and individual issues may be more relevant to sustainability in an organization that has not had that traumatic experience. With different histories, a management style that elicits enthusiastic commitment in one setting can trigger cynicism and resentment in another.

A processual perspective has three features which address those limitations.

- Processual accounts rely on *narrative explanations* (Langley, 1999). A narrative provides the necessary broad frame of reference, gives coherence to a complex sequence of events, recognizes the status of qualitative evidence, and captures the range of factors leading to observed outcomes. Those factors may suggest a 'cumulative effects' explanation, where pressures build up to produce the outcome, or a 'conjunctural causality' explanation, where a particular combination of factors supports the outcome of concern. Process narratives contrast with traditional variance explanations which rely on establishing the quantifiable and enduring impact of independent variables on dependent variables (Mohr, 1982).
- Processual accounts recognize the *significance of context*. The same change initiative may lead to different sets of outcomes in organizational settings which differ with respect to their general histories, past experiences of change, and current structures. Process explanations generalize beyond individual cases, through accumulating comparable instances of similar event sequences (Abbott, 1990), through analytical generalization informing theory (Tsoukas, 1989), and through naturalistic generalization in which readers make links to their own experience (Stake, 1994).
- Processual accounts assume *path dependency*, which means that current conditions can be explained partly in terms of the events which led up to them (Poole *et al.*, 2000). This perspective explores critical junctures triggering patterns of action, the decisions of key actors over time, and patterns of response (positive and critical) to those decisions. Path dependency also assumes that temporal factors (timing, sequencing, pacing) are significant explanatory factors contributing to outcomes.

We will return to those theoretical concerns in Chapter 12. Meanwhile, a simple tabulation of factors is a useful first step. But those factors just identify the context, set the stage, provide the cast of characters, establish motives, trigger the action, generate the plot, define the pace, shape decisions, condition responses, produce outcomes, trigger further action. In relation to processes of sustainability and decay, Figure 2.2 presents a provisional model of this process, the possible event sequence, the elements of the narrative.

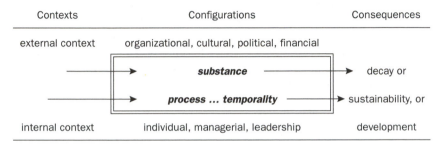

Figure 2.2 *The process of sustainability in context*

This model first suggests that change is influenced by events beyond the organization's boundaries. A turbulent external context, for example, may jeopardize attempts to stabilize internal arrangements, or to maintain a constant programme of change (Ansoff, 1997). Change is also influenced by the internal context, by past events, and by anticipated futures. Another dimension of internal context, discussed in Chapter 3, is receptiveness to change (Pettigrew *et al.*, 1992). The issues at the heart of this model are:

substance the change itself, centrality to organizational performance, perceived as acceptable or threatening to key stakeholders

process implementation structures and methods, involvement of those affected

temporality timing, pacing, and sequencing of events, rush or delay, time to adapt

The narrative unfolds, in a given context, in relation to a particular change, implemented in a particular manner, following a sequence in which timing and pacing are significant, leading to a series of outcomes conditioned by organizational, cultural, financial, political, individual, managerial, and leadership issues. This model is just a guide, for research, for management action to safeguard sustainability, and to themes emerging in the following chapters.

This discussion implies that sustainability and spread are independent. But these processes are linked, to the degree that respondents in this research programme had difficulty making a distinction. One set of issues linking these phenomena concerns social convention, popular opinion. As we have seen, change is more likely to be sustained where it is perceived to be 'swimming with' rather than against current practice, and contributes to an organization's external image. This argument again reverses the assumption that spread precedes sustainability. Ideas that do not have widespread support, that are unlikely to be sustained, or that are not sustained by early adopters are unlikely to spread elsewhere. There are also practical linkages. The manner in which change is spread can influence the degree to which change will be sustained. For example, changes which are introduced hastily, without staff involvement and adequate training time, may be quickly abandoned.

The concept of path dependency allows us to explore these issues further. One typical event sequence might involve implementation at first location, spread to other locations, then sustaining those practices for an appropriate period. An alternative event sequence concerns implementation at first location, demonstration of sustainability at that site, followed by spread to a limited set of other locations, which may or may not demonstrate sustainability, followed by wider spread (or not) depending on prior experience. The research findings suggest that 'implement, spread, sustain' relies on a particular combination of contextual, change substance, and organizational factors. The sequence of 'implement, sustain, spread some, demonstrate sustainability, spread some more' may be more typical.

Implications for practice

No simple prescription for managing sustainability emerges from this account. Any process that is dependent on the continuing presence of such a diverse range of factors is potentially at risk. It is therefore appropriate to recommend strategies that are sensitive to complexity, ambiguity, and uncertainty, and to the range of supportive and damaging issues and stakeholders. It is also evident that sustainability depends on a number of 'externalities', beyond direct management control, but which may need to be addressed in some manner. These observations suggest a diagnostic approach and constant vigilance, scanning for potential threats to sustainability, and bolstering supports, while monitoring the desirability of decay. We will return to the practical implications of the studies reported here in Chapter 13.

Where appropriate, therefore, the questions that chapters in Part II will seek to answer include:

- Under what conditions are changes more likely to be sustained or to decay?
- In what ways might circumstances, issues, and factors accumulate, leading either to sustainability or to decay?
- Are there particular combinations, or types of combinations, of factors that are more likely to lead to sustainability or decay?
- What typical event sequences, or narratives, are suggested by the evidence to explain sustainability and decay?

Critical debates

1 Given the pace of change, new working practices, procedures, policies, structures, and processes are bound to become obsolete faster than they might have done in the past. In this kind of rapidly shifting context, to what extent are efforts to sustain organizational changes valuable or doomed?

2 In what ways do narrative explanations for the process and outcomes of organizational changes differ from conventional explanations based on independent and dependent variables? For explaining organizational processes, what are the strengths and limitations of narrative accounts?

3 If the sustainability of organizational change relies on such a broad range of factors, under 11 main headings, what are the practical managerial implications for sustaining major changes in the complex, professional, organizational setting of public sector healthcare?

3 The best practices puzzle: why are new methods contained and not spread?

David A. Buchanan and Louise Fitzgerald

Chapter aims

1 To introduce the problem of spreading organizational change and innovation.
2 To explore theory and evidence concerning the diffusion of change and innovation.
3 To consider the theoretical and practical implications for spreading desirable changes.

Key point summary

- The problem of spreading ideas, the 'best practices puzzle', is not new, but has acquired a new urgency in the context of healthcare modernization.
- While rapid spread of effective new working practices is in principle desirable, this can have damaging implications; slow diffusion can be beneficial in many contexts.
- There are different types of innovation. We are concerned with a combination of sustaining and disruptive operational innovations.
- Innovations are more attractive to potential adopters where they are clearly advantageous, compatible, understandable, observable, testable, and adaptable.
- The source, credibility, and non-threatening nature of evidence supporting a new idea can be as important to adopters as the quality of the evidence.
- Individual behaviour change can be a protracted process, passing through the stages of precontemplation, contemplation, action, maintenance, and possibly relapse.
- Diffusion of new ideas depends initially on innovators and early adopters, and subsequently on how quickly the early and late majority can be persuaded to shift.
- Formal and informal networks, opinion leaders, and weak ties are important mechanisms for disseminating information about new ideas.

- New ideas are more likely to be adopted successfully in organizations with an innovative culture, a creative climate, receptiveness to change, and absorptive capacity. Evidence suggests that healthcare is not a context receptive to innovation.
- As a multi-dimensional process that unfolds over time, spread is best understood through a processual perspective that focuses on theoretical narratives, cumulative effects, conjunctural causality, and path dependency, concepts that are also valuable in understanding the linked process of sustainability.

Why contained?

> The history of acceptance of new theories frequently shows the following steps: At first the new idea is treated as pure nonsense, not worth looking at. Then comes a time when a multitude of contradictory objections are raised, such as: the new theory is too fancy, or merely a new terminology; it is not fruitful, or simply wrong. Finally a state is reached when everyone seems to claim that he had always followed this theory. This usually marks the last state before general acceptance.
>
> *Source*: Lewin (1951, p.43)

With sustainability, a related problem facing the Agency in 2001 concerned spreading 'best practice' more widely across the health service. Research has focused on the diffusion of product innovations in pursuit of company profitability, while innovations in working practices in public sector service settings, such as healthcare, have been overlooked. Related terms include adoption, transfer, dissemination, and assimilation of best practice, process redesign, good ideas, new working methods, and so on. In this volume, our usage has three features. First, from the following lists, any combination of terms on the left with terms on the right has the same meaning. The spread of new working methods, the adoption of innovation, and the transfer of best practice, are thus synonymous in the following treatment.

spread	good practice
diffusion	innovation
adoption	best practice
transfer	redesigned processes
dissemination	new ideas
assimilation	new working methods

Second, rather than legislate on one precise definition, we will argue that, as with sustainability, the 'correct' definition of spread or diffusion is the one that applies in the context under analysis. Greenhalgh *et al.* (2004) make a distinction between diffusion (passive spread) and dissemination (planned efforts to stimulate adoption). But in common usage, those terms are interchangeable, and can have different meanings and connotations in different settings, particularly in healthcare. It is inappropriate to reject a term that is locally significant in favour of one that is consistent with an abstract theoretical framework.

Third, also in common with our understanding of sustainability, we will regard spread of best practice, diffusion of innovation, and other similar expressions as convenient labels for a broad category of organizational problems which share common properties, the details of which vary from one setting to another. Those properties relate to a concern that methods, systems, and working practices that are effective in one setting are not being adapted for or used in other settings where they could also be beneficial. The problem is that these new methods remain in use only where they were first implemented, as 'islands of improvement'. The absence of spread was thus another threat to modernization. But this is neither a new nor a 'modern' problem. Describing organizational knowledge that stays in one place and does not spread further as 'sticky', Szulanski (2003) dates 'the best practices puzzle' from the 1970s. The problem of 'containment' is much older than that. Berwick (2003) describes how the treatment for scurvy, identified in 1601, did not become universal practice in the Royal Navy until 1865, over 260 years later. Most healthcare organizations today will not wish to wait that long. A more recent example concerns delay in the use of thrombolytic drugs to treat acute myocardial infarction or heart attack (Ketley and Woods, 1993).

Commentary on organizational change tends to adopt a 'pro-innovation bias' (Robertson *et al.*, 1996), assuming that 'new' must be better. However, the rapid spread of 'good ideas' can be damaging. One good idea may not work as well as even better ideas that have been sidelined. What works in one context may not work well in another. Organizational research has consistently shown that 'best practice' is contingent, that there is no 'one best way'. While some commentators advocate 'accelerated' methods, the rapid spread of new ways of working may not allow staff adequate time to learn new skills. Some rapid changes (such as near-patient testing, reducing the timescale from referral to diagnosis to treatment) can alarm patients. Locock (2001, p.42) argues that:

> Repeating the learning locally – re-inventing the wheel – is not intrinsically wasteful, as sometimes assumed. On the contrary, it can be a vital part of creating a climate for change and gaining ownership, and ensure changes are embedded rather than superficially grafted onto the existing culture.

The interesting, but more complex, questions thus concern the spread of *potentially* valuable methods, at an *appropriate* pace, taking into account the need for *adaptation* to local circumstances.

Star envy and the politics of spread

From his research, Walton (1975, p.21) predicted 'relatively little diffusion of potentially significant restructuring in the workplace'. He followed successful work redesign experiments from the 1960s in eight organizations, including two American, two Canadian, one British, two Norwegian, and one Swedish. There was little or no diffusion in seven companies, and only at Volvo (a pioneer in work redesign) was the diffusion 'truly impressive'. Why was diffusion not more extensive? Walton identified the following difficulties, particularly in maintaining momentum in the pilot or demonstrator projects:

- projects decayed through internal design inconsistencies, loss of top management support, union opposition, and premature turnover of key staff such as project leaders;
- crises encouraged a return to authoritarian management;
- there was lack of participant involvement following success and publicity;
- experiments and their leaders became isolated from the rest of the organization;
- some pilot projects lacked credibility and were seen as poor models for change elsewhere;
- there was confusion over what was to be diffused, stated in terms that were either too operational or too conceptual, and the concepts employed were not seen as realistic;
- inadequate resources, such as training;
- vested interests in existing routines, and the threat to those whose skills would no longer be required;
- 'star envy', causing resentment when pilot sites attracted publicity, visitors, and management attention.

Walton also identified two 'political' issues, although he did not use that term. The first was that, while innovators received considerable credit, those who subsequently adapted their ideas received less praise, even though they too were successful (and had they failed, they probably would have lost more standing than the pioneers would have lost had they failed). Second, the leaders in innovative units were involved in arguments with superiors and staff groups, where they had to defend their positions aggressively, damaging their careers as a result. Colleagues observing this wished to avoid a similar fate. Consequently, 'The more successful the pioneer, the less favourable are the payoffs and the greater the risks for those who follow' (Walton, 1975, p.21). Those barriers and deterrents help to explain why, although lack of diffusion undermines a demonstrator project, a successful pilot project does not necessarily diffuse. Walton offers the following practical advice:

- introduce several projects at the same time;
- avoid over-exposure and 'glorification' of those projects;
- ensure that the programme is identified with top management from the start.

Diffusion is a process, not an event, and different factors and sets of conditions may become more or less significant, with respect to spread or containment, at different stages. The ways in which changes spread or are contained cannot be seen as isolated, time-bounded events.

Spread and diffusion

That it [the stethoscope] will ever come into general use, not withstanding its value, I am extremely doubtful; because its beneficial application requires much time, and it gives a good deal of trouble both to the patient and practitioner, and because its whole hue and character is foreign, and opposed to all our habits and associations. It must be confessed that there is something ludicrous in the picture of a grave physician formally listening through a long tube applied to a patient's thorax, as if the disease within were a living being that could communicate its condition to the sense without.

Source: John Forbes in Preface to Laennec (1821)

Despite a substantial literature, there is no agreement over the use of terms such as spread and diffusion. Definitions of innovation are also controversial. One reason for these disagreements is that the topic has interested several disciplines, including the psychology of addiction, the sociology of farming, communication studies, network analysis, organization theory, change management, and product (and service) marketing. Greenhalgh *et al.* (2004) identify 13 separate lines of disciplinary interest in diffusion of innovation. Concern with diffusion in healthcare has traditionally focused on new technology, clinical practice, and health advice.

In psychology, sociology, marketing, and healthcare studies, the unit of analysis is the individual. Will individuals change their behaviour, adopt that method, buy that product? Explanations focus on attributes of the innovation, on the nature of the interpersonal communications through which information is shared, and on personality traits that predispose individuals to seek novelty. In network studies, organization theory, and change management, the focus lies with the team, department, the organizations, or society. Those studies focus on changes to organization structures, systems, procedures, technologies, and working practices. Explanations here tend to concentrate on the interaction of change substance, implementation processes, organization politics, and the wider social context.

The concept of spread thus has a spectrum of meanings (Figure 3.1). It can refer to the use at site B of methods developed at site A. This is the 'copy exact' model of Szulanski and Winter (2002), which assumes that the receiving and sending contexts are similar. Spread can also imply the tailored application of broad principles, such as process re-engineering, total quality management, or the guiding framework of an improvement model (Kerr *et al.*, 2002). Between these extremes lies a continuum of selectivity and adaptation, involving processes of 'reinvention', and 'appropriation', through which ideas are modified to fit local contexts, or what Fleck *et al.* (1990) call 'innofusion'.

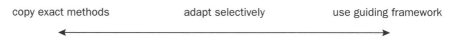

Figure 3.1 *The spread continuum*

A related issue concerns the unit of spread. This could involve the spread of ideas from one organization to another, or from one department to another within the same organization. In healthcare, other options arise, such as 'region to region', 'network to network', 'trust to trust', 'clinical service to clinical service', and 'consultant to consultant'. It may be that the further the change has to travel, geographically and organizationally, the more complex the processes involved and the more challenging the barriers (but in healthcare, anecdotal evidence suggests that spread between even close geographical neighbours is problematic).

Concerned with the spread of change in healthcare, Fraser (2002, p.vii) argues that 'It's much easier to improve by adapting the systems and processes we already have in place, than to completely replace them.' She thus advocates 'cherry picking' and 'reinvention', choosing and adapting good ideas from elsewhere, and she identifies four types of spread, as in Table 3.1.

Table 3.1 *Types of spread*

Type of spread	Definition	Reinvention issues
Scatter	One simple behaviour or practice is disseminated to and adopted by many	*Not much*: ideas are simple and obviously better
Switch	Transferring good practice from one sector to another context	*Significant*: ideas from outside require a new language
Share	Copying practices in one division to others in the organization	*Moderate*: practice hard to share due to internal competition
Stretch	Expanding good practice across internal divisional boundaries	*Significant*: crossing boundaries increases complexity of process

Scatter can happen fast, Fraser argues. *Switch*, however, depends on the scale of change, although individuals may pilot changes rapidly if no extra resources are required. *Share* is slower, involving departments with different working arrangements. *Stretch* crosses organizational and professional boundaries, involving a lengthy decision-making process.

While much of the literature uses the term innovation, we are thus also concerned with leveraging advantage from existing practices, which may be new, and innovative, in settings where they remain untried. One useful definition of innovation, therefore, is 'new *here*'. To map what is known about spread and diffusion, we will outline four research strands, drawing on a comprehensive review commissioned by the NHS Service Delivery and Organisation Research Programme (Greenhalgh *et al.*, 2004). The four strands concern:

1 the substance of innovation;
2 the psychology of behaviour change;
3 the role of networks;
4 the contribution of context.

The substance of innovation: what are we trying to spread?

Innovations come in a variety of forms, such as new technologies, ideas, products, tools, methods, services, business models, and organizational practices. Christensen *et al.* (2000) distinguish between sustaining and disruptive innovations:

sustaining innovations   making improvements to existing processes, procedures, services, and products

disruptive innovations   the development of wholly new processes, procedures, services, and products

Those are just convenient labels for categories of novel ideas, and they must be used with care, to avoid misunderstanding. With sustaining innovations, for example, it is often the underlying theme, concept, way of thinking, or pattern of behaviour that is sustained, but supporting systems and processes may change. With disruptive innovation, it is traditional ways of thinking that are disrupted, rather than (or as well as) organization arrangements; such ideas may not lead to chaos and upheaval. The distinction between 'improving what we have' and 'creating something new' is what matters, rather than category labels. However, truly disruptive innovations may be harder to manage, because they are riskier, and because there are no established routines for handling them.

Commercial organizations have traditionally been preoccupied with innovations concerning new technology, products, services, and business models. In contrast, Hammer (2004, p.86) discusses the benefits of operational innovations:

operational innovations   the invention and deployment of new ways of
doing work

The modernization agenda for healthcare, expressed in these terms, thus primarily involves a combination of sustaining and disruptive operational innovations. Greenhalgh *et al.* (2004, p.7) use the following definition, encompassing not only the varied substance of innovations, but also the style in which they are implemented, and the intended outcomes, indicating the close linkages between those issues:

> We defined innovation in service delivery and organization as a novel set of behaviours, routines and ways of working, which are directed at improving health outcomes, administrative efficiency, cost-effectiveness, or the user experience, and which are implemented by means of planned and coordinated action.

The modernization agenda thus sought to combine sustaining and disruptive operational innovations. From his influential review, Rogers (1995) concludes that the probability of an innovation being adopted is increased when it is perceived to display six properties:

- advantageous when compared with existing practice;
- compatible with existing practices;
- easy to understand;
- observable in demonstration sites;
- testable;
- adaptable to fit local needs.

Individual and context factors are as important as the innovation itself. Unless you perceive that an innovation will help you to improve on current methods, you are unlikely to be persuaded. You also need to see how an idea can be adapted to fit local conditions. Diffusion thus depends on characteristics of adopters and the context, as well as the innovation.

Dopson and Fitzgerald (2005b) analyse the diffusion of clinical innovations in 49 case studies based on over 1,400 interviews. It is useful to note that a number of clinical innovations also had organizational dimensions: allocating responsibility for clinic management, arranging patient recall systems, cost monitoring, and so on. Their findings suggest that an innovation must be more than attractive, and that the role of context, social networks, and evidence also play a part in determining whether and how innovations spread.

The role of context

As a relatively sweeping and vague concept, 'context' has a poorly
understood influence on diffusion. For example, multi-dimensional change,
plus the need for collaboration between organizational units or agencies,
plus high cost and a history of unsuccessful innovation, may lead to slow
adoption. Context must also be regarded as more than just the stage on
which the action is played out. Not only do context attributes influence the
spread process, but context features are themselves actively shaped by
ongoing events (Dopson and Fitzgerald, 2005b).

Dopson and Fitzgerald emphasize the role of opinion leaders, who can either champion
or block change, depending on their perspective and sense of self-interest. Their
evidence suggests that opinion leaders can be found at different points on a number of
axes, such as:

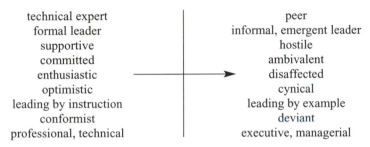

technical expert	peer
formal leader	informal, emergent leader
supportive	hostile
committed	ambivalent
enthusiastic	disaffected
optimistic	cynical
leading by instruction	leading by example
conformist	deviant
professional, technical	executive, managerial

Clearly, it is difficult to predict the impact of an opinion leader without an
understanding of their profile (professional expert, optimistic, and supportive, or
management peer, ambivalent, and cynical), and also of how their position will be
perceived by and thus influence others.

Source: Dopson and Fitzgerald (2005b, p.95)

The role of interpersonal exchange

Professional social networks, peer comparisons, and the advice of colleagues
can shape individual behaviour in ways that are more significant than
external agencies. However, professional boundaries and organization
structures can inhibit the movement of knowledge. Evidence does not
always flow easily across those boundaries. The role of opinion leaders as
change facilitators and inhibitors is also critical, if complex; opinion leaders
can block as well as encourage change. In a processual perspective, the role
of the change agent is to build a coalition behind a new idea, through power
plays, bargaining, negotiation, and other political influence tactics (Kanter,
1983; Dawson, 2003a).

The role of evidence

One might expect that evidence generated by clinical trials would persuade doctors readily to change their practice. However, this study revealed differing concepts of what counts as 'good research' and 'good evidence'. Even 'strong' evidence may be ignored if it challenges entrenched professional autonomy and training. Evidence is differentially available to different medical professions, and is not always shared. Other sources of evidence are important, including tacit and experiential knowledge, and craft skills, which are difficult to codify and transfer. Robust evidence, therefore, does not alone lead to diffusion. The source, nature, credibility, and timing of that evidence are also critical.

If clinical evidence can be contested, how much greater a burden of proof must evidence carry with regard to organizational change, where causality is difficult to establish, given the complex range of factors interacting over time? While product innovations may be well defined and visible, operational innovations affect processes straddling occupational and functional boundaries, are more likely to evolve with experience, and are only visible and demonstrable when they are being performed. The features of many complex operational innovations may therefore not be apparent before they have been implemented.

Operational attributes

In addition to Rogers' 'standard attributes', Greenhalgh *et al.* (2004) identify a number of operational attributes that complex organizational and technological innovations in particular benefit from in terms of diffusion. These include relevance to the user's work, value in improving performance, feasibility for use in a particular context, few barriers to be overcome, the option to adopt incrementally, and the ease with which the relevant knowledge can be codified and transferred to a different context.

We are considering in this volume the spread of multi-faceted operational innovations in healthcare, and not product innovations in a commercial context. The 'target' for diffusion efforts may include individuals, clinical teams, service departments, and whole healthcare provider organizations, rather than exclusively individual adopters. It seems clear that efforts to spread those kinds of changes in this kind of context are not going to be guided effectively by any straightforward checklist.

The psychology of behaviour change

The enthusiastic roles of opinion leaders and change champions have been widely recognized. However, most managers have stories of new structures, systems, and procedures undermined by individuals who refused to change their behaviour. Diffusion of innovation is thus a matter for individual psychology, considering attitudes, interests, fears, anxieties, values, beliefs, understandings, and perceptions. One influential model, developed by Prochaska and DiClemente (1984), from addiction psychology, identifies five stages of behaviour change, which unfold at a different pace, and in different sequences, depending on the person (this model underwent later, minor, modifications; see Chapter 5):

1 **Precontemplation**: the individual is not ready to discuss or consider change.
2 **Contemplation**: the individual is willing to listen and to consider a change.
3 **Action**: the individual is now ready to do something concrete.
4 **Maintenance**: the individual strives not to slip back to old behaviours.
5 **Relapse**: old behaviours are resumed.

Considering audience needs when designing a message, and choosing methods appropriate to the 'target', are standard advice for persuasive communication. Advocates of innovation must therefore tailor their strategies to each individual's stage in the change process. Plsek (2000) suggests four strategies for moving someone past precontemplation: avoid rational appeal based on evidence from elsewhere; capture their emotional attention; provide feedback based on the behaviour of peers; and dramatize the bad experiences of others.

Rogers (1995) argues that the adoption of innovations follows a pattern. Initially, small numbers adopt, followed by 'take-off', then achieving a critical mass of adopters. Finally, the pace slackens as saturation is reached, typically short of 100 per cent (you can never convince everyone). This is usually shown as an S-shaped diffusion curve. Recognizing that the shape of the curve depends on local circumstances, Rogers argues that this pattern is influenced by the attributes of five broad personality types:

1 **Innovators**: usually the first in their social grouping to adopt new approaches and behaviours, a small category of individuals who enjoy the excitement and risks of experimentation.
2 **Early adopters**: opinion leaders who evaluate ideas carefully, and are more sceptical and take more convincing, but take risks, help to adapt new ideas to local settings, and have effective networking skills.
3 **Early majority**: those who take longer to reach a decision to change, but who are still ahead of the average.

4 **Late majority**: even more sceptical and risk averse, these wait for most of their colleagues to adopt new ideas first.
5 **Laggards**: viewed negatively by others, the last to adopt new ideas, even for reasons that they believe to be rational.

Diffusion relies initially on innovators and early adopters, and subsequently on the pace at which the early and late majority are swayed. One criticism of this approach is that these are not personality types at all. An individual may be an early adopter of one idea, but a late adopter of another, depending on circumstances. To be an innovator or a laggard depends as much on the social or organizational context as on the individual. This perspective suggests two conclusions, however. First, behaviour change is rarely a sudden event, but a protracted process, triggered and developed by contextual factors as well as individual perceptions and interpersonal communications. Second, there is no 'one best way' to influence people to change; interventions must consider individual needs and perceptions.

The role of networks

The one-way transmission of ideas from a sender to a receiver, Rogers (1995) argues, is oversimplified. The diffusion process depends on the joint creation and exchange of information across social networks. The idea that adopters make rational decisions is also oversimplified, overlooking the selective and often biased nature of the available information.

Using evidence from medicine and farming, Valente (1995) develops a mathematical modelling approach to diffusion as a process dependent on communication and interpersonal influence in social networks. Diffusion relies on imitation, and the speed of diffusion depends on network characteristics. Where it is risky to 'go it alone', collective behaviour reduces uncertainty. An idea is 'contagious' if individuals adopt it when they see someone else doing it. Contagion occurs through direct ties, social proximity, popularity, and formal networks. Networks do not operate in one direction, and innovations are subject to decay, as individuals discontinue, defect, or leave, those defections reflecting network effects in reverse.

Also adopting a communications perspective, focusing on processes of information exchange, Robertson *et al.* (1996) studied the adoption of computer-aided production management (CAPM) in British manufacturing during the 1980s. Their findings demonstrate the role of interpersonal and inter-organizational networks through which adopters learn about technologies. The concept of network here refers to formal and informal social arrangements, within and across organizational boundaries, involving information exchange, concerted action, and the joint production of information, knowledge, and expertise. They note, however, that the manner in which 'knowledge' that was diffused through the networks of interest to their study was influenced by technology suppliers. The information circulating through those networks was not necessarily neutral and unbiased.

Networkers are also known as 'boundary spanners' (Robertson *et al.*, 1996, p.336), and while some network activity relies on contractual relationships and alliances, less formal networks also contribute to diffusion. Granovetter (1973) argues that formal social arrangements do not expose network members to fresh ideas, and that 'weak ties' linking marginal acquaintances (sporadic meetings with distant colleagues) are more likely to expose participants to new thinking. Weak ties can thus strengthen diffusion. Robertson *et al.* conclude that there is no guarantee that network processes will lead to the spread of appropriate ideas and practices. The combination of pressures may be such that suboptimal solutions will be adopted in some instances. Networks are just as capable of diffusing less effective ideas.

The contribution of context

It is useful to ask whether the organization as a whole is ready for innovation and change. The answer lies with innovative cultures, creative climates, ready and receptive contexts, and absorptive capacity.

Innovative cultures and creative climates

What are the features of an innovative organization culture? Burns and Stalker (1961) contrast rigid, hierarchical *mechanistic* management systems with adaptive, flexible *organic* systems. Organizations in stable, non-threatening environments can operate effectively with mechanistic systems. Those facing turbulent and unpredictable environments must adapt rapidly and creatively, thus requiring organic systems. This argument remains influential, reworked by Kanter (1983) who contrasts *integrative* with *segmentalist* organization cultures. Integrative organizations are innovation stimulating, while segmentalism is innovation smothering. The characteristics of integrative cultures include:

- holistic problem solving;
- team orientation and co-operation;
- mechanisms for ideas generation and exchange;
- sense of purpose and direction;
- ability to overthrow history and precedent;

- use of internal and external networks;
- person and creation centred;
- results orientated.

Segmentalist structures display different attributes:

- compartmentalized problem solving;
- preoccupation with hierarchy;
- emphasis on efficiency and rules.

Ekvall (1996, p.105) has developed the related concept of creative climate, which is regarded as an attribute of the organization, a collection of attitudes, feelings, and behaviours which exist independently of the perceptions and understandings of members. The 10 dimensions in this perspective are:

1 **Challenge**: people experience joy and meaning in work and invest high energy.
2 **Freedom**: people make contacts, exchange information freely, discuss problems, make decisions, take initiative.
3 **Idea support**: people listen to each other, ideas and suggestions are received in a supportive way by bosses and colleagues.
4 **Trust and openness**: high-trust climate, ideas can be expressed without fear of reprisal or ridicule, communications are open.
5 **Dynamism and liveliness**: new things happening all the time, new ways of thinking and solving problems, 'full speed'.
6 **Playfulness and humour**: relaxed atmosphere with jokes and laughter, spontaneity.
7 **Debates**: many voices are heard, expressing different ideas and viewpoints.
8 **Conflicts**: conflict of ideas not personal, impulses under control, people behave in a mature manner, based on psychological insight.
9 **Risk taking**: decisions and actions prompt and rapid, concrete experimentation is preferred to detailed analysis.
10 **Idea time**: opportunities to discuss and test fresh ideas that are not part of planned work activity, and these chances are exploited.

Organizations where the culture displays more of those attributes are more likely to adopt, and to generate, creative ideas for change and innovation.

Receptive contexts

From research in healthcare, Pettigrew *et al.* (1992) identify eight attributes of the organization receptive to change and innovation:

1 **Clear strategy**: broken into actionable elements, with clear benefits which win commitment, focusing on the long term.

2 **Skilled leadership**: not 'macho' management, but team builders, with interpersonal skills which matter more than status or rank, combining planning with opportunism and good timing.

3 **External pressures**: used to trigger change, without creating crises and draining energies.

4 **Supportive culture**: challenges beliefs, encourages cross-boundary working, supportive human resource management policies, risk-taking approach, positive self-image.

5 **Good managerial–clinical relations**: seeking common ground, involvement of key players, efforts to build climate of trust, honesty, and communication, fostering alliances.

6 **Co-operative inter-organizational networks**: opportunities for trading and exchange, bargaining and deal making, trust building, informal and purposeful.

7 **Clear goals and priorities**: limited set of change priorities, insulated from short-term pressures, agenda divided into manageable action elements.

8 **Fit between change agenda and organization**: nature of workforce, local political culture, nature of local population, other context factors that shape perceptions.

Those factors in combination influence the level of receptiveness to change. Where they are present, they increase the probability of innovation being adopted and successfully implemented. The continuing configuration of those attributes may also contribute to the sustainability of change.

Absorptive capacity

First developed by Cohen and Levinthal (1990), this concept is also used by Szulanski (2003) to express an organization's ability to acquire, assimilate, and apply new knowledge. This concept incorporates the organization's:

- stock and level of knowledge, including basic skills, shared language, and experience;
- up-to-date information about relevant areas of knowledge;
- awareness of where relevant expertise can be found: who knows what, who can help;
- ability to exploit external sources.

These properties imply that an organization possesses 'learning organization values', concerning the creation and sharing of new ideas. Szulanski argues that an organization which lacks absorptive capacity is less likely to recognize the value of new ideas, less likely to recreate that knowledge, and less likely to apply it successfully.

Rules for stifling innovation

1 Regard a new idea from below with suspicion, because it's new, and because it's from below.
2 Insist that people who need your approval to act first go through several other levels of management to get their signatures.
3 Ask departments or individuals to challenge and criticize each other's proposals. That saves you the job of deciding; you just pick the survivor.
4 Express criticism freely, and withhold praise. That keeps people on their toes. Let them know that they can be fired at any time.
5 Treat identification of problems as signs of failure, to discourage people from letting you know when something in their area isn't working.
6 Control everything carefully. Make sure people count anything that can be counted, frequently.
7 Make decisions to reorganize or change policies in secret, and spring them on people unexpectedly. That keeps people on their toes.
8 Make sure that requests for information are fully justified, and make sure that it is not given out to managers freely. You don't want data to fall into the wrong hands.
9 Assign to lower-level managers, in the name of delegation and participation, responsibility for figuring out how to cut back, lay off, move people around, or otherwise implement threatening decisions you have made. And get them to do it quickly.
10 And above all, never forget that you, the higher-ups, already know everything important about this business.

Source: Kanter (2002)

Implications: theory and practice

From this overview, it appears that the diffusion of innovation, and the spread of change, depend on more than just good ideas and eager adopters. As with sustainability, several factors, at different levels of analysis, influence the process, in theory and in practice. It is also important to note that, while this and the previous chapter might imply that sustainability and spread are distinct processes, they are closely intertwined and mutually influential.

Implications for theory

Factors affecting the spread or diffusion of change and innovation appear to include:

substantial	attractive, contagious ideas sustaining, disruptive, operational adaptability to local needs and circumstances
individual	stage in behaviour change process: innovator, adopter, or laggard response to tailored influence and persuasion tactics perceived benefit and/or threat to autonomy

social	role of formal and informal networks in diffusing
	   information
	change champions, opinion leaders, boundary spanners,
	   weak ties
	source and perceived credibility of supporting evidence

political	if first adopters damage their careers, others will not
	   follow
	pioneers get more praise for success and less blame for
	   failure
	late adopters get less praise for success and more blame
	   if they fail

contextual	innovative culture, creative climate, avoidance of 'star envy' organizational readiness and receptiveness absorptive capacity of the organization

The diffusion process is likely to be lengthy, and dependent on the scale and complexity of the changes. Here, we are considering operational innovations, involving the transfer of knowledge concerning policies, performance targets, job specifications, role relationships, structures, procedures, working practices, and in some cases physical facilities. That it is problematic to implement and spread such changes rapidly is hardly a damaging criticism. Locock (2001, p.42; original emphasis), citing cases of effective service redesign, argues that:

> It is important to stress that these examples have been arrived at *by going through a redesign process*; lifting the outcome off the shelf to re-use somewhere else without going through the redesign process may or may not work, but would miss the point that redesign is about analysing what is done in each local context now, and how local staff believe it could be done better in the interests of their patients.

The process of spread is highly contingent. Operational innovations require adaptation to fit the local setting, and the factors which influence the nature, pace, and success of the diffusion process depend on local circumstances. Operational innovations are resistant to codification beyond broad guiding principles or frameworks, they are visible only when they are active, and they evolve as those working with them learn from experience. Diffusion of these kinds of changes thus makes demands on transmitters and adopters significantly more complex than innovations which involve single tangible products or standardized methods.

Implications for practice

Healthcare may be resistant to change and innovation, for three sets of reasons. The first concerns size. Large organizations are often non-innovative due to the functional barriers, administrative routines, management controls, and internal tensions that accompany size (Dougherty, 1996). Created in 1948, and employing around 1.3 million people, the NHS has had half a century to refine those routines, controls, and tensions; the website for a typical healthcare organization in 2005 lists around 25 separate external monitoring agencies. The second concerns organization culture. In public ownership, the NHS is subject to constant media attention; the careers of government ministers, and administrations, can turn on performance figures. Healthcare is thus risk averse, and the probability of litigation following error strengthens the desire to follow procedures, rather than to experiment.

The third set of reasons concerns characteristics of the professional organization, in which powerful occupational groups police their respective role boundaries. Clinical professionals are more likely to challenge ideas that appear to conflict with their values and threaten their autonomy. This makes it difficult for general managers unilaterally to implement even minor changes to structures and working practices (Powell *et al.*, 1999).

From a review of total quality management applications in Europe, Øvretveit (2000) confirms the stereotype, that healthcare organizations are not receptive to change, and that the spread of quality initiatives faces barriers including:

- cost (time and money) and uncertain returns;
- management resistance to employee empowerment;
- professional resistance based on loss of autonomy, scepticism, and lack of time;
- lack of incentives for change;
- absence of adequate measures of quality improvement;
- the complexity of healthcare.

Despite an extensive literature on organizational change, there is little advice on spreading operational innovations. There is no simple checklist of factors that will smooth the rapid diffusion of complex organizational changes. The question of pace and timing is also problematic; while the rapid spread of new working practices appears to be desirable, hasty action can damage the outcomes and threaten the sustainability of changes driven at too fast a pace. We will explore the practical implications in more depth in Chapter 13.

The process of spread seems to be influenced by a similar array of conditions and factors as sustainability. It therefore seems relevant to explore these issues using the theoretical apparatus discussed in the previous chapter. This involves conceptualizing spread, or diffusion, as a process that unfolds over time, where the sequence of events is potentially influenced by cumulative effects, conjunctural causality, and path dependency. Where appropriate, therefore, the questions that chapters in Part II will seek to answer include:

- Under what conditions are changes more likely to spread, or to be contained?
- In what ways might circumstances, issues, and factors accumulate favouring either diffusion or stickiness?
- Are there particular combinations, or types of combinations, of factors that are more likely to support the spread of new working practices?
- What typical event sequences, or narratives, are suggested by the evidence to explain spread and stickiness?

Critical debates

1 Why should operational innovations in healthcare be more or less easy to spread or diffuse than, say, product innovations such as new mobile phones and music players?
2 How can organization politics interfere with the spread of obviously useful ideas and methods?
3 From a personal perspective, what are the advantages and dangers in being an 'early adopter' in your organization with regard to an operational innovation?

Part II
Experience

4 View from the top: opening the box on sustainability and spread

Jane Louise Jones, Elaine Whitby, and Rose Gollop

Chapter aims

1 To outline why spread and sustainability were identified as crucial issues for success and worthy of research.
2 To describe the first Research into Practice study that identified key factors that help or hinder the spread and sustainability of new NHS practices.
3 To explore the views and experience of 'key informants' working in leading national and regional roles associated with two NHS Modernisation Agency Programmes.
4 To examine the theoretical and practical implications of these findings.

Key point summary

- The use and understanding of the terms 'spread' and 'sustainability' varies.
- Spread and sustainability are distinct concepts, but they are contiguous and linked processes.
- The factors that influence spread and sustainability are broadly similar, their presence or absence acting as either facilitators or inhibitors respectively.
- A complex set of interrelated factors contribute to spread and sustainability:

  - nature of the improvement programme
  - organizational context
  - process of engaging individuals in change
  - importance of key roles
  - existence of influential relationships
  - time necessary to make successful change.

- Spread and sustainability are dependent not merely on the presence of a given set of factors, but also on the context, sequence and timing of events.
- Planning for spread and sustainability should be considered from the outset of an improvement initiative.

- Variation in the level of adoption and sustainability may only become evident some time into improvement programmes.
- There is a clear need for integrated working to achieve widespread adoption, spread, or sustainability. Initiatives must be cohesive, linked with, and made relevant to each organization's priorities and agendas.
- Collective leadership is significant: key actors, working in partnership, can exert greater influence and encourage more effectively both the spread and sustainability of improvements.
- A better understanding of appropriate timescales for sustainable change in healthcare is required by policy makers at all levels.

Opening the box

The chapter reports the findings from interviews with senior clinical and managerial staff who were involved in implementing two of the Agency's first major national service improvement initiatives, the Cancer Services Collaborative, and the National Booking Programme. Interviews concentrated on their experience of those programmes, and in particular on the factors they considered to be influential in sustaining and spreading those initiatives. The Agency aimed to produce measurable improvements in patient care. However, the size and complexity of the service made this challenging. Both initiatives were ambitious, and were designed to introduce rapid service-wide improvements. Less than 18 months after the launch of the booking initiative, while much progress had been made, concerns had also been raised. There were wide variations in achievements between pilot sites, and there had been problems in sustaining improvements beyond the pilot stage (Ham *et al.*, 2003). Why were some pilot projects more successful than others? Why had some initiatives flourished and been sustained, while others struggled to survive or failed to maintain their early achievements? What were the critical success factors? How should future improvement programmes be nurtured? The Agency commissioned a study of staff experience and opinion to identify the factors that facilitated spread and sustainability in national improvement programmes.

The study focused on staff who were leading these service improvement initiatives, holding a mix of national and regional management and clinical roles. The aim was to learn from the experience of this senior group, to explore 'the view from the top'. In addition, although working in different parts of the country, this group all held Agency employment contracts, and were relatively easy to contact. Participants were asked to identify and discuss factors which they believed influenced the spread and sustainability of new working practices in the parts of the health service with which they were familiar. Data were collected between January and May 2002 through

39 semi-structured interviews, 13 with booking and 26 with Cancer Services Collaborative staff. Interview transcripts were subjected to thematic template analysis, and findings were presented in three reports, one for each programme, and one dealing with the specific issue of 'scepticism' (Gollop *et al.*, 2004; Chapter 5, this volume).

Exploring the terms

It was apparent from the related literature that there were few definitions of the terms 'spread' and 'sustainability' and that multiple interpretations were in use (Osborne, 1998; Berwick, 2003). Consequently, the data were explored to identify how participants in this study themselves understood and used these terms. Although this was a relatively homogeneous participant group, with regard to their contacts with and experience of these national initiatives, there was little consistency in their use of the terms 'spread', 'roll-out', and 'adoption', which were in common use at the time. Some used these terms interchangeably, while others gave them specific meanings. There was some consistency in the use of the term 'roll-out', referring to a planned approach to dissemination. However, the substance of what was being rolled out differed, with some participants referring to improvement methodology, while others focused on new working practices. Others differentiated between spread and roll-out, assigning responsibility for these processes to different parties, for example:

> Spread, we have said, if you've maybe looked at one clinician in this project, and say you've got four, that's about spreading the practice or the change that we make in that unit or department to the other consultants. That's different from how some people are interpreting it. So we've said that, roll-out we will help you with, and the network is responsible for that, but spread is actually the Trust's responsibility. Everybody you talk to will say something different.
>
> (Regional facilitator)

Echoing the discussion in Chapter 2, participants also defined sustainability in different ways. One regional director outlined sustainability in relation to achieving and maintaining targets. Another defined this in relation to continuous improvement, observing that 'changes have been sustained, but they've also been built upon'. Others viewed sustainability as the continued structured use of an improvement methodology:

> It's about sustaining the kind of formality of the process really. Which is quite a disciplined process about constantly reviewing where they are at, constantly making improvements. It is the kind of discipline and the formality that that kind of approach to methodology gives.
>
> (Regional director)

Does it matter that people have different interpretations and uses of these terms? Arguably it does for those who are collaborating on improvement work, as this could influence goals and behaviour, since people may be working towards different goals. With respect to sustainability, working to sustain performance to meet targets is quite different from aiming for continually improving services – which may then exceed those targets. It requires a different approach, and different measures of evaluation. While variation in usage is an interesting theoretical observation, clarity and agreement over the meaning of terms among close colleagues are important. These variations in apparently cohesive groups have been noted elsewhere (Greenhalgh *et al.*, 2004).

From the outset of the study, spread and sustainability were considered as two discrete processes, and interview questions reflected this. While some participants differentiated clearly between the two, many could not:

> I don't buy into this, the model of 'project' and 'roll-out'. I think you have to start thinking about sustainability from the very beginning.
>
> (Regional clinical lead)

A relationship between the two processes became evident. When spread was specified as an explicit goal, for example achieving national coverage with a particular programme in a short time, the chances of sustainability were thought to be jeopardized:

> They want completion, and that's within two years. That's where there has been a lot of debate around, do you have coverage or completion, and trying to achieve both is very difficult. This whole business of doing it to themselves and not being done to, that's what gives you the sustainability, but it does make things a lot slower.
>
> (Regional facilitator)

While sustainability and spread can be seen as distinct analytical concepts, they are mutually influential processes which are difficult to separate in practice. This raises a number of questions concerning sequencing and effect. Should an innovation be embedded in one area before it is spread to another, or is it better to spread as widely as possible, as quickly as possible, so that saturation contributes to sustainability? In the context of national service improvement programmes, change leaders found that phased implementation challenged their vision of planned and rapid spread and sustainability. Successful roll-out from the pilot sites depended on new working practices being accepted and embedded, so that the focus could switch to new areas without jeopardizing early success. Spread and sustainability would thus proceed in tandem, building an irreversible pressure for change. In practice, some pilot areas found that new methods took longer to become routinized than anticipated. Subsequently, they struggled to maintain momentum as resources and attention moved on to other issues. In particular, in situations where a long-term approach to supporting service improvement had not been developed, for example in terms of permanent administrative arrangements, early gains were likely to be lost. As this research showed, rapid spread does not automatically lead to sustainability; focusing first on sustaining early successes may prove to be a better strategy.

Fateful factors

What factors did participants identify as 'fateful' in influencing sustainability and spread?

The findings highlight a complex set of processes, suggesting that the sustainability and spread of new working practices are influenced by interrelated factors that cannot be listed in a simple 'recipe' or checklist format, or explained neatly by a set of conventional causal relationships. Consistent with other evidence, and also with dimensions of the processual perspective introduced in Chapter 2, this suggests a model of conjunctural causation, where sustainability and spread are explained by the occurrence of particular *configurations* of factors. The configurations identified were similar for both sustainability and spread; where differences were noted, this was more a matter of emphasis. Factors were often described as both facilitating and inhibiting, and were viewed on a continuum depending on their relative presence or absence. These have been grouped under broad headings in Table 4.1.

1 The improvement programme

The substance of the initiative, and in particular the perceived benefits and integration of the programme, were felt to affect the sustainability and spread of new practices and methods.

Perceived benefits

Demonstrating the benefits arising from the programme was identified as key. Demonstrating benefits for patients was seen as particularly powerful, as well as essential, with many respondents referring to *The NHS Plan*, and the policy to develop a service around the needs and choices of patients. However, additional benefits for staff and their working practices were also seen as important. One national clinical lead said:

Table 4.1 *Fateful factors for sustainability and spread*

Themes	Influencing factors	Potential impact
1 The improvement programme	Perceived benefits	Demonstrating patient benefits and the promise of additional resources can help spread an initiative
	Programme integration	Spread and sustainability are more likely if the programme is consistent with other initiatives, and is linked to core business and priorities
2 The organization	Balancing priorities	Adoption at a local level is facilitated if there are no other competing priorities
	Organization culture	Supportive culture and readiness for change are important for both spread and sustainability
3 Engaging staff		Widespread staff engagement leads to a sense of ownership, contributing to sustainability
4 Key roles	Leadership and facilitation	Strong, effective, and credible leadership provides direction, focus, and momentum
	Chief executive	Senior management support is essential
	Clinicians	Clinicians have a key role at national and local levels in supporting and sustaining changes
	Project managers	Project managers steer projects and facilitate adoption and longer-term ownership
	Middle managers	Middle managers are 'gatekeepers' to change
5 Power and influence	Collective leadership	Widespread staff involvement facilitates spread
	Professional organization	Role boundaries and hierarchies can stifle progress
	Opinion leaders	Opinion leaders can be identified at all levels, influencing adoption, and later sustainability
6 Time for change	Time to focus	Dedicated time to focus on new programmes is essential for spread and sustainability
	Pace of change	Rapid change can facilitate spread and meet targets, but can jeopardize sustainability
	Time to learn	Phased implementation with incremental successful changes can facilitate spread
	Beyond the short term	Phased implementation hampers sustainability as short-term funds and project status lose momentum
	Time to embed	Volume, pace, and frequency of change leave little time for consolidation and embedding of improvements

> It's got to be a win-win type thing. It's no good just being absolutely
> brilliant for the patients. It's got to have advantages for virtually
> everybody involved.

This is broadly consistent with Rogers' (1995) argument that an innovation
is more readily adopted if it is seen as 'attractive' by those who will be using
it. Altruism is no more or less likely to be found in public sector healthcare
than in any other type of organization. The potential benefits of adoption
included the promise of increased resources and support, including funding,
staff, equipment, and access to educational events. Interestingly, however,
the perceived high cost of large national programme events such as
conferences and briefings was seen as 'distasteful' to some, thus potentially
limiting spread.

Demonstrating success from the pilot sites was thought to be a useful
strategy for increasing spread. Having a body of evidence to illustrate the
benefits was important, and this included robust case studies as well as
quantitative performance data. However, the effect of the credibility of
evidence on diffusion is ambiguous and contested, as often well-evidenced
practice does not spread (Dopson *et al.*, 2002; Fitzgerald *et al.*, 2002).

Simplicity of message and methods was also thought to be important,
although differences of opinion were evident, underlining the need for
appropriate communication tailored to each audience. For example, while
some praised the practicality of the collaborative approach, others perceived
it as being unfamiliar and too complex.

In summary, it appears important not only to identify the benefits, but also
to establish the most appropriate way to demonstrate those advantages to the
intended audience. How the benefits were presented, the type and credibility
of evidence, and the use of appropriate communication methods were all
regarded as influential.

Programme integration

Concerns that programmes were seen in isolation, and given priority over
other services, or implemented in a way that compromised other services,
highlighted potential threats to both spread and sustainability. For example,
booking was seen by some as relevant only to administrative and clerical
staff, while some staff believed that the focus of the cancer collaborative was
inappropriate:

> Why am I seeing these patients and treating them quickly, when these
> other patients are waiting for ages with equally serious problems, but just
> don't happen to have cancer?
>
> (Cancer Services Collaborative clinical lead)

Some participants cited the large number and fragmented nature of Agency programmes, suggesting that, rather than focus on stand-alone projects, a whole-systems approach should be developed. Consequently, if modernization was not integrated nationally, how could trusts be expected to make useful links between programmes? Suggestions for integrating initiatives at a local level included integrating programmes into local planning processes, and incorporating programme targets into individual and service objectives. Established local and regional modernization teams were felt to improve co-ordination, by balancing organizational pressures while maintaining a focus on improvement.

2 The organization

Organization culture was seen as an important influence on spread and sustainability. It was felt that, regardless of the programme, the local context helped to determine whether initiatives would be adopted, sustained, and spread. Key aspects of culture were identified, including local priorities, multiple agendas, and readiness for change.

Balancing priorities

Competing priorities were identified at all levels. Many respondents felt that trusts were faced with so many priorities, and Agency programmes were not high on their agendas. Several trusts were undergoing mergers and large-scale reorganizations that diverted attention from improvement initiatives, a point confirmed by other recent studies (Garside, 1999; Appleby, 2005). Other pressures such as star ratings, performance targets, Commission for Health Improvement (CHI) audits, and Private Finance Initiatives were also seen as obstacles:

> Unfortunately, the chief executives of trusts are worried about stars, waiting times, numbers of patients on trolleys in casualty, and those that have suffered when CHI visits. We've had a bad CHI visit and my chief executive is worried about his job, I suspect. He's not really giving a toss about me trying to tweak the patient pathway. As long as CHI doesn't measure it, he probably doesn't want to know.
>
> (Regional clinical lead)

A chief executive's role in balancing priorities was acknowledged as being complex, and it was particularly difficult to allocate priority to one service over another. The prioritization problem was compounded by differences in values and beliefs concerning how to improve the quality of the health service. Some felt that the Agency's initiatives were unwelcome simply because the service was experiencing 'initiative fatigue', and some chief executives wanted to maintain the status quo. However, some trusts were criticized for taking on too many initiatives (often in order to gain from the additional funding), and then not being able to meet targets. The 'fit' of an initiative with current local needs and day-to-day pressures was also felt to impinge on opportunities for improvements. For example, if bed occupancy rates were high, the ability to develop an effective patient booking system was reduced.

To facilitate spread and sustainability, improvement programmes must be linked to an organization's current priorities and agendas. There was a felt need for 'a change in working and a change in thinking', to ensure a coherent approach. Initiatives are less effective when viewed in isolation rather than as complementary: 'waiting times and booking go hand in hand'. Some felt that it was the responsibility of programme leaders 'to let the chief executive realize that this actually can work for them, rather than being another nuisance'.

Organization culture

It was recognized that a culture with an informal atmosphere, a non-hierarchical structure, participative rather than dictatorial management, and a lack of entrenched working practices facilitates both spread and sustainability. A history of successful change in the organization was also regarded as a predictor of future success. For example, it was felt that organizations where booking had previously been used successfully were more likely to develop and sustain this approach. In contrast, where booking had previously failed, it was much harder to introduce the approach again. Organizational readiness for change was also important, that is 'being open and willing to accept things coming from the outside'. Although many trusts were involved in improvement programmes, trusts where modernization methods had been fully embraced were reported to be very rare, depending to a large degree on the influence of the chief executive and the trust board (Pettigrew *et al.*, 1992):

> If the chief executive leads, and leads in a way that creates a 'can do' culture, a 'want to do' culture, then you get utterly different results in terms of adoption of practice, spread of practice, than you do in other organizations.
>
> (Regional manager)

One tangible aspect of organizational readiness concerned resource availability, whether staffing, funding, or computing. For instance, if an investment need was identified, but the necessary computing resources were not available, this constrained both sustainability and spread. The same applied to the recruitment and retention of appropriate staff, at all levels.

The existence of entrenched working practices was also believed to be an obstacle to change. It was acknowledged that 'medicine has been delivered in virtually the same way for a century', and that medical culture is 'good at debunking things, which is destructive rather than creative'. One respondent, a doctor, observed that:

> Nobody's ever done this sort of thing before. We've all been working the same way since 1948. There's no tradition of ever changing the way doctors work. There's all the traditions of changing the managerial structure, but doctors still work in exactly the same way. Everything's always been organized around them, because their time is precious, so as long as they are fully occupied. Organizing time around patients, because patients' time is precious, I think is a very, very difficult concept for them, and we really want both their times to be precious, so that they line up and nobody's wasting anything. That's the ideal.
>
> (National clinical lead)

If this response reflects the experience and perceptions of most doctors, it is perhaps difficult to overemphasize the degree of challenge to traditional ways of thinking and working presented by the scope and novelty of the modernization agenda since 2000.

3 Engaging staff

The importance of engaging staff in modernization was recognized, with terms such as sign-up, involvement, commitment, support, influence, and championing used interchangeably. Although an exploration of the concept of engagement is beyond the scope of this chapter, the findings raise questions about degree of engagement in service improvement. The nature of personal engagement varies, from negativity (active resistance, scepticism, disinterest), to enthusiasm. However, enthusiastic engagement may also sit on a continuum, from intellectually engaged (thinking about it), to actively engaged (doing something about it).

Beyond individual engagement, involving the whole team in planning and implementing new practices was felt to facilitate both their spread and sustainability through developing a sense of ownership and responsibility. The danger of alienating staff, particularly medical staff, by 'telling' them what to do was highlighted. One respondent noted that 'clinicians don't readily adopt solutions that have come from outside'. But the philosophy of 'adopt, adapt, or reject', where problems and potential solutions are shared, and methods are modified to suit local practice, was seen to aid spread. Early involvement, many argued, would lead to staff having a vested interest in further development. Indeed, in the booking programme, it was felt that the lack of early clinical engagement had been a mistake, causing subsequent problems:

> We tend to start programmes in this country by devising the programme at some sort of policy level, amongst people who usually are politicians. They take that to people that are in regions or trusts who are managers. Some may have clinical backgrounds, most will not. Hardly any, if any, will be clinicians. What happens then is that those managers take the scheme, work it up into guidelines and structures, and then plonk it in front of their consultants at some point, usually as late as possible, because too many people are far too uncomfortable about talking to clinicians.
>
> (Regional manager)

Timing is discussed in more detail later, but it was evident that people engaged with change at different periods, depending in part on when it became meaningful to them:

> I think first of all it is about timing for people when they first hear about it. Not interested at that particular time. Then, for some reason, when they have heard about it for a number of days, weeks, months it suddenly becomes real to them, and they can see it applying to their work practice.
>
> (Regional facilitator)

Without this desire to change, attempts to engage people were challenging, and could result in significant effort being made by the change agent for minimal gain. However, many participants reported a personal sense of excitement at becoming involved in new initiatives. Particularly strong in the early stages of the booking programme was the sense of 'fun and energy', and this enthusiasm promoted spread. However, one clinical lead observed that enthusiasm resembling evangelical zeal could instead antagonize.

The degree of ongoing engagement with service improvement programmes also appeared to vary depending upon individuals' perceived needs at any one time. This is illustrated by one participant's experiences following the publication of annual performance ratings. Some trusts with a zero star rating were felt subsequently to have 'embraced' the collaborative initiative, whereas three-star trusts were reluctant to admit that there was anything wrong with their service.

Levels of individual engagement could also be influenced by the message, as well as its source (Fraser, 2002). Perceptions of a programme can be formed at an early stage. For example, at one programme launch event, some participants were 'turned off' by the presentation style and the use of unfamiliar jargon. The power of language was also seen in relation to the naming of the Booked Admissions Programme, signalling an administrative focus. Many respondents said that this did not appeal to clinicians, as there was no obvious 'hook', unlike the Cancer Services Collaborative with its clear clinical focus. It is apparent that the message should target specific audiences, incorporating their needs and values, be compatible with existing practice, and be communicated through appropriate channels.

In summary, widespread early engagement of staff across all disciplines and at all levels within teams was seen to lead to a sense of ownership, which contributed to sustainable change. Individuals engage when there is a recognized need or desire to change, and this can be influenced both by an appropriate message and by the context.

4 Key roles

Leadership was described as crucial for both spread and sustainability of modernization programmes, and was described in terms such as 'strong', 'effective', 'clear', and 'credible'.

Chief executive and senior management

A chief executive who sees modernization as a priority and is able to make the strategic decisions necessary to ensure that improvements continue to spread within the organization was seen as pivotal. However, varying degrees of such support had been experienced, ranging from chief executives who expressed no interest, through those who were interested but not involved, to those who were actively involved and gave clear messages concerning priorities. Difficulties in engaging senior staff, obtaining their support, and accessing their time, were also reported. A few participants agreed that having an effective project board was also important for sustaining booking as it 'policed' the process.

Clinicians

Clinicians play key roles in healthcare service improvement, even with respect to changes that appear to be primarily administrative (such as patient booking). For most respondents, 'clinicians' meant hospital consultants, who can hold both national and local roles. Support from enthusiastic clinicians ensured that change happened, that sceptical colleagues were more likely to be influenced, and that a programme gained credibility:

> It's those projects that have got groups of clinicians on board, and have
> then used those clinicians to sell the project to other clinicians, that have
> been the really successful ones.
>
> (Regional manager)

With sustainability in mind, 'buy-in' from consultants was viewed as
essential for knowledge retention, as they generally stay with an organization
for longer than project managers. The concept of 'leadership' was
challenged by one clinical lead who argued instead that the consultant's role
was facilitative, describing it as 'making connections', and as 'networking
and supporting rather than providing a lead for the process'. Other studies
have found that clinicians are more often seen as a group resisting change
and blocking progress (Plsek and Kilo, 1999; Edwards and Marshall, 2003).
The issue of scepticism is explored in Chapter 5.

Project managers

A 'good' project manager was regarded as someone who could steer projects
and influence others to take ownership of the changes. Qualities such as
dedication, enthusiasm, persistence, tenacity, experience, and credibility
were all mentioned as important. Being 'rooted within the organization',
having local knowledge and the ability 'to get below the surface and know
the politics', were also seen as significant attributes. Project managers
were thought to aid the spread of the booking programme through 'working
closely with staff, identifying the movers and shakers in each particular
area so that they can influence their peers'. They were seen as key in helping
administrative and clerical staff to understand the concept of booking, and in
facilitating changes in working practices and procedures.

Middle managers

The role of middle managers in promoting or limiting spread was
particularly identified with the cancer collaborative experience. One
participant said that 'they just come along and say, no, we're not doing that,
end of story'. It was suggested that the collaborative initiative had focused
on clinical teams and chief executives, and that general managers had
received less information, resulting in an initial feeling that this was
'challenging their services':

> We have had some managers that were quite obstructive at the start, who,
> in going to conferences and in getting the training then got confidence
> and started to really enjoy it.
>
> (Regional facilitator)

With regard to key roles, it is important to observe that, despite programme benefits and organizational support, service improvement initiatives can be affected by the actions of key individuals in positions from which they can effectively delay or block change.

5 Power and influence

The strength of working relationships was perceived as crucial to the successful spread and sustainability of service improvement.

Collective leadership

One regional director explored the concept of 'whole leadership' rather than individual leadership; whole leadership concerned all staff being involved in making change happen. The presence of collective leadership was often beneficial:

> One of the key things for me is a combination of clinical and managerial leadership working together. You get two committed individuals, or a set of committed individuals working together like that, and I would say that they are virtually unstoppable.
>
> (Regional director)

Change can be implemented in many different ways, with positive results. Approaches vary depending on individuals, teams, and organizations. The presence of a multidisciplinary team, working co-operatively with common goals and priorities, was seen as key. The ability to establish personal relationships, gain an understanding of others' agendas, utilize a no-blame, non-threatening approach, and achieve a joint search for solutions was identified as a positive influence on spread.

Professional organization

The difficulties of working in professional organizations were acknowledged by participants, with role boundaries and hierarchies often stifling real progress, a point made by others (Powell *et al.*, 1999; Øvretveit, 2000). Leadership for modernization could be provided by a number of personnel, but it was felt that clinicians remained the most influential. One interviewee observed that consultants 'are the people who are really going to decide whether or not the change will run through'. In other words, consultants frequently hold ultimate decision-making power and authority.

Recent attention has been focused on manager–clinician relationships (Degeling *et al.*, 2003) and their inherent tensions. Similarly, in this study, clinicians' perceptions of general managers were reported as being historically negative, with managers viewed as an 'expensive tier of administration', rather than as leaders, 'working by instructions, utilizing tick-boxes'. On a more positive note, there was recognition of the different but complementary skills clinicians and managers contribute, and the need to identify common areas of interest and develop collegial relationships.

Opinion leaders

The role of opinion leaders in healthcare has been widely recognized (Greenhalgh *et al.*, 2004). They often work with social networks rather than through formal positions of authority. In our study, a number of stories illustrated the powerful influence of the medical profession. Some accounts were positive:

> The fact that a clinician is standing up there, being quite enthusiastic and saying, 'I thought I had a great service, but actually this has really helped us, and we now understand why pre-booking is good'.
>
> > (Regional facilitator)

Some were negative:

> If the staff around them do not see their clinician taking a real lead on this project, if they see any form of scepticism, it has a knock-on effect. They say, 'Well, our clinician isn't bothered about this so why are we?'
>
> > (National lead)

It was also interesting to note that apart from 'consultant innovators', it was often senior nurses who introduced new ideas:

> If you leave it to the consultant to initiate changes, without exception you will fail in my experience. You have to get the nurse practitioner involved.
>
> > (Clinical lead)

Opinion leaders are often regarded as individuals in particularly influential positions (Locock *et al.*, 2000), and studies of collective leadership have tended to concentrate on small senior elites (Denis *et al.*, 2001). Comments from participants in this study suggest that leadership and influence are much more widely dispersed.

6 Time for change

Respondents discussed a number of temporal issues, and in particular:

- having adequate time to focus on and become involved in a change initiative;
- dealing with the pace of change implementation and meeting targets;
- the threat to sustainability from staff looking for new challenges after a while;
- innovators, creating and implementing, moving on to the next project;
- having time to learn from experience;
- sustaining change initiatives beyond short-term projects;
- having enough time to embed change, influencing the organization culture.

Time to focus

Day-to-day time constraints were identified as a significant factor inhibiting spread, particularly if the change was regarded as additional work. Dedicated time, away from operational demands and stress, to meet, plan, develop, and undertake improvement activities was seen as essential for spread and sustainability:

> It is about time. One of the things that came out of the clinical lead sessions over the last couple of weeks was actually, I don't have time. If I had time to sit back and breathe and think, then actually we could start to make some of the changes that people want to make.
>
> (National clinical lead)

Pace of change

The fast pace of implementation of some programmes encouraged spread, but inhibited sustainability. Also important was the role of project managers in skilfully pacing initiatives, 'pushing, but not pushing people too hard; going at a pace, but knowing the limits'.

Often, rapid change, where several initiatives were being pursued simultaneously, threatened sustainability. 'Initiative fatigue' was the result. However, one clinical lead attributed the lack of sustained practice to people enjoying new challenges and continual change, because 'most of us have a very brief attention span, and it needs to be continually stimulated with something different'. This observation perhaps also applied to many Agency staff, whose role as innovators, focusing on creation and implementation, diverted them from sustainability.

Time to learn

The phased and incremental implementation of initiatives was seen to facilitate spread. This approach was used in booking, starting with one clinical area, then encouraging those consultants to introduce booking elsewhere. At a national level, the success of early 'waves' helped to spread similar changes elsewhere. Time to learn from the success of pilot sites was needed, so that positive stories could be spread to those involved in later phases. Interestingly, it was acknowledged that spread through phased implementation gradually became more difficult, as it was introduced to those not necessarily involved by choice, in contrast with those who had been eager to innovate in early waves.

Beyond the short term

Although phased implementation helped spread, the 'wave-phase' model, marked by short-term funding, hampered sustainability both at national programme and local project level. The gap in funding between phases often resulted in a loss of momentum, with attention being diverted to securing further funding as short-term contracts ended. The wave structure also encouraged staff to think in terms of short-term projects. Participants recounted experiences of organizations undertaking projects, then reverting to old ways of working, an example of 'initiative decay' (Buchanan *et al.*, 2005). The project label may also have discouraged other staff from assuming responsibility:

> Rather than take individual responsibility for a system or a process, they attribute it to the person who lit the blue touch paper. They're not here any more. It doesn't matter, they've gone.
>
> (National clinical lead)

Skills and knowledge could easily be lost when project leads left:

> One of the criticisms of health service managers, and it usually comes from clinicians, is 'You'll be gone in two years.' And the reality is, that's right.
>
> (National clinical lead)

Trusts where booking worked well were those that regarded it as a long-term process. The evidence from this study and others, therefore, suggests that policies must support new processes, ensuring they become 'mainstream', and that they continue when key staff leave.

Time to embed

The volume, frequency, and pace of change in healthcare were thought to leave little time for embedding improvements or consolidation:

> Where they are sustained, when they are embedded, where they are rooted in normality, when they are mainstream. Once it's embedded and it's normal practice, that's where it is sustained.
>
> (National clinical lead)

Another national lead commented, 'It is going to take a huge amount of time because we are talking major cultural shifts'. Ham *et al.* (2003) also note that improvement often takes longer than expected to take hold, and longer still to become firmly established.

Implications for theory and practice

This study captured the experience of senior clinical and managerial staff involved in implementing national change programmes. While these key informants may not answer for staff closer to 'the front line', they offer a privileged perspective on the formation and implementation of change strategy. The findings from this group echo issues raised in the literature, and reveal the complexity of sustainability and spread, and suggest that, while these processes can be regarded as analytically distinct, they are in practice closely intertwined.

The reviews in Chapters 2 and 3 prompted questions concerning the conditions, combinations of factors, and sequences of events that could explain the sustainability and spread of new working practices. One key finding concerns the number and variety of factors potentially influencing sustainability and spread, relating to the nature of the change initiative itself, organization culture and current priorities, the engagement of staff, senior and project management and related roles, the ways in which power and influence are exercised, and a range of temporal issues. A second observation is that sustainability and spread appear to be affected by a similar range of facilitating and inhibiting factors. A third point is that it is difficult to weight those factors in terms of impact; each could assume significance depending on timing and context. In addition, while all of those conditions appear to be necessary, none on their own would appear to be sufficient to implement, sustain, and spread these kinds of change initiatives. Different conditions are likely to assume significance at different times; leadership providing direction may be a prerequisite for adoption, but project management and adequate time may be more significant in terms of durability.

The processual perspective introduced in Chapter 2 argues that it is necessary to understand the interaction of change substance, context, and process. This broad theoretical claim also appears to be illustrated by the evidence from these interviews, suggesting that sustainability and spread depend on the following combinations of conditions:

substance   perceived benefits to patients and staff; promise of additional funds; initiative integrated with other current activities

context   no competing organizational priorities; supportive culture with high readiness for change; absence of professional boundaries and traditional hierarchies

process   effective leadership, focus, and direction; senior management support; national and local clinical support; skilled project management to encourage adoption and long-term ownership; middle management gatekeepers; time to focus, to learn, to embed; pace of change; phased implementation

It would seem to be unlikely that initiatives could be sustained and spread where only some of these conditions applied: where, for example, there were perceived benefits, no competing priorities, and senior management support, but when an initiative was not integrated with other activities, and there was strong clinical resistance, inability to recruit skilled project leads, and lack of time. This suggests that all, or most, of those conditions must be met for the processes of sustainability and spread to function, taking into consideration context and timing. In most cases, a condition has to be present at the appropriate time (perceived benefits; skilled project management), but in some instances these processes are more likely to develop where certain conditions are absent (low initial readiness for change; emphasis on boundaries and hierarchies; rapid pace of change; focus on short-term project completion). Similarly, a sequence of events in which phased funding comes to an end, project staff leave, senior management attention is diverted to other priorities, and staff are now suffering from 'initiative fatigue' is more likely to lead to initiative decay, and to an absence of the further spread of those new practices.

Seasoned change agents may see in Table 4.1 a list of more or less familiar headings. However, experience suggests that it is helpful to remind practitioners of these issues, and in particular the combinations of issues that explain why some service improvements are sustained while others decay, and why initiatives either spread or do not spread to other units. In this respect, three issues appear to be of particular significance: integrating initiatives, collective leadership, and temporal factors.

Integrating initiatives

One question raised by this study is that, if modernization at a national level is not integrated, how can local providers be expected to achieve this? Most programmes were seen either as isolated stand-alone projects or as artificial priorities which compromised other services. A related question concerns the relevance of national programmes to local needs, and whether the Agency's model was appropriate in facilitating sustainable change at the point of healthcare delivery. To facilitate sustainability and spread, programmes must be relevant to and linked with an organization's agendas and priorities. Improvement programmes thus need to be seen as complementary, rather than as separate and competing. Local modernization teams can help in this respect. By 2004, many trusts and health authorities had appointed directors of modernization, demonstrating that a more coherent and integrated approach was required.

Collective leadership

The roles of chief executives, clinicians, project managers, and middle managers were identified as especially important. Their support, example, and influence encouraged both the sustainability and spread of modernization programmes. One practical implication is that these key roles operating in partnership can exert considerable influence, emphasizing the value of collective rather than individual leadership.

Widespread and early engagement of staff across all disciplines and levels fosters a sense of collective ownership, an observation widely accepted. However, this also contributes to sustainable change. People engage when there is a recognized need or desire to change, and this is influenced by the message itself as well as the context. It is therefore important to demonstrate programme benefits. How to present benefits effectively, the types of evidence required, the credibility of evidence, and the use of appropriate communication channels and methods need to be considered. Professional organizations create their own barriers to effective communication and integration. Dopson *et al.* (2002) noted that professional boundaries inhibit the transfer of knowledge, as most forums for information exchange are either based on single disciplines or led predominantly by clinicians. Mintzberg (2003) argues that innovation in the professional organization, especially when it cuts across specialist boundaries, requires a degree of co-operation that is not often evident among autonomous professionals (Locock, 2001). Integrated working in multi-professional teams is one solution to this problem, again underlining the importance of collective leadership.

In addition to those in formal leadership positions, opinion leaders also exert a powerful influence, facilitating or disrupting the adoption of new practices and the probability of their being sustained. Opinion leaders can be found across an organization. Professionals tend to mix with those who have similar backgrounds and values (Quinn *et al.*, 2003), and Rogers (1995) indicates that homophily, where individuals share personal and social characteristics, including education and beliefs, promotes the transfer of ideas. Dopson *et al.* (2002) noted that clinical behaviour is shaped by experience, peer comparisons, and reliance on colleagues for support and advice, as much as by scientific evidence, and that medical opinion is unlikely to be challenged by other professionals.

Temporal factors

Do centrally driven national programmes with specific targets and widespread coverage inhibit sustainability, routinization, or 'normalization' of service improvements? Rapid change, in a context where several initiatives are introduced simultaneously, appears to jeopardize sustainability. Efforts are not consolidated; there is no time to 'anchor' changes (Kotter, 1995). Indeed, the future of such ambitious national programmes appears to be in doubt, reflected in the delegation of delivery and responsibility for the programme to health authorities and individual providers, and the subsequent transition of the Agency into another role (Chapter 1). This delegation was considered appropriate, given the degree of skills development in front line staff, which was not present when the national programmes began.

The significance of temporal issues was consistently underlined in this study. Cultural shifts often take longer than anticipated, and longer still to become firmly established. Dedicated time for staff to meet, share experiences, think through, plan, focus, develop, and undertake improvement activities is essential to facilitate spread and sustain ongoing improvement. Over time, staff become habituated to new working practices and seek fresh stimulation and challenge, particularly those whose job definition involves creativity and innovation (such as, in this case, some national Agency staff). Learning from the experience of pilot sites also takes time, to assess the approaches and the benefits, and identify how best to tailor and apply those methods elsewhere. Knowledge management and knowledge transfer have acquired the status of management fads, but it is important to observe that these are complex social and political processes which have to unfold at an appropriate pace if they are to be effective.

The 'waves' implementation model used by many Agency programmes created the perception that these changes were temporary, terminating when that project and the associated funding came to an end. The concept of learning from pilot projects before committing the wider organization is a widely accepted change strategy. However, for sustainability and spread to be effective, projects driven in 'waves' may need to be managed in a manner that avoids the perception that they are transient. Given the scale and complexity of the modernization agenda, that was problematic. Sustainable improvements may be more likely to result from changes developed at the point of delivery, rather than changes delivered from a national body.

The language of these issues, and the related literature, encourage an approach which focuses first on implementation, with sustainability and spread as later stages. As indicated earlier (Preface), this does not necessarily reflect the temporal logic in practice. It seems more helpful to plan for sustainability and spread from the start, rather than managing these issues as afterthoughts. We know, broadly, the conditions in which sustainability and spread are more or less likely to occur. While we cannot make firm predictions and guarantees in this regard, we know enough about the nature of these processes to be able to influence the odds.

A final linguistic issue: members of the widely informed group on which the findings in this chapter are based appeared to have no common understanding of the key terms, which may require clarification among front line staff, to encourage broad agreement about goals and methods. Misunderstandings and lack of clarity could inhibit the sustainability and spread of service improvement initiatives.

Critical debates

1 There is no agreement across the health service concerning the meaning of the terms 'sustainability' and 'spread' with regard to new working practices. Is that lack of consensus significant or not, and why?
2 Some major changes are centrally driven, across the whole organization, by a national agency. Some are developed locally, by provider units. Which are more likely to be sustained and to spread more effectively, and why?
3 You are a change leader responsible for a major service improvement initiative. Should you first attempt to engage a wide group of colleagues to establish 'critical mass'? Or would it be better to work initially with a small group of enthusiasts?

5 Shades of resistance: understanding and addressing scepticism

Rose Gollop and Diane Ketley

Chapter aims

1 To introduce the concepts of scepticism and resistance towards modernization initiatives in healthcare.
2 To describe the findings of research that explored scepticism and resistance towards two national programmes.
3 To relate the research findings to a behavioural model of change.
4 To question negative assumptions about scepticism and resistance.

Key point summary

- Changes introduced as part of the process of modernization have met with both scepticism and resistance from some healthcare staff.
- The history and culture of the NHS, characterized by the dominance of powerful staff groups, have contributed to scepticism and resistance towards change.
- NHS Modernisation Agency research has demonstrated that these reactions slow the spread of service improvement and jeopardize its sustainability.
- The roots of scepticism and resistance lie in a complex mixture of factors that include elements of the change itself, individual reactions, and issues of timing and context.
- Sceptics can become supporters, and even public champions, of change, but newly won support is sometimes fragile and may require nurturing to be sustained.
- People choose to become involved in change for many reasons, most notably because they begin to understand the benefits that will result.
- Skilled and experienced change facilitators can influence the process of engagement with change through the use of a range of tailored techniques designed to match individuals' concerns.
- A number of conceptual models exist that help to explain the process by which individuals become engaged with change.
- Although scepticism and resistance are often described in negative terms,

some organizational change theorists argue that these responses contribute positively to the debate and creativity surrounding change. In this study, that view was not shared by most change agents dealing with these issues on a day-to-day basis.

The nature of scepticism and resistance

In 2000, *The NHS Plan* set out an ambitious agenda for improving the quality of care offered to patients, to be supported by significant additional funding for the service, and by a new central 'organization development' agency. How could anyone working in healthcare be opposed to developing better patient care with more money? The aim of this chapter is to report the findings of a study which explored the nature and sources of that opposition.

Anecdotal tales of scepticism and resistance towards change are common in the NHS, but they have been the subject of relatively little research. The nature, causes, and effects of scepticism and resistance, and indeed the differences between those concepts, have received only passing attention. This is perhaps surprising, given that the success of change initiatives depends heavily on the way in which people perceive and respond to them. The terms 'scepticism' and 'resistance' are often used interchangeably, as natural language labels that describe opposition towards something unwelcome or new. The *Oxford English Dictionary* defines these terms differently. The sceptic questions or doubts accepted opinions. The resistor tries through actions and arguments to prevent someone from doing something, or something from happening. These definitions imply a range of attitudes and behaviours.

In practice, making a clear distinction between the two sets of responses implies an unrealistic degree of separation. These terms are more appropriately viewed as a continuum of attitudes and behaviours, encompassing resistance at one end and active involvement at the other (Gollop, 2004a; Research into Practice, 2004). It is possible to move along this continuum in either direction, depending on circumstances (Figure 5.1). This perspective indicates that both attitudes and behaviours need to be influenced to gain a person's active involvement in change.

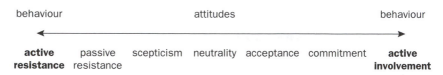

Figure 5.1 *The scepticism continuum*

Whether an individual's opposition expresses itself as resistance or scepticism may depend, at least in part, on the nature of the change, and whether it is perceived as being voluntary or imposed. The choices open to individuals in organized settings may be constrained in several ways (Rogers, 1995). Change can be *collective* (everyone in a particular group must decide to adopt or not), *authoritative* (the individual is told to adopt), or *contingent* (the individual cannot choose to adopt until the organization has sanctioned it). Imposed and authoritative changes are constant features of centralized public services. Changes to the structure of the service cannot be resisted, but attempts to introduce change to processes and, even more subtly, to the culture of healthcare provision, have been, to date, voluntary, and have faced both scepticism and resistance. The NHS is a professional organization, and the dominant position of powerful groups such as doctors enables them to resist such changes with ease. The history and development of the evidence-based medicine movement is one example of an initiative that has progressed unevenly as a result of resistance from those it was intended to influence. The cherished notion of clinical autonomy has led some doctors to reject those imposed changes to processes and organization culture on the grounds that they remove their right to unchallenged decision making, reducing the status of clinical practice to technical 'cook-book' medicine (Dopson *et al.*, 2003).

The comprehensive evaluation by McNulty and Ferlie (2002) of the business process re-engineering programme at Leicester Royal Infirmary highlights the limited impact of a model of change that aspired to 'whole hospital redesign'. Although introduced as a strategic choice by senior hospital management, with the support of influential medical staff, it did not result in the anticipated transformation. Their findings underlined the view that professional staff are not passive recipients of policy-inspired change, and that resistance to these kinds of changes was not confined to medical staff:

> Findings of the study confirm the indifference and resistance that
> planned, programmed, top-down change strategies may face, not just
> from clinical professionals in this case, but also other managers.
>
> (McNulty and Ferlie, 2002, p.331)

Their conclusions with respect to the impact of the re-engineering programme noted that doctors held the most power either to block or adopt change.

Being sceptical or resistant towards one particular set of changes does not necessarily imply blanket opposition to all initiatives in any circumstances. With regard to response to the new, Rogers (1995) distinguishes between innovators, early adopters, early majority, late majority, and laggards. However, Greenhalgh *et al.* (2004) warn against interpreting these labels as fixed personality traits, since responses to change vary with context.

Describing someone as 'resistant' or 'laggard' may not only be inaccurate, but is also likely to antagonize.

What's the problem?

That example (from McNulty and Ferlie, 2002) of resistance to high-level change provides some background to understanding how staff have responded to the broader modernization movement. The agenda has included some radical changes to structures, such as the introduction of foundation hospital status, but these have taken place along with more fundamental changes to processes and ways of working. While many have welcomed the modernization agenda as an opportunity to reform and streamline services, and to experiment with new working practices, some have viewed it with suspicion and have resisted involvement. However, the underpinning philosophy of modernization is that it will transform healthcare in ways that business process re-engineering (in that particular case) failed to do. Success would involve widespread involvement from staff across the whole service, a challenging requirement. One study estimated that only 15 per cent of front line staff were participating in formal improvement activities (Bate *et al.*, 2004). While the failure of the majority to become involved cannot be assumed to be due simply to scepticism or resistance, opposition to the philosophy of modernization has clearly been a factor.

Research undertaken by the Research into Practice team studied the existence, impact, and management of scepticism and resistance as part of the broader study into spread and sustainability. As described in Chapter 4, senior staff from two national programmes, the Cancer Services Collaborative and the National Booked Admissions Programme, were interviewed for this study, which was carried out in 2002. (The collaborative was later renamed the Cancer Services Collaborative Improvement Partnership, and booking was renamed the National Booking Programme.) The findings demonstrate how scepticism and resistance among all staff, and medical staff in particular, slow the spread and jeopardize the sustainability of new working practices.

High-profile initiatives

Scepticism, particularly among medical staff, was known to be an issue facing change leaders during the early stages of the cancer collaborative and booking programme initiatives. Both programmes were high-profile examples of national initiatives designed to spearhead the drive to modernize service delivery, and aimed, at least in part, towards meeting government targets. Both required the involvement of doctors, but the clinical focus of the collaborative was thought from the outset to require closer clinical engagement than the booking programme which aimed to improve patients' access to services.

The National Booking Programme

This was the first, and largest, of the national service improvement programmes supported by the Agency as a key element of *The NHS Plan*. The focus was on access and choice for patients, and it aimed to allow patients in England to choose and pre-book the date of their healthcare appointment or hospital admission. The functions of this programme were subsequently assumed by the National Programme for Information Technology.

The introduction of a system of booked appointments moved the locus of control from clinical and secretarial staff to dedicated booking administrators and patients. Running a successful booking system might involve the introduction of 'pooled' waiting lists, where referrals are directed to a team of consultants rather than to a named individual, the replacement of paper-based with electronic appointment systems, and staff being required to give longer advance notice of their annual leave plans, to enable clinics to be booked well in advance. While this programme appeared to be little more than an expensive administrative refinement, it had significant consequences for managerial and clinical practice.

The Cancer Services Collaborative

The collaborative was another national programme, designed to improve the experience and outcomes of care for patients with suspected and diagnosed cancer, through redesigning healthcare services. Although nationally led at the beginning, this initiative was more devolved in later phases, becoming aligned with services at local levels through a system of cancer care networks. Changes introduced as a result of the collaborative involved the extension of traditional roles, as for example nurse-led clinics, and the development of common diagnostic pathways agreed by a group of doctors who had each previously followed their own preferred methods.

The research described in this chapter (and Chapter 4) was conducted using confidential semi-structured interviews to elicit the views and experiences of clinical and managerial staff working with the programmes at regional and national levels. Two questions formed the focus of enquiry:

- Why are some staff sceptical or resistant towards these improvement programmes?
- What influences staff to change their minds?

The sample of 39 staff included 5 former self-proclaimed sceptical consultants working as clinical leaders in the cancer collaborative. Their interviews provided a personal view, adding another dimension to the perspectives of the other participants who discussed their experience of managing colleagues' scepticism and resistance. The main findings of this study concern the nature and prevalence of scepticism and resistance, its sources, and the processes through which staff became supporters of the programmes (Gollop *et al.*, 2004).

Study findings

The findings from this study showed that scepticism and resistance slow the adoption of changes designed to improve services, negatively affecting their spread and sustainability. Staff employed to lead and facilitate change found that they spent a considerable amount of time and effort persuading colleagues to become involved. This was time that might otherwise have been spent facilitating further change. Furthermore, sceptical staff sometimes influenced others not to become involved, in effect spreading the opposite message. The findings are summarized here under four headings concerning the nature and prevalence of scepticism, sources of scepticism, moving towards support, and influencing personal change.

Nature and prevalence

Almost all of the staff interviewed, from both programmes, had experienced scepticism and resistance among colleagues, especially medical colleagues, thus confirming anecdotal accounts. Although the findings were broadly similar for both programmes, some interesting differences in emphasis emerged. Those working in the booking programme experienced opposition from administrative staff as well as clinical and managerial staff, an observation not made by those in the cancer collaborative. Booking staff also referred more frequently to scepticism and resistance as being widespread and difficult to manage. However, this does not necessarily indicate that either scepticism or resistance was more prevalent in the booking programme than in the cancer collaborative.

The ways in which the two programmes were established and subsequently developed, one focusing on clinical issues and the other on patient access, may help to explain these differences in emphasis. In 1998, the booking programme was the first national improvement programme to be established; little was known among NHS leaders about how to spread and sustain such a large-scale initiative. It was also established to be led locally by booking managers, initially without clinical leadership at national or local levels, being seen principally as an administrative initiative. Although the need to involve doctors in leading and developing the programme was recognized, national clinical leads were not appointed until the third wave of the programme in 2000–2001. Administrative staff were also not involved in planning, as it was believed that managers would implement the changes.

The evolution of the booking programme contrasts with that of the cancer collaborative, which began a year afterwards, in 1999. Its leaders were familiar with the collaborative methodology from the beginning, adapting it from the approach developed by the Institute for Healthcare Improvement in the United States (Kerr *et al.*, 2002). The approach centres on the capacity of clinical teams to spread small-scale changes to other teams, passing on their experience and learning, and eliminating the need for reinvention. Clinical leaders are therefore prominent members of improvement teams, and their contribution is key (Parker *et al.*, 2001). Doctors were thus involved in the collaborative from the outset, at both national and local levels. Although it still encountered much scepticism and resistance, this was, in essence, a clinically centred improvement programme, focusing on changes in a specific disease group. Many of its original clinical sceptics were involved from an early stage, working through their scepticism in public and private debate, some eventually to become supporters and leaders. While opposition continued to be a factor in its adoption, the more widespread network of clinical leadership probably helped to support change managers to spread and sustain the collaborative's messages.

One of the issues emerging from this study was that, even when support is won, it may not be permanent, and can prove to be fragile. In particular, support depends upon the continuing provision of positive evidence of outcomes. Some participants described how support began to waver when anticipated benefits were slow to be realized, or failed to meet expectations:

> One of our clinicians, who really got us into phase one here, has seen no benefits at all for his service, and he's very cynical about phase two.
>
> (Clinician)

This potential loss of support has implications for the sustainability of initiatives of this kind. It could be argued that the subsequent opposition of someone who was previously closely involved as a supporter is more damaging than that of someone whose objections have always been made from a distance.

Sources of scepticism

This study showed that the roots of scepticism and resistance lie in factors that relate both to the change substance and to individuals' responses. Factors related to the change itself include its nature, the context and timing of its introduction, and the way in which it is promoted. Factors related to individual response include levels of knowledge and understanding, past experience of change, and interpretations of personal meaning and perceived impact. It is difficult and unhelpful to attempt to isolate these factors, since they are often interconnected and cumulative (see Chapter 12). For example, some of the early opposition to the booking programme was founded in a climate of suspicion that arose from a mixture of factors including incomplete knowledge and assumptions about the nature and purpose of booking.

The findings suggest that some scepticism and resistance stems from personal and deeply held anxieties about freedom and autonomy to practise in ways of one's own choosing, fears about loss of power and influence, and forced changes to job role. These reactions were not confined to one staff group. Staff in all disciplines feared the impact of change for them personally. Some had spent many years developing and refining systems that they felt served them very well, and they were reluctant to accept new systems for booking, especially when those were seen as being imposed on them. Some participants hinted at the existence of perverse incentives to maintain unreformed systems that ensured longer waiting lists. This was later echoed in an evaluation of the early waves of the booking programme, which found that some clinical resistance related to fears that an improved system of booking appointments would reduce the likelihood of patients choosing private treatment (Ham *et al.*, 2003). An evaluation of staff experience and perceptions of the fourth wave of the booking programme confirmed continuing opposition, especially among clerical and medical staff (Neath, 2004b). Interestingly, this later work identified clerical staff, including medical secretaries and administrative staff, as both the most and least receptive to the introduction of booking, and also found that medical staff were the least receptive. Some of these reactions reveal a fundamental tension between the impact of change on individual staff, and potential benefits to patients. There was no evidence that staff were so altruistic as to accept change that would benefit patients if it was perceived as being detrimental to their own working lives.

Some of the medical participants in this study voiced the opinion that doctors now face a barrage of challenges to their authority and autonomy, whether from government, managers, the media, or an increasingly informed public. This was making them less inclined to embrace the modernization agenda, contributing to the perception that it was a movement that would further erode their position and influence.

The origins of these programmes thus triggered a measure of opposition. This was more apparent in the booking programme, perceived by some to be a centrally led initiative that should be rejected on principle because it was politically inspired. Scepticism towards government health policy and its implementation is not new (Horton, 2000; Winyard, 2003) and was particularly evident among medical staff in this study:

> They saw it as a way to manipulate waiting lists. That's all it is. Another government initiative to fiddle the figures.
>
> (Regional booking manager describing the reactions of medical colleagues)

The booking programme was also understood by some clinicians as essentially administrative in nature, and therefore not requiring their involvement, a response perhaps less associated with scepticism and more with lack of interest. In contrast, the cancer collaborative was opposed in some quarters because of its specific clinical focus, which was interpreted by some as inappropriately prioritizing cancer above other, and more prevalent, diseases.

Such responses do not necessarily indicate opposition to the need for service improvement per se, but to the focus of specific programmes. That opposition was also based, in part, on a lack of full understanding about the benefits of involvement with initiatives such as these. Staff who did become involved found that they learned improvement tools and techniques that could be readily transferred to other, high-volume areas of the service. In some situations, the boundaries between specific patient groups were removed, so that collaborative funding began to be used to make changes across a whole system or department.

The context and timing of the introduction of these programmes was a significant factor in the way in which they were received. Trusts were under pressure from government to meet performance targets, and these improvement programmes were seen by some staff as a source of competing priorities. The booking programme in particular was perceived in some quarters as a diversion rather than as a means of helping to achieve targets. Sceptical managers did not consider it as integral to their organization's core business. Staff also felt overwhelmed by the pace of change, and some believed that they could ignore invitations to become involved, because they would soon be superseded by other workload imperatives.

In the cancer collaborative, there was a specific negative reaction to the way in which the programme was introduced to staff at early national conferences. This response centred on the style, content, and source of material used to explain the collaborative methodology. The national team had invited American collaborative experts to present the programme's philosophy and methods. However, the reactions of clinicians in particular demonstrated the gulf that existed at that time between front line healthcare professionals in Britain and American ideas. One of their objections reflected their preference for hearing new ideas about healthcare from tried and trusted sources, in other words their domestic peers:

> We recognised almost nobody on the platform as having any authority or clout in our own craft organizations. I would have expected to see somebody who was on [my professional] section of the Royal Society of Medicine, or somebody well known for their research output.
>   (Lead cancer clinician, and former self-confessed sceptic)

Moving towards support

The process through which staff became more receptive towards these programmes was generally described as gradual, although several participants recalled specific events that led them to experience something approaching a damascene conversion. One of the most powerful examples of this was involvement in a multi-professional team exercise known as process mapping, in which the path through the healthcare system experienced by a 'typical' patient is unpicked, step by step, and shared by all. This commonly reveals process delays and duplications, as well as illustrating the role of each team member. The dramatic effect this exercise had on some staff, especially doctors, seems to have stemmed from its illumination of the complete patient pathway. Healthcare tends to be 'episodic', with those providing the service witnessing only the patient interactions at which they are personally present. Some medical staff confessed that they previously had only a general idea of what happened to patients when they left their consulting rooms. Exposure to process mapping acted as a catalyst for subsequent involvement for some sceptical staff, as this demonstrated failings in the current system, and how simple but effective improvements could be made.

Another common scenario for moving from scepticism to support appears to have been one of slow and often assisted progress along the continuum of behaviours and attitudes. Sceptics sometimes adopted the position of sideline observer for a time, as others embraced the programmes with varying degrees of enthusiasm and success.

Our study found that attitudinal (and subsequently behavioural) change was prompted by a number of factors. The most powerful factor was an appreciation of the benefits that the changes would bring (Berwick, 2003).

Participants frequently referred to the impact of evidence, whether in the form of rigorously gathered objective measures, or a more subjective feeling that matters were indeed better than before. Even when the assessment of benefit was measured in negative terms (a new system of booking was not actually *worse* than the system it replaced), this could be sufficient to persuade someone to try it again.

Some staff expressed irritation with the terms 'modernization' and 'service improvement'. These labels implied criticism of current practice. However, others were induced to become involved because they were aware that existing methods were inefficient in various ways, and that to continue working as before was no longer an option:

> He said to us, 'Can you come and talk to us?' It was clear from the problems he was alluding to, they had got to do something. That's an example of someone who has been resistant, but has heard about it, and out of the situation of chaos and crisis he has said, 'Can you come and help?'
>
> (Lead cancer clinician, describing the response of a medical colleague to the cancer collaborative)

A more pragmatic response was to be attracted by the extra resources that participation in the programmes brought, demonstrating a readiness to become involved while at the same time remaining sceptical. Several of the consultants who went on to become clinical leaders of the collaborative programme started from this position. Taking a longer-term view, they foresaw that the programme would expand, requiring their eventual involvement, and decided to take the opportunity to join at the outset, arguing that they would be in a better position to influence from within. While clearly not resistant, neither were they champions at that early stage, but their willingness to become involved contrasted with the responses of many of their peers. Their subsequent move to become champions resulted from their personal experience, and a growing awareness of the benefits of working in different ways.

Influencing personal change

Many of the staff interviewed for this study were responsible for promoting the spread and sustainability of modernization through their roles as managers, facilitators, or clinical leads. This required them to influence sceptical and resistant colleagues to become involved in the programmes. They described using a range of skills and techniques which involved initially identifying the source of individuals' objections, then gauging their state of readiness to change, and finally using tailored strategies to win support.

Taking time to listen to people's objections allows an assessment both of their readiness to change and the triggers that might prompt them to begin that process. Participants described how they deliberately concentrated their efforts on staff who were more receptive, after making little progress with the truly resistant. The effect of transferring attention away from people who were not ready to change was to allow them to observe from a distance, before moving to a state of readiness to become involved themselves:

> He just watched it from the sidelines for long enough to see how it could meet his needs, and then thought, 'I'll do it.'
>
> (Regional facilitator, cancer collaborative, describing how a colleague's support was won)

This staged reaction reveals the complexity of personal decision making, with differing concerns dominating at different stages of the process (Greenhalgh *et al.*, 2004).

Modelling behaviour change

There are several conceptual models that attempt to explain the process through which individuals choose to adopt changes. The extent to which these models highlight resistance as part of the process varies. Those relating to the psychology of change demonstrate a more sophisticated understanding of the process than did early models that sought to explain the adoption of simple innovations (Greenhalgh *et al.*, 2004). Psychological models that reflect motivations include the concerns-based adoption model (Hall and Hord, 1987), and the transtheoretical model originally developed to explain individual addiction behaviour (Prochaska and DiClemente, 1984). The transtheoretical model has more recently been tested in controlled workplace experiments, with the aim of applying this perspective to the field of organizational change (Prochaska *et al.*, 2001). It specifically recognizes the impact of resistance on change initiatives, and relates the stages of change to practical interventions designed to influence adoption. For these reasons it will be discussed in some detail here, with reference to our own findings.

The later transtheoretical model describes how people progress through a series of five stages when modifying behaviour, either on their own or with input from others. The stages are:

1 **Precontemplation**: the individual is not ready to discuss or consider change.
2 **Contemplation**: the individual is willing to listen and to consider a change.
3 **Preparation**: the individual gets ready to do something concrete.
4 **Action**: the individual starts to work with the change.
5 **Maintenance**: the individual strives not to slip back to old behaviours.

Prochaska and colleagues note that, at any one time, 80 per cent of those in the stages before action are in either precontemplation or contemplation, with only 20 per cent in preparation mode. They argue that these 80 per cent are likely to view change as imposed, and that they can become resistant if forced to take action before they are ready. In a further development of this model, they identify 10 processes that produce individual behaviour change, described in Table 5.1. Their research suggests that stage-matched interventions can have a far greater impact than standard or generic methods, because they can be tailored to correspond with the individual's readiness for involvement with change. They can also be tailored to correspond to individual motivations. In this way, resistance can be reduced, resources to support change better focused, and change implemented more quickly.

Table 5.1 *Processes and activities for influencing behaviour change*

Processes	Activities
Consciousness raising	Becoming more aware of a problem and potential solutions
Dramatic relief	Emotional arousal, such as fear of failure to change, and inspiration for successful change
Self re-evaluation	Appreciating that the change is important to one's identity, happiness, and success
Self liberation	Believing that a change can succeed, and making a firm commitment to it
Environmental re-evaluation	Appreciating that the change will have a positive impact on the social and work environment
Reinforcement management	Finding intrinsic and extrinsic rewards for new ways of working
Counter-conditioning	Substituting new behaviours and cognitions for the old ways of working
Helping relationships	Seeking and using social support to facilitate change
Stimulus control	Restructuring the environment to elicit new behaviours and inhibit old habits
Social liberation	Empowering individuals by providing more choices and resources

In our study, participants used tailored strategies spontaneously, deliberately, and successfully. The strategies they employed were both overt and covert, dependent on their assessment of individuals' receptivity towards that particular change. They represent an impressive range of techniques and 'hooks' for gaining initial interest and support, and demonstrate the value of an experienced project manager or clinical lead. Strategies included:

● **Appealing**
  – making direct appeals to focus on something already identified by staff or patients as an important area for reform;
  – asking sceptical staff for help with something known to be of interest to them, for example an IT issue, in order to draw them into a project;
  – asking reluctant staff to become involved as a personal favour, 'just for me'.

● **Demonstrating**
  – presenting data to illustrate current activity;
  – demonstrating a particular improvement technique, such as process mapping.

● **Bribing**
  – ensuring the immediate success of a trial of a change by offering a temporarily increased level of resource;
  – providing resources such as small items of clinical equipment, or computing hardware, or funding for additional posts.

● **Shaming**
  – ensuring that sceptical staff were exposed to pro-change peers at meetings, sometimes by deliberately seating sceptical staff with a group of enthusiasts;
  – focusing efforts on pro-change staff, which had the effect of gradually isolating sceptical members of the team.

● **Hiding**
  – avoiding the use of terminology associated with improvement when inviting sceptical staff to work on improvement projects, for example describing a 'plan–do–study–act' or 'PDSA' cycle (Langley *et al.*, 1996) as 'a pilot study';
  – testing a change without directly involving sceptical staff, and telling them about it only after it had proved successful.

Many of these tactics echo the successful organizational activities described by Prochasksa and colleagues. Table 5.2 outlines how the stages and processes of change can be used by change leaders engaged in modernization work in healthcare organizations.

If attempts to understand resistance in terms of psychological change models are to be criticized, it may be on the basis that they present overly rational explanations of motives, behaviours, and potential intervention strategies. In contrast, some explanations for opposition provided by participants in our study demonstrated the habitual or instinctive nature of some responses to national change interventions; for example, some will probably always tend to resist new ideas on principle, simply because they were government inspired.

Table 5.2 Stages, processes, and change interventions

Stages	Precontemplation	Contemplation	Preparation	Action	Maintenance
Processes	Consciousness raising	Dramatic relief Self re-evaluation	Helping relationships Self-liberation Environmental re-evaluation		Counter-conditioning Helping relationships Reinforcement management Stimulus control Social liberation
Actions	Communicate change issue widely, to encourage awareness, understanding, and debate Focus efforts on enthusiasts Listen to objectors	Communicate information about the success of similar changes elsewhere Highlight the benefits to patients and staff Emphasize the consequences of doing nothing Emphasize the importance of individual participation Address individual concerns	Emphasize the importance of individual participation Establish teams to develop change plans Encourage mutual support and networks Identify individuals' and teams' training, support, and resource needs Be visible	Provide identified support, training, and resources Link new 'converts' to experienced peers Ensure benefits are measured and widely communicated	Remove processes and protocols that support old practices Support the development of networks and communities of practice Devolve responsibility and decision-making powers to lowest possible level

The value of scepticism and resistance

A further criticism of models that explain the way people behave is that some treat resistance as a force to be overcome. Organization theorists (Prochaska *et al.*, 2001) often argue that resistance to change stems from poorly planned change implementation, and that conflict occurs when change leaders make mistaken assumptions about employees' readiness to become involved. Such logic implies that good planning is all that is required to ensure full participation, and that understanding sceptics' and resistors' views is important for the purpose of influencing them either to change their minds or to adopt a positive stance with regard to the change initiative from the start.

But other studies have found value in negative reactions. Commercial practice, for example, often interprets resistance to change as a natural and necessary force for exposing and resolving conflict, and consequently for planning and implementing change effectively (Mabin *et al.*, 2001). This perspective advocates that those who challenge and question proposed change should be encouraged, and that different opinions (often including other good ideas) should be encompassed. Schön (1963) argued that organizations need resistance to change in order to prevent bad and poorly developed ideas from being implemented. This viewpoint acknowledges that resistance helps to draw attention to the potential pitfalls of change, thus encouraging the development of other options that could prove to be superior to the original plan (Wadell and Sohal, 2001).

In healthcare, policy researchers have started to question the appropriateness of 'overcoming resistance' to change in such a one-dimensional manner. The alternative perspective identifies resistance as necessary for the development of 'bottom-up' energy, debate, and power that can ultimately lead to widespread, sustained change (Bate *et al.*, 2004). Unquestioning compliance with reform is interpreted as being incompatible with the development of grass-roots ownership of change. However, our research uncovered relatively little evidence of positive feelings about scepticism and resistance at operational levels. Despite these idealistic (and often realistic) claims concerning the value of negative questioning and challenging responses, change agents and leaders in this study found that dealing with and attempting to resolve those reactions was difficult and time consuming.

Implications for theory and practice

The findings from our study indicate that scepticism and resistance towards national service improvement programmes are common, exist among all staff groups, and are being managed at service delivery level by project managers and clinical leads. They have adopted a behavioural approach to the challenge, using tailored strategies that have much in common with the techniques advocated by behavioural researchers. In practice, positive interpretations of resistance to change found little support among respondents. The view that resistance can be a creative challenge did not resonate with the experiences of most of those in change agency roles who encountered some form of resistance daily. With few exceptions, they saw resistance damaging the adoption, spread, and sustainability of healthcare modernization, and consuming much of their time and resources. The few who did welcome the challenge interpreted it as an opportunity to reflect on the process of change, and used this as a check on the viability of their plans. The study did not explore why individual change agents reacted in different ways to resistance, but it is likely that the experience, skills, and credibility of change leaders influence the way they react to colleagues' responses.

The findings also demonstrate that individuals' acceptance of change is affected by a complex and connected set of social and organizational factors, including the nature of the change itself as well as issues of context and timing. These powerful influences on decision making are summarised in Figure 5.2. They represent a conundrum for those who are considering change but are not convinced of its value. How are those factors perceived and weighted in terms of significance and priority with regard to shaping the individual's ultimate decision and the timing of that outcome?

The complex nature of the decision process through which individuals choose to adopt or become involved with change presents change leaders, drivers, agents, and facilitators with a significant challenge. As large-scale, phased national programmes were replaced by locally managed modernization initiatives, this perhaps altered the balance between involvement that was perceived to be imposed and that which was voluntary. Indeed, if the NHS is to succeed in developing a mass movement for change, involvement must be viewed as voluntary, desirable, and achievable. If staff possess a better understanding of the need to change, and more control over how to achieve it, this is more likely to happen. Meanwhile, understanding why people resist or are sceptical is an important part of managing the modernization agenda, whether through welcoming such responses or attempting to change them.

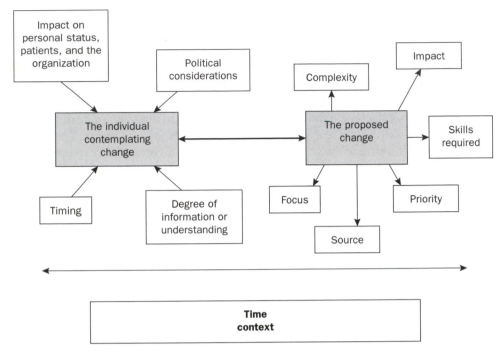

Figure 5.2 *The involvement conundrum*

Critical debates

1 To what extent does the history and culture of Britain's publicly funded national healthcare system inevitably contribute to a climate of scepticism among staff with regard to government service improvement and modernization ideas?

2 Are stage-specific interventions to accelerate the process of converting sceptics into supporters of change dubious, manipulative, organization political tactics or valuable change agency skills and techniques?

3 Opposition to change, in the forms of questioning scepticism and active resistance, can be either helpful or damaging. Construct a 'balance sheet' to help decide whether the benefits of such disruptive behaviours outweigh the drawbacks – or vice versa.

6 Tracking sustainability: lessons from the patient booking timeline

Annette Neath

Chapter aims

1 To describe the national structure and funding of the Booked Admissions Programme, the first and one of the longest-running initiatives sponsored by the NHS Modernisation Agency.
2 To identify factors influencing the sustainability and spread of booking initiatives.
3 To consider the achievements of this programme between 1998 and 2003, examining national, organizational, patient, and staff perspectives.

Key point summary

- The National Booking Programme, from 1998 to 2003, was the first, the largest, and one of the longest-running modernization programmes linked to *The NHS Plan* change agenda. It was implemented through four overlapping waves, which cost a total of £115 million.
- Giving patients the opportunity to choose appointment and admission dates increases certainty and patient satisfaction, reduces anxiety and the time between referral and treatment, and can reduce the number of patient-initiated cancellations.
- For booking to work well, waiting times in a clinical service first have to be cut to six months or less, which was another benefit from this initiative.
- While the aims of this programme seem straightforward, defining 'a booked appointment' for the purposes of measuring performance was one of the most problematic and controversial aspects of this initiative.
- Despite the apparently straightforward goal of making the booking of a hospital appointment as simple as booking an airline ticket, significant process redesign was required if targets were to be met. This involved new roles and administrative procedures, changes in clinical practice, new computing and management information systems, new forms of collaboration between primary and secondary care, and new physical facilities (typically daycase surgical units).

- Realizing that the service has become more flexible, some patients are more likely to rearrange appointments at short notice, disrupting a system that now has less slack, making it more vulnerable to disruption from unplanned emergency admissions, and making less effective use of resources.
- The organization structure of this programme was multi-layered and complex, involving the Department of Health and its 'Waiting and Booking' Policy Branch, the NHS Executive, regional offices which were abolished in 2001 and replaced by strategic health authorities, the Agency which inherited support of the programme from the National Patients Access Team in 2001, the national booking team whose clinical leads assumed the responsibilities of the regional office booked admissions leads, and the hospital-based booking project leads and teams. In 2003, responsibility for the initiative was devolved to the health authorities and local teams.
- The spread of booking practice was to be informed and encouraged by the implementation structure of the programme, with subsequent waves learning from previous experience. Spread was inhibited, however, by medical scepticism, confusion concerning definitions and goals, changing reporting requirements, the complexity and cost of the process changes required, and frequent shifts in national priorities which caused attention and resources to be diverted to other issues.
- Sustainability of booking practice was reinforced by the patient, organization, and staff benefits, but was jeopardized by the short-term project-based nature of the waves of the programme and by those shifts in national priorities.
- Patient booking is costly, complex, and time consuming to implement, but it is not clear whether patients rate choice of appointment dates more highly than shorter waiting times, and it also questionable whether booking improves quality of patient care or the overall patient experience of care.

Background and aims

> The concept of booking did more to shake the medical model than any number of policy papers and government targets, in that it prioritized the patient as an active partner in planning health care. One response we got in a patient survey still sticks in my mind: 'Doctors' time is precious, so is mine'.
>
> (Redesign coach)

The National Booking Programme was the first, largest, and one of the longest-running modernization programmes. While the concept of offering patients a choice of appointment or admission date seems relatively simple, this involved a complex series of changes and significant redesign of services. Chapter 7 explores the sustainability and spread issues affecting this programme, exploring the experience of one acute hospital. Chapter 8 considers change leadership and interpersonal influence in developing the booking programme. This chapter provides background information on the initiative, and explores in particular the contextual and temporal issues relevant to a national programme of this scale and substance. In particular, the chapter describes the programme's history, outlines the national changes that affected its progress, and its achievements, seen from national, organizational, patient, and staff perspectives.

The National Booked Admissions Programme began in July 1998, two years before publication of *The NHS Plan*, as part of the government's strategy for modernizing healthcare. The programme was launched by the National Patients Access Team (NPAT), established to examine ways to reduce hospital waiting lists and waiting times, and experience with booking contributed to the vision to design the heath service around patient needs. When it was formed in April 2001, the Agency assumed responsibility for the programme. Staff involved in this research used a range of terms such as 'national booked admissions', 'national booking', 'national booked', and 'booking' when discussing the initiative. For consistency, the terms 'booking' and 'booking programme' are used throughout this chapter, except in direct quotes from publications and interviews.

Booking allowed patients to choose the date and time of their outpatient clinic appointment or hospital admission. *The NHS Plan* indicated that this would be extended to every service in every hospital. This would make booking a hospital appointment as easy as booking an airline ticket, with the target that all outpatient appointments, daycase, and inpatient elective admissions would be pre-booked by December 2005. Following the publication of *The NHS Plan*, the booking programme was supported and facilitated by the Agency. In addition to benefits for patients, booking systems were expected to result in more efficient use of resources, through reductions in hospital- and patient-initiated cancellations, and a drop in the number of patients not attending their appointment.

Traditional approach

While practice varied between hospitals, the following example is typical of the patient experience before the introduction of a booking system. Following a decision to refer a patient to a specialist, the general practitioner (GP) writes a referral letter to the relevant hospital consultant, asking the consultant to see the patient, and to confirm the diagnosis and treatment. Some GPs write their referral letters once a week, resulting in a delay between the decision to refer and the consultant seeing the patient.

On receipt of the letter, either the consultant's medical secretary or a waiting list clerk sends a written reply offering an outpatient clinic appointment, perhaps in several months' time. If the appointment date is inconvenient, the patient has to contact the clinic to ask for another appointment, and then wait for another letter to arrive, hoping that the new date will be suitable.

During the clinic appointment, the consultant may decide that diagnostic tests are necessary, in which case the patient has to wait for a further appointment date so that these tests can be performed. If the consultant decides that surgery is necessary, during the first examination or following diagnostic tests, the patient's name is added to the surgical waiting list, and the patient may have to wait for another letter giving a date to attend a pre-operative assessment clinic, to check that they are fit for surgery. In the clinic, the patient will be given only a vague idea of how long this might take, but it could be several more months. When the appointment letter arrives, the patient either confirms that the date is suitable or contacts the clinic to rearrange. Assuming that the assessment confirms suitability for surgery, if not already on the surgical waiting list, the patient will be added to it at this stage. When the consultant decides to schedule surgery, the patient receives a letter to confirm the date and time of the operation. Once again, if not suitable, the patient will again have to contact the hospital to rearrange this.

This process has disadvantages. The number of steps leads to administrative errors and duplication of effort, and to long, uncertain, and anxious delays. Patients are given no say about their appointment dates, which increases the probability that these will have to be rearranged, causing further delays. Another consequence is that many patients simply do not turn up for appointments, which wastes hospital time and money. The patient also has to make several hospital visits, incurring travelling time and costs. When the time between pre-assessment and operation is protracted, the assessment may have to be repeated as the patient's condition may have changed. This process is inefficient, and is not patient focused. Moreover, the system was designed around the convenience of the hospital, and not the patient. The booked appointments system is more consistent with the concept of 'patient-centred' healthcare.

Booked appointments system

With patient booking, the GP refers patients to their local hospital, and often to a 'pool' of relevant specialists. When patients are 'pooled', the waiting times for all consultants in a particular specialty are the same, which means that patients are more likely to be seen in order of referral. With an electronic online booking system, the GP can arrange the referral while the patient is in the consulting room, accessing the outpatient clinic appointments system, ensuring that the date and time are suitable. In some cases, the practice clerk arranges this appointment while the GP sees the next patient. More often, however, the GP will refer by letter or fax, in which case a hospital clinic clerk, or central call centre, will telephone the patient (or the patient may call them) the next day to arrange a suitable date and time. Knowing the date and time in advance, uncertainty is reduced, and patients can make plans in the meantime.

At the clinic appointment with the consultant, if further tests or treatment are indicated, then those diagnostics and surgical pre-assessment may take place on the same day. If the patient is fit for the procedure, then a date for treatment is either agreed that day, with the surgeon or with clinic staff, or the patient may telephone the next day to arrange a convenient date. In other words, patients either leave the clinic knowing when their operation will take place, and that this date is convenient, or will be given an appointment within one working day.

This process works well when waiting times are short, and usually less than six months. Appointments booked more than six months ahead are more likely to have to be changed. Consequently, for booking to work effectively, hospitals had to reduce long waiting times, often involving the appointment of new staff as well as other process improvements, and sometimes including the construction of new daycase facilities.

Table 6.1 shows the differences between the conventional referral and treatment pathway and booking systems for patients requiring daycase surgery. This 'before and after' account does not adequately represent the difference in elapsed time between the two systems. Time to admission was reduced with booking for five reasons. First, hospitals had to reduce waiting times before introducing a booking system to a particular specialty. Second, co-ordination between primary and acute care was improved. Third, hospital doctors changed their practices by pooling patients, and by seeing patients more than once on the day of an outpatient clinic appointment. Fourth, the number of hospital visits that patients had to make was cut. Finally, patients negotiated appointment times, reducing the need to rearrange these.

Structure and development

In 1998, just over a year after the election of the Labour government, the new ministerial team in the Department of Health announced its commitment to streamlining services, reducing waiting times, and making the health service more responsive and accessible to patients. Patient booking was regarded as one method for achieving this, and it was decided

Table 6.1 *Patient booking: before and after*

Traditional

1 GP refers patient to hospital specialist by letter; patient returns home to wait to hear from hospital

2 Consultant specialist's secretary adds patient's name to outpatient clinic waiting list; patient still waiting

3 Letter sent to patient giving date (decided by hospital staff) of outpatient clinic; if date is inconvenient, patient telephones hospital to rearrange

4 Consultant examines patient in hospital outpatient clinic, and decides what further tests and treatment may be required; patient returns home to wait to hear from hospital, and may have to visit hospital again to attend for those tests

5 Medical secretary adds patient's name to pre-operative assessment clinic waiting list; patient still waiting

6 Letter sent to patient giving date (decided by hospital staff) of pre-operative assessment; if date is inconvenient, patient telephones hospital to rearrange

7 Patient attends pre-operative assessment clinic; patient returns home to wait to hear from hospital

8 Medical secretary adds patient's name to surgical waiting list; patient still waiting

9 Letter sent to patient giving date (decided by hospital staff) for admission and surgery; if date is inconvenient, patient telephones hospital to rearrange

10 Patient admitted to hospital for treatment

Booking

1 While in the surgery, the GP refers patient to group of specialists, agreeing date for outpatient clinic appointment with the patient either during surgery or by telephone the following day

2 Consultant specialist sees patient in hospital outpatient clinic, arranging any further diagnostic tests, and a pre-operative assessment on the same day; patient discusses and agrees date for admission and treatment

3 Patient admitted to hospital for treatment

to pilot this approach in 24 trusts. The intent was to develop booking incrementally, so that early experience and lessons could be incorporated as the approach was disseminated more widely. Booking, like other modernization programmes, was thus implemented in waves. Each of the four waves ran for 18 months, and was launched at annual intervals, which meant that the waves overlapped. The number and complexity of projects increased with each wave.

Funding for the programme was allocated by the Department of Health, and held by the Policy Branch's 'Waiting and Booking' unit. There were annual increases in budget as the programme expanded, starting with £5 million for the first wave in 1998, rising to £50 million in 2001 for the fourth and final wave. This core budget had two elements, one to support local project teams, and the other to fund the national booking team, the latter including budgets for conferences and publications as well as staff. The national director of the programme had responsibility for the core budget, allocating funds to local healthcare organizations, and liaising with the policy team at the Department of Health. In other words, the organization structures of this initiative were multi-layered and complex.

Table 6.2 summarizes developments over the four waves of the programme, identifying two additional projects ('continuous improvements' and 'pre-operative assessment') which were designed to accelerate progress with booking. Two other modernization programmes, the Cancer Services Collaborative and the Coronary Heart Disease Collaborative, were associated with the second and third waves of booking. Both aimed to enable service providers to work in collaboration to improve access in areas of high priority for the NHS.

First wave: pilot

The programme began in October 1998 with 24 pilot sites. At that time, the NHS in England had eight regional health authorities, and guidelines from the NHS Executive, following a statement by the Minister for Health, required three pilot sites from each region. The sites would be supported by a budget of £5 million, and each site expected to receive between £100,000 and £300,000 for the six months to March 1999. Similar funds would be available for the following year, subject to satisfactory progress. The funds provided over the 18 months of this wave ranged from £165,000 to £756,000 for each site, the average being £413,655. All trusts were invited to apply for funding. Applicants were asked to show how their projects would:

● increase the percentage of patients who receive a booked admission;
● reduce 'did not attends' (DNAs) and cancellations;
● improve communication with patients and general practitioners;
● be integrated with other hospital systems and support systems;
● use resources in an innovative way, including process redesign;
● help to reduce the number of patients waiting and the time they waited.

Around 70 applications were received, and regional selection panels chose the 24 pilot sites.

Booking was not new, but previous initiatives were confined to enthusiastic clinicians. However, there was little evidence that their methods increased capacity or reduced waiting times, and booking alone could not be expected to improve access and convenience. From the outset, therefore, the programme focus was on system redesign, and sites selected for the first wave were those considered to be most capable of making booking work because they already had short waiting times. Most of the 24 pilots reported previous experience of booking, another reason for their selection.

Table 6.2 Development of the booking programme

Phase	Dates	Sites	Funds	Aims	Scope
Wave 1: pilot	October 1998–March 2000	24	£5m	Pilot the concepts of redesign and booking	Daycase, inpatients, general practice, 3 electronic booking sites
Wave 2: rapid replication	October 1999–March 2001	60	£20m	Extend lessons to more sites and prove the concepts are replicable	Adding diagnostics and 10 electronic booking sites
Wave 3: spread	October 2000–March 2002	197*	£40m	Spread widely; all acute trusts to book at least two daycase specialties or high-volume procedures	Adding outpatients and 30 electronic booking sites
Wave 4: moving to mainstream	October 2001–March 2003	**	£50m	Develop whole-community working, with booking and choice across whole patient journey; meet NHS Plan targets	Growing to 50 electronic booking sites
Continuous improvement of booked admissions, wave 1	1999–2000	12	–	Explore in detail issues raised in the main programme	Team coaching, inpatient booking, capacity and demand analysis
Pre-operative assessment project	1999–***	8	–	Explore the potential for redesign in this area	Pre-operative assessment for inpatient and daycase procedures

* Wave 3 extended the programme to all acute hospitals in England.
** Wave 4 extended the programme to all health communities in England.
*** Pre-operative assessment project was ongoing, transferred to theatres project in 2001.

The first-wave emphasis was also directed to booking patients for daycase treatment, because previous initiatives had involved that area rather than inpatients, and because there had been a recent increase in the number of patients waiting for daycase surgery. Daycase waiting times tended to be shorter anyway, and the pilot sites chosen had waiting times of less than six months, or were approaching that target. The pilot sites used additional funds to appoint project managers, administrative staff, and pre-operative assessment nurses, along with more clinical sessions, training, and new technology, and attendance at national and regional 'sharing events'.

Second wave: rapid replication

In April 1999, the government announced a second wave, and trusts were again invited to bid for funding, for three purposes. The first concerned the continuous improvement of booking at the existing pilot sites, and this became a programme in its own right, the Continuous Improvement of Booked Admissions Programme. The second was to introduce around eight pilot schemes to develop booking systems for cancer services, as part of a wider redesign, a project that became part of the Cancer Services Collaborative Programme. The third was to increase the number of pilots by at least 50, by replicating the experiences of first-wave sites. Following a similar selection process, a further 60 sites were identified, and this wave ran until March 2001 with an additional £20 million to fund the second year of the first wave along with this additional work to develop and disseminate booking practices.

Third wave: spread

In April 2000, a further £40 million was allocated to a third wave, beginning that October, and running until March 2002. The purpose at this stage was to spread the practice more widely, and to develop the continuous improvement programme. The Coronary Heart Disease Collaborative was also established that year. The target was that, by the end of March 2002, every acute trust in England would be booking in at least two specialties or high-volume procedures. This wave involved 197 sites, and that target was met. *The NHS Plan* was published in July 2000, announcing that, by the end of 2005, waiting lists for hospital appointments and admissions would be abolished and replaced with booking systems giving patients a choice of a convenient time within a guaranteed maximum period.

Fourth wave: moving to mainstream

The fourth wave was announced as part of *The NHS Plan* targets for 2005, and covered health communities, including mental health trusts, social services, and health authorities as well as acute and primary care. 'Moving to mainstream' ran from October 2001 to March 2003. The intent was to develop booking from local projects to standard practice across the service. Redesign was emphasized, and the programme supported health communities to build on improvements made in previous waves. The goals of the fourth wave were to:

- work towards 100 per cent booking of daycases by March 2003;
- significantly increase booking from and within general practice;
- significantly increase booking for inpatient elective admissions;
- roll out booked admissions changes widely across the NHS;
- introduce widespread electronic booking by 2005.

All healthcare providers were required to meet these targets by March 2003. Those that had successfully run projects in the previous waves were expected to extend booking further, for example to include arranging diagnostic investigations. An evaluation of the first wave had highlighted the significance of senior leadership in the development of booking systems. The identification of a lead chief executive was compulsory in fourth-wave applications.

The first three waves were based in acute hospitals. However, the national team felt that better progress had been made in projects that involved primary care. Consequently, the development of booking in general practice became a fourth-wave priority. In addition, teams had to identify other local modernization projects, and to indicate how they intended to work together. The documentation also indicated that primary care providers should play an influential role in further developments. Applications for funding thus had to represent the whole local healthcare community, and bids from single providers were not accepted. As with previous waves, the release of funds was subject to achievement of clear milestones.

The booking programme ended in March 2003, and responsibility was devolved to strategic health authorities, with support from a smaller national team. In April 2004, the Agency's remaining responsibilities were transferred to the national programme for information technology and strategic health authorities.

NPAT and the MA

A prior review of methods concluded that the development of a full booked admissions system would require significant organizational and cultural change (Bensley *et al.*, 1997). That review influenced the way in which the National Patients Access Team (NPAT) designed the booking programme. This was to be a major initiative, supported with additional funds and expertise in organization development. Booking was the first in a series of initiatives led by NPAT aimed at improving access to services, patients' experience, and the use of health service capacity. NPAT's role was distinctive in emphasizing the proactive sharing and dissemination of best practice, and the provision of expertise in service redesign.

An evaluation of the first wave (Ham *et al.*, 2002) concluded that staff involved in the programme acknowledged that the leadership provided by NPAT had been crucial, and it was particularly regarded for its skill and expertise in service redesign and waiting list management, and in forging links between NPAT staff and booking sites. NPAT was also praised for encouraging learning and development to bring about service improvements:

> [this] derived from the philosophy that underpinned NPAT's work and its position outside the main structure of NHS performance management. The credibility of NPAT's staff and their background in the NHS reinforced its influence and enhanced its standing among those involved in the first wave.
>
> (Ham *et al.*, 2002)

The booking programme pioneered a systematic attempt to redesign services from the patient's viewpoint. This experience influenced further developments in NPAT's work, and shaped the subsequent role of the Agency. As Ham *et al.* (2002, p.28) indicate:

> It is only a slight exaggeration to suggest that the vision behind *The NHS Plan* of a service designed around the patient, and its focus on reform as well as investment as the means of implementing the vision, owed not a little to the work of NPAT in its first two years, including the development of booked admissions.

The NHS Plan brought NPAT, and eight other organizations involved in service improvement, under the umbrella of the Agency, which was formed in 2001. The Agency continued to develop the booking initiative through a new national team.

The National Booking Team

The National Booking Team was formed in 2001 to support local teams to implement booking through promoting local ownership and commitment to improving care services. Over the first few months, a programme director, three associate directors, administrative and analyst support, and programme managers were recruited to the team, which continued to grow rapidly over the following two years.

As indicated, the importance of clinical leadership in implementing and sustaining booking projects was a theme emerging from early evaluations. Relationships were forged with the Royal Colleges, considered to be opinion leaders, to engage their support in communicating the programme's aims and benefits to their members. National clinical leads (including GPs and other specialists) were employed to bring a professional perspective to this work. In partnership with the national clinical leads from other programmes, their role was to:

- provide clinical leadership;
- exploit opportunities to promote and communicate the principles and practice of booking amongst clinicians and managers;
- provide support and guidance to the team and project sites.

In 2001, the government announced that the eight regional offices were to be abolished, and replaced by 28 new strategic health authorities, which would provide leadership and co-ordination in their respective health communities. Previously, each office had a regional office booked admissions lead (ROBAL), co-ordinating and managing booking in its area. ROBALs had links with the national team, and provided information about local problems and achievements. They also offered tailored support to local initiatives. Additional national programme managers were appointed, as there were no ROBALs in the new structure. A new role for national redesign coaches was also developed, covering specific geographical areas, and linked to the national programme managers. Their role was to provide support, training, and guidance for a specific period and with specific aims as agreed with local organizations.

The aims of the national team, with the Department of Health's Waiting and Booking unit, were to develop the booking programme by providing support so that, at a local level, there were the skills, expertise, and resources to meet the national targets.

The national team also provided training in redesign techniques:

- process mapping followed the patient journey, to see how this could be streamlined;
- with 'plan–do–study–act' (PDSA) cycles, improvements were tested and developed in small-scale experiments;
- capacity and demand analysis was used to manage waiting lists and resources more effectively;
- five change principles, which from experience had the greatest impact, were developed (Table 6.3; note that these are distinct from the 10 high-impact changes identified in Chapter 1).

Table 6.3 *Five high-impact change principles*

1 *Focus on patients' needs*
   Design booking processes that match patients' needs
   Involve patients in decisions, and give them real choices about their care
   Give patients a choice of appointments or admission dates at every stage of their journey
   Enable staff to operate as a team across the whole patient process

2 *Improve the booking process*
   Redefine and agree the patient process
   Redefine roles and skills
   Introduce partial booking as a first step towards full booking
   Book appointments in advance

3 *Match demand and capacity*
   Identify the true demand for your service
   Identify the actual capacity of your service
   Match demand and capacity for your service on a day-to-day basis
   Plan annual leave in advance to support the booking process

4 *Improve communication*
   Review and redesign all written patient communication
   Review and redesign other methods of communication: personal, electronic, telephone
   Establish effective communication within the booking team
   Promote communication about booking throughout your health community

5 *Make it mainstream*
   Make booking part of the regular monitoring system for your organization
   Build booking targets into organizational and personal objectives
   Ensure booking is included in your health community business planning process
   Make sure everyone knows what booked admissions mean

The booking programme had its own section of the Agency's website, where updates, news of local and regional events and training, and 'good news stories' were posted. However, not all booking staff had Internet access. Local teams could join 'listserve', an email group, to access up-to-date programme information. Listserve also enabled trusts to share experiences and learn from the others. Questions could be posted to which any subscriber could respond. Case studies were published in *Ready, Steady, Book!*, an implementation guide with a range of examples from primary and acute care. The national team hosted conferences for the booking community to learn about new developments and techniques, and share experience. Local teams thus had significant and varied forms of support throughout the programme.

Definitions of booking

Defining a 'booked appointment' appears to be straightforward, but this was one of the most difficult and controversial aspects of the programme. To collect valid and comparable data, a standard definition was required. One measure of success was the proportion of patients who were able to book their appointment or admission date. As part of the national reporting mechanism, all trusts were expected to provide monthly figures to the programme analysts, who collated those data for the Policy Branch of the Department of Health. The areas in which data collection were required, such as referrals, daycases, inpatients, and diagnostics, were specified by the Department, but these changed several times during the programme.

The definition of booking in *The NHS Plan* was: 'All patients and their GPs will be able to book outpatient appointments and inpatient elective admissions for a date, time and place that is convenient to the patient.' However, a more detailed definition was developed at the start of the first wave, when the focus was on daycase services:

> For a patient to be considered to be booked, the healthcare provider will offer booked appointments and/or admissions within 24 hours of a mutual agreement of the decision to refer. This mutual decision will be made by the patient and healthcare provider/practitioner.
>
> (National Patients Access Team, 1998)

As the programme developed, teams implemented booking in other specialties and in more complex ways. That definition was no longer comprehensive, and did not reflect progress. Project teams identified five problem issues:

1 An appointment could only be counted as booked if it was made within 24 hours of the decision that an appointment was necessary. This created problems over weekends and bank holidays, and some patients wanted more time to reflect and make arrangements.
2 Teams were booking patients at multiple stages of the patient journey. Some teams counted every separate patient appointment, whilst others counted only patients, resulting in inconsistencies in local and central reporting methods.
3 Some teams did not redesign the care process, adding booking to traditional systems. Although appointments were pre-booked, patients could not choose a date or time.
4 Some teams booked appointments more than six months ahead. While these were counted, this increased the number of patient- and hospital-initiated cancellations.
5 Some teams used 'partial booking' to reduce waiting times as a step towards full booking. Partial booking was excluded by the standard definition and was not counted.

This prompted a policy change in 1999. The new definition of a booked appointment was:

> The patient is given a choice of when to attend. For full booking, the patient is given the opportunity to agree a date at the time of, or within one working day of, the referral or decision to treat. The patient may choose to agree the date when initially offered, or defer their decision until later.

It was expected that services would be redesigned to support full booking, while taking into consideration the ability to guarantee that a date offered could be honoured. Where that would not be possible, 'partial booking' was appropriate; during the consultation, the patient would be told the approximate waiting time (which would typically be more than six months), and would then be contacted about a month before that time to choose the appointment or admission date. Partial booking thus also gave patients certainty and choice, offering some of the benefits of full booking, such as reducing cancellations and 'did not attends'. This approach also reassured consultants who were reluctant to book patients more than six months ahead. The official definition of partial booking was:

> The patient is advised of the total indicative waiting time during the consultation between themselves and the health care provider/practitioner. The patient is able to choose and confirm their appointment or admission approximately four to six weeks in advance of their appointment or admission date.

Partial booking was only regarded as an interim measure. As waiting times were reduced through other service improvements, full booking was to be established. Following these revised definitions, booking could be counted for performance monitoring purposes at each point in the patient pathway where a clinical decision was made about subsequent treatment:

- decision to refer, and booking into an outpatient clinic;
- decision to investigate, and booking into diagnostics, such as radiology;
- decision to operate, and booking onto a theatre list;
- decision to refer, and booking into tertiary care;
- decision to discharge from one organization, and booking into follow-up care;
- decision to begin a course of treatment or investigation, and booking for each attendance.

That review was intended to provide clear advice on what a booked admission or appointment represented, and to ensure a national standard for booked admissions and appointments.

Hitting the target, missing the point?

In 1999, the Department of Health commissioned an evaluation of the first wave. The initial report (Meredith *et al.*, 1999) concluded that process redesign and booking were under way in the 24 pilot sites but the second observed that 'there was some slipping back' (Kipping *et al.*, 2000, p.3). The final report (Ham *et al.*, 2002) identified two problems. First, sustainability was jeopardized, with some trusts reverting to traditional methods. Second, local teams were encountering opposition, from doctors and from other colleagues. There was no second-wave review, but the Agency conducted its own evaluation of the third and fourth waves. From that evidence, this section considers the impact of the programme from national, organizational, patient, and staff perspectives. Five years and £115 million later, had booking been sustained, and how widely had it spread?

National policy

Political commitment to the booking programme both helped and hindered its implementation and development. The policy framework provided the stimulus for the programme, and the NPAT provided support and co-ordination for pilot sites. The lead given by government ministers enabled managers and clinicians to demonstrate that improvements could be introduced in this context, indicating the importance of booking relative to other government healthcare priorities. National targets meant that all trusts had to become involved, eventually, and the 'waves' gave local project teams clear structures and objectives. Consequently, time and energy were focused on booking as an element of a wider strategy to redesign care processes and improve access to services. As the programme developed from pilot to mainstream, it was confirmed as policy in *The NHS Plan*, and the Department of Health demonstrated significant interest in learning from this experience. The programme achieved some significant milestones:

- by January 2002, every healthcare community was involved in process redesign incorporating booking;
- by September 2002, more than 9 million patients had received a booked appointment or admission date;
- by March 2004, total booking had reached 90 per cent (target 67 per cent), outpatient booking had reached 77 per cent (target 67 per cent), and daycase booking stood at 97 per cent (target 100 per cent).

This implies substantial cultural change over the duration of the programme, as it became more widely accepted that patients should be able to choose appointment dates and times convenient for them.

However, that political commitment also generated problems. Some doctors did not attach the same priority to booking as did government ministers, believing that other aspects of the service were more important. This was a national, policy-driven, 'top-down' change, delivered through a national programme with national targets; many staff felt that this was not the best approach to stimulating improvements in patient care. Project managers reported that some staff felt strongly that the purpose of this initiative was political gain:

> I think it is an appalling use of taxpayers' money. Instead, the money should be directed towards serious diseases and not towards a gimmick. This is wallpapering by the government.
>
> (Consultant surgeon)

In some cases, doctors used ministerial support as justification for *not* supporting the programme; this cynicism meant that the influence of political motives was not entirely positive. Other tensions arose when, during this programme, other issues were given equal, if not more, government attention, such as reducing waiting times in accident and emergency departments (see Chapter 11). The shifting pool of national priorities meant that local attention and resources were frequently diverted to fresh issues, jeopardizing the sustainability of existing projects. The areas where attention was focused tended to reflect changing definitions of activities, and deadlines for meeting targets, rather than patient needs. For example, as the 2003 daycase target deadline approached, hospitals focused on booking daycase patients, and other areas (inpatients and diagnostics, for example) were neglected.

The unstable policy environment encouraged potentially dysfunctional behaviours. For example, some trusts implemented partial booking, and met targets without redesigning services. Patients would have 'a booked appointment', removing them from the waiting list figures, when they had only been advised of approximate waiting times. Full booking usually involved some process redesign. The Department of Health regularly changed performance measures, requiring trusts to submit data from new areas. Staff were not motivated to book patients if this did not matter for meeting targets. Some chief executives withdrew resources from areas where booking targets no longer contributed to their performance rating. On the other hand, other trusts had invested resources in booking, such as running more clinics and additional theatre sessions, to meet the ambitious targets. But it proved difficult to sustain this diversion of resources, and time pressures often inhibited effective process redesign.

Consequently, while interim targets were met, some changes were inevitably not sustained. More significantly, patient services were not always improved.

In the booking community, this outcome was widely described as 'hitting the target but missing the point'.

The patient's perspective

A mental health patient, faced with a professional group arguing about booking, said, 'I want speedier access and I want choice, therefore I want booking'. This immediately ended the professionals' debate.

(National booking manager)

For the patient, a booked appointments system has several advantages. The service is more convenient, waiting times are reduced, there is certainty over appointment dates, anxiety is reduced, patients are more involved in the planning of their care, and the number of hospital visits is cut. Hospitals can plan clinic and theatre sessions more precisely, ordering equipment and scheduling staff in advance, reducing hospital-initiated cancellations. Redesign led to other benefits, such as better hospital signposting, the provision of booked admission lounges, and improved (multilingual) information leaflets. In some cases, patients played a major role by calling the hospital's call centre to arrange appointment dates and times, reducing patient-initiated cancellations, and (from survey evidence) increasing satisfaction with services.

However, it is questionable whether a booked appointment improves the quality of care, especially where no other redesign has occurred. That firm appointment date may be less important for patients than shorter waiting times. Anecdotal evidence from national programme managers revealed that, while some hospitals claimed to be offering booked appointments, they were simply offering patients the next available date, rather than a choice. The 24-hour qualifying window for booked appointments is not always convenient. Some patients want time for reflection and family discussion before making an appointment, and others need to rearrange commitments before confirming a date.

The organization's perspective

With booking, the number of patients who did not attend their appointment (DNAs) fell significantly, as dates had been confirmed with patients as convenient. This also reduced the number of patient-initiated cancellations. Hospitals that also redesigned services achieved the best results, and their improvements were more likely to be sustained. Staff and facilities were used more efficiently: there was no need to repeat pre-operative assessments, and operating theatre use was maximized. Staff leave was planned in advance, reducing hospital-initiated cancellations. Hospitals also found that, maximizing capacity by planning appointments and admissions in advance, waiting times were consequently reduced. Third-wave evaluation (Sharpe, 2002) concluded that process mapping influenced staff appreciation of the benefits of booking, and showed that staff were also applying this approach to redesign in other areas.

However, the programme also presented challenges, particularly with regard to budget allocations. Booking became one of the indicators contributing to a hospital's star rating, and trusts were encouraged to divert resources from other aspects of patient care to ensure that booking targets were met. As changes were made in clinical and administrative practices, booking administrators were appointed, and consultants, nurses, theatre staff, and booking clerks required training in new procedures. As indicated earlier, waiting times had to be reduced before full booking could be developed. This often involved the establishment of dedicated daycase facilities (which for some hospitals meant major construction work), the introduction of online appointments systems, and new information systems to monitor patient referrals and pathways. These changes had significant cost implications.

Even booked appointments were subject to hospital-initiated cancellation. Appointments could only be guaranteed where clinic and theatre sessions and beds were available. However, it was not always possible accurately to predict the time that would elapse for each stage of a patient's treatment, such as a diagnostic procedure, a surgical intervention, length of hospital stay, and discharge. If any step took longer than anticipated, this created a backlog, increasing the probability that the hospital would have to cancel another patient's booked appointment at short notice. Booked appointments were also cancelled because of emergency admissions.

Booking did not necessarily lead to more effective use of resources. Once booking was working, some patients saw the service as more accessible and flexible, and assumed that it would be as easy to change an appointment date as to arrange one. One unanticipated consequence, therefore, was an increase in requests to change appointments at short notice. However, if appointments were already booked, it was difficult to rearrange those patients. Also, if there were no gaps in the system, it was difficult to accommodate urgent cases. If gaps were left for possible emergencies, but not used, then resources were wasted. Previously, patients on the waiting list, or those who had been cancelled, would simply be contacted to see whether they could be available at short notice, and that slot would probably be filled.

The timing of the programme 'waves' caused problems. Significant process redesign takes time to develop and then to implement. A window of 18 months limited what could be achieved, especially as there were no guarantees that a project would continue into the next wave. There were also no guarantees that the 18-month contracts for newly appointed project managers and administrative staff would be renewed, so recruitment to those positions was difficult. Some project managers were recruited externally, and needed time to familiarize themselves with the issues, and to determine how best to approach the process. End of project meant end of employment contract, and it was not surprising when their focus shifted to job search in the closing months. Evidence suggests that one major threat to sustainability of booking projects concerned the loss of key staff, such as project managers.

The staff perspective

More than just a new appointments system, the booking programme had a significant impact on the roles and working practices of doctors, nurses, managers, and other staff (Ham *et al.*, 2002). These changes were seen as beneficial. The role of nurses was enhanced where they assumed responsibility for patient assessment as well as booking appointments, and some nurses became more involved in pre-operative assessment. New and broader administrative and clerical roles were designed, with responsibility for arranging appointments directly with patients, and much less time was spent dealing with patient enquiries and rearranging dates.

Agency evaluations of the third and fourth waves concluded that increased patient satisfaction had a positive impact on morale. Staff felt that they had more control over their work, and valued the opportunity to develop new skills and be involved in redesign, particularly where this involved exploring the whole patient process, and not just one isolated segment. As the programme developed, booking was more likely to be seen as an ongoing process, a part of the modernization agenda, than as an isolated short-term project.

Staff reactions were not all positive. One concern was the lack of time to adapt to new methods and to gain necessary skills. It was also difficult for staff to find time to focus on process redesign to support booking, which was one initiative among many other priorities. The 'waves' approach with targets and deadlines meant that booking retained its project status, and although this perception weakened over the duration of the programme, some staff felt that it was easy to ignore, knowing that, like many other programmes, it would end.

The most significant resistance to booking came from hospital consultants, some of whom resisted the imposition of government-inspired targets on principle. Booking works well when patients are 'pooled', referred to a specialist group rather than a named individual. Some consultants preferred patients to be referred to them, did not want colleagues to treat patients who were referred to their clinic, and did not want to treat patients referred to other consultants. Long waiting lists were also a sign of being 'in demand'. However, shorter waiting times and a more convenient service reduce the demand for private treatment. Doctors had other concerns. Some early initiatives ran into difficulties, and doctors and other staff had to cope with disappointed patients whose 'booked' treatment was rescheduled; they were reluctant to repeat the exercise until convinced that, this time, things would be different. Some doctors also felt that they were relinquishing control by making a commitment to see patients on given dates. Many doctors disliked the fact that they would not be able to take holiday breaks and conference trips at short notice. Annual leave had to be booked well in advance to allow patient appointments to be booked with confidence. These concerns were exacerbated by transferring the management of doctors' diaries to nurses and booking clerks. One of the most significant threats, therefore, to the development and sustainability of booking was lack of medical support (Ham *et al.*, 2003).

Booking also met with resistance from administrative, clerical, and secretarial staff. While some welcomed the broader role, others did not want more responsibility. Some did not want to deal directly with patients, or felt unprepared for this. Lack of training for administrative and clerical staff was thus identified as a major drawback. Some medical secretaries, who managed their consultants' diaries and organized patient appointments, felt threatened. They were reluctant to relinquish these responsibilities and the patient contact, and some were concerned that their roles would be downgraded.

Conclusions

The booking programme developed from 24 pilot sites to cover the whole service. The benefits to patients, staff, and hospitals were many. As the first modernization programme on this scale, it reinforced the role of process redesign in meeting apparently straightforward targets. The lessons from this experience influenced other initiatives. While political commitment was advantageous, this experience highlighted tensions between government policy and practical realities. With public and media pressure for rapid improvement, with hindsight, a national programme, driven by national targets, may not have been the most appropriate vehicle. In particular, the time required to meet policy expectations was greater than anticipated, and this finding was repeated with other modernization initiatives. With a programme of this nature, scale, and time frame, it is difficult to distinguish clearly between the processes of sustainability and spread, as they are closely interlinked, and influenced by similar issues. Nevertheless, the main influential factors appear to have been the following:

1 *Sustainability supports*:
   - performance targets, which focused attention on the development of booking, and which motivated staff when achieved;
   - wider system and process redesign, in which booking was one embedded element;
   - acknowledged benefits for patients, staff, and provider organizations.

2 *Sustainability threats*:
   - performance targets which kept shifting, in terms of definition, and areas of coverage, which moved attention away from areas that were no longer measured;
   - the 'waves' structure of the initiative, which encouraged a short-term project focus with temporary project staff;
   - lack of evidence that quality of patient care was improved, combined with operational difficulties in maintaining a fully booked system.

3 *Spread contributors*:
   - political commitment to giving patients choice in planning their care;
   - the 'wave' structure of the initiative, in which subsequent adopters could learn from the experience of pilot sites;
   - national support in the form of expertise, training, and funding.

4 *Spread inhibitors*:
   - the perception that booking was being promoted for political gain, without improving quality of patient care;
   - job redesign, which allocated unwanted tasks and responsibilities to some key members of hospital staff;
   - insufficient time to develop the necessary process redesign to support booking.

Critical debates

1 If you had £115 million to spend over five years, what other models of change implementation would you consider for the effective sustainability and spread of patient booking in the NHS?
2 To persuade a sceptical doctor, what are the best arguments for implementing patient booking? To persuade a hospital chief executive to allocate resources to another project instead, what are the best arguments against patient booking?

3 For a large-scale national change initiative, a complex organization structure is necessary in order to monitor the effective use of public money. But what are the disadvantages of such a structure, and do those outweigh the benefits?

7 Sustaining and spreading change: the patient booking case experience

Jane Louise Jones

Chapter aims

1 To explore the experience of implementing the National Booking Programme through an in-depth case study of an acute hospital, Parkside NHS Trust.
2 To reveal the complexity of sustainability and spread processes.
3 To expose the multiple factors, at different levels of analysis, that influence whether an initiative is sustained over time and spreads to other areas.

Key point summary

- As a processual perspective argues, the wider organizational context is a key factor contributing to the adoption, sustainability, and spread of the improvements associated with booking. In addition, aspects of the change itself, such as substance, process, and timing, can influence that wider context.
- Parkside Hospital was introducing change at several levels: individual, team, clinical specialty, organizational. Characteristics of a receptive context included the availability of key people in leadership roles, good relationships between managers and clinicians, a supportive culture that had been established over many years, good relationships with external organizations, and clear fit between the change agenda and the organization's policies and goals.
- Parkside's redesign team was seen as an important resource for implementing and sustaining change initiatives, and provides a model that could be adopted elsewhere.
- The process and timing of change (planning, introduction, implementation) contribute to successful adoption, sustainability, and spread. Improvements were piloted on a small scale in receptive areas, evidence of success was gathered, and principles of improvements were then shared between teams.
- Booking was implemented and sustained in several specialties, and continued to spread to other areas at Parkside. The 'pockets' where these changes had taken place, compared with areas where they had not, were explained by

varying degrees of receptivity to, and compatibility with, booking in different clinical specialties.

- The development of common service improvement goals relies on understanding individuals' differing perceptions of and responses to change.
- Service improvements can be routinized and sustained through supporting changes in policies, procedures, and job descriptions, which can also help to provide a sense of security and continuity for staff.
- A focus on implementation and results may overlook the need for preplanning and development of change, and for subsequent consolidation. Effective preplanning and consolidation are critical in influencing others to participate, and these steps take time. Preparation time was one resource for which national targets did not allow.

Booking at Parkside

Chapter 6 explored the national structure and funding of the booking programme, identifying the general implications for patients, staff, and hospitals. In contrast, this chapter moves into a single hospital, to explore in more detail the issues influencing the development of booking from an organizational perspective. *The NHS Plan* made a commitment that, by the end of 2005, all patients requiring an outpatient clinic appointment or a daycase or inpatient admission would be offered a choice of dates. Overall responsibility for booking was devolved from the national team to strategic health authorities in 2003. Booking was thus included in the performance targets for individual hospitals, contributing to their star rating.

In addition to describing how booking systems function, the previous chapter identified three characteristics of this approach. First, while the objective appears to be straightforward (give patients a choice of appointment dates), the changes that need to be put in place to achieve this are many and complex, and take time to develop and implement. Second, while booking appears to have advantages for patients, staff, and hospitals, not all patients want to be rushed into an appointment, some staff do not welcome the new responsibilities they are asked to assume, and booking does not always lead to a more effective use of hospital resources. In addition, booking may not improve the quality of patient care, and may instead divert attention and resources from patients with the greatest clinical need (Ham *et al.*, 2003, p.430). Third, as the definition of booking changed during the national programme, as the Department of Health changed the areas where performance monitoring was required, and as booking could only operate effectively if supported by redesigning surrounding systems, different hospitals implemented booking in different ways. This chapter describes how one hospital addressed these issues.

Service redesign involves scrutinizing existing processes, challenging taken-for-granted assumptions, and changing processes to eliminate unnecessary steps that cause duplication, errors, and delays. As Locock (2003, p.121) observes, the process of redesign involves questioning how things can be done better, whether they need doing at all, and by whom.

As Chapter 6 observed, booking has required the development of complicated systems, leading sometimes to inconsistencies and confusion. This may partially explain the protracted timescales that have been required to get people and organizations working effectively in this way. However, booking is easier to implement in some clinical services than in others. Apart from length of waiting list, issues that make booking difficult to implement include:

- the need for elective inpatient treatment (rather than outpatient appointments);
- long duration and unpredictability of diagnostic procedures or interventions;
- unpredictability of length of stay in hospital;
- overall unpredictability of patient admissions and discharges.

Orthopaedic and urology services tend to have those properties, and present challenges with regard to the development of booking. To achieve something as apparently simple as giving patients booked appointments, major changes in clinical and administrative practice, new forms of co-ordination between primary and secondary care, and in some cases new buildings were required. Often, this meant the recruitment of dedicated booking administrators or co-ordinators, the use of 'pooled' waiting lists (referrals to teams of consultants rather than named individuals), the establishment of dedicated new facilities (for daycase surgery, for example), and the introduction of electronic appointment systems.

For staff, this required changes to working practices and the development of new roles and responsibilities. General practitioners experienced increased workload through pre-booking hospital appointments during consultations, and hospital consultants had to agree to shared ('pooled') waiting lists, instead of personal referrals. Previously, long waiting lists may have been perceived as a sign of being 'in demand', leading to lucrative private consultations, which could thus be threatened by more efficient processes. Consultants' annual leave and study leave had to be booked well in advance to allow appointment slots to be pre-booked confidently. Medical secretaries had to relinquish their key role in patient administration to booking co-ordinators, and to 'call and book' centre staff. The creation of new roles for booking centres and co-ordinators required additional acclimatization and training time.

Parkside Hospital Trust was a 'three-star' acute hospital providing services to around 280,000 residents of the city in which it was located, and the surrounding area. Most services were provided from two sites, the main district hospital in the city centre (420 beds), and another site (250 beds) 2 miles (3.2 km) away. A small hospital (90 beds) was incorporated by merger in 2002. Parkside was larger than average, employing 2,300 staff (whole-time equivalents), with 63,000 finished consultant episodes per annum. According to an internal audit in 2000, resources (staffing and beds) were higher than average, while average income was lower. Parkside joined the booking programme in the second wave, in October 1999. Booking patients was not new at Parkside, as several specialties had been offering patients a choice of appointment or admission date before the programme was first launched. However, participation in the national programme provided opportunities to build on that earlier work.

The research at Parkside used a qualitative multi-methods case study design. It is important to note that the unit of analysis involved a complex nested arrangement of clinical services in a wider organizational context. The study focused on booking in two multi-professional services, daycase and gynaecology, both of which worked in collaboration with local primary care. Data were collected in 2003 from several sources:

1 Interviews, recorded and transcribed, with 26 hospital staff including:

  • director of organization development;
  • six consultants and general practitioners;
  • six secretarial, administrative, and clerical staff;
  • five clinical nurse managers and nurses;
  • three information technology systems staff;
  • four members of the redesign team;
  • one other member of staff.

2 Three focus groups involving 12 staff:

  • two focus groups with administrative and clerical staff;
  • one focus group with the redesign team.

3 Observation of meetings involving the hospital booking team, the redesign team, the booking steering committee, and a consultants' meeting.
4 Inspection of documents such as hospital reports, newsletters, and performance data.
5 Ongoing feedback from staff, concerning clarification of issues and the provision of further information.

Data analysis was based on the identification of recurring themes through content analysis, and validity checks were performed with a number of hospital staff who had taken part in the study. Final reports were produced for both the hospital and the Agency.

Organizational context

The context of change can influence the process, but in turn, aspects of the change, such as the substance, implementation process, and timing, can affect the context. Parkside presented a receptive organizational context. By 2003, booking had been implemented and sustained in many specialties, and was continuing to spread to other (but not all) areas of the hospital. In other words, receptiveness differed between individuals and teams in the same organization. It is necessary, therefore, to explore change at different levels, including the wider health service, the hospital, clinical specialties, and individuals.

The findings suggest that organization culture plays an important role in the sustainability and spread of booking. It was acknowledged that Parkside had a 'can do' culture, a readiness for change illustrated by a nurse who said, 'We never say no. We say we will if we can.' Interviewees highlighted that this had not always been the case, and that the culture had changed gradually, but significantly, over several years.

How does organization culture influence the sustainability and spread of new working practices? Organization culture is usually defined broadly in terms of shared beliefs, values, attitudes, norms of behaviour, routines, rituals, ceremonies, traditions, rewards, and meanings (Mannion *et al.*, 2003). Shared ways of thinking and behaving, 'the way things are done around here', define what is legitimate and acceptable in an organization. However, some commentators have focused on particular aspects of culture related to organizational change. Cohen and Levinthal (1990) and Szulanski (2003), for example, develop the concept of 'absorptive capacity', defined as an organization's ability to acquire, assimilate, and apply new knowledge (see Chapter 3). Others have been concerned with assessing an organization's readiness for change (Ingersoll *et al.*, 2000; Narine and Persaud, 2003). Consequently, if absorptive capacity is low, sustainability will present a challenge, and where readiness is low, the spread of new working practices will be inhibited.

From their studies of organizational change in Britain in the 1980s, Pettigrew *et al.* (1992) found that some parts of the healthcare community were more receptive to change than others. Their concept of the receptive context has eight dimensions:

1 external pressures
2 skilled leadership
3 good managerial–clinical relations

4 supportive culture
5 clear policy and strategy
6 co-operative inter-organizational networks
7 clear goals and priorities
8 fit between change agenda and organization.

They argue that those attributes combine to determine how receptive an organization will be to innovation and change. These attributes are used to structure the findings from this study with respect to issues affecting sustainability and spread, summarized in Table 7.1. This table first identifies five broad themes: organizational context, the redesign team, the change process, the roles of specialties and teams, and individual receptivity. The factors influencing sustainability and spread are then identified in detail under those headings.

External pressures

The health service environment is moulded, in part, by government policy, which can change dramatically. The stability of the external context can thus jeopardize the sustainability and spread of new working practices (Ferlie and Shortell, 2001; Appleby, 2005). Parkside had been proactive and progressive with respect to modernization, achieving high standards of patient care reflected in its 'three-star' ranking. Parkside was also to become one of the first of only 10 foundation hospitals, in 2004. The National Booking Programme, therefore, did not trigger booking initiatives at Parkside, but was seen as a source of additional funding and support for local initiatives already under development. Resource dependencies can render an organizational vulnerable to changes in the external environment (Issel *et al.*, 2003). Recognizing this, Parkside allocated specific funds to booking to reduce reliance on the national programme, to secure organizational stability and staff security should that additional funding be withdrawn.

Most respondents in this study felt that healthcare policies and priorities had been imposed on front line staff. Health service staff had experienced other significant changes in the recent past, some of which had not been sustained (Sheaff *et al.*, 2003). While this hospital's aims and values were broadly aligned with national policy, some doctors experienced a conflict between meeting government targets and providing quality of patient care:

> Some people you hear saying, 'government this, and government that', and I'm sure that causes resentment. Some people think this is just another thing from the government, and they'll change their mind next week.
>
> (Consultant)

Table 7.1 *Sustainability and spread at Parkside*

Theme	Factors	Parkside status
Organizational context	External pressures	High-performing hospital; involvement in National Booking Programme develops existing work; measures to minimize resource dependency on programme
	Skilled, stable, dispersed leadership	Visionaries in key positions; supportive management; continuity of senior staff; opinion leaders at all levels
	Good management–clinical relations	Early engagement of clinicians and other staff; effective communications; relationships and trust built prior to change
	Supportive culture	'Can do'; no formal hierarchy; managers recognize achievement; emphasis on participation; strong loyalty and morale; shared priorities; pride in the organization
	Clear, coherent policy	Clear strategy and shared vision based on high standards and patient focus
	Good inter-organizational networks	Partnership working is recognized; rapport across health and social care community
	Clear goals and priorities	Clarity over desired future state and goals; awareness throughout the organization
	Fit between change and organization	Modernization agenda perceived central; booking complements goals and existing practice
Redesign team		Seen as key component of modernization process; key to supporting, implementing, and sustaining improvements
Change process	Implementation methods	Methods adapted to fit specialty; small-scale pilots targeting receptive individuals and specialties; observable processes broken down into simple changes
	Demonstrating improvements	Emphasis on data and evidence; access to 'live' waiting lists

Table 7.1 *continued*

Theme	Factors	Parkside status
	Spread and integration of booking	Redesign team as 'linking pin'; spreading principles, not 'copy exact'; organization-wide agenda, not isolated projects; embedding in normal practice
	Change takes time	Timing, pacing, flow of events; sufficient time allowed to implement and to achieve sustainable change
Specialties and teams	Receptivity	Receptivity within specialty team; shared values and priorities; good relationships
	Compatibility	Compatibility between change and specialty; conditions such as short waiting times, outpatient procedures
Individual receptivity	Perceptions of booking	Expectations, emotions, other responses to change

While external pressures provided support and funding for service improvements, the very source of those pressures could stimulate a cynical response.

Skilled, stable, dispersed leadership

Another attribute of a receptive context concerns visionary individuals leading change in key positions (Pettigrew *et al.*, 1992). The staff at Parkside emphasized the significance of leadership and support for service improvement initiatives from senior staff. Top managers were seen as approachable and supportive. For example, the chief executive regularly visited areas of the hospital to talk to staff. A recent audit report concluded that the overall impression was of an effectively managed organization, with a highly visible and enthusiastic chief executive, who demonstrated strong leadership. The trust board and management team set the strategic direction, while the hospital's redesign team (described below, p.136) provided support and expertise in implementing desired changes. The redesign project had been created and was led by the director of organization development, a well-respected and long-standing senior member of the hospital management.

The continuity of key staff was also acknowledged as important. The previous chief executive had been in post for seven and a half years.

The current chief executive had been recruited internally in 2002, and demonstrated the same commitment to the organization. Credibility was often earned by showing loyalty, insight, and an understanding of the culture, through having worked in the organization for a substantial period:

> The leaders have to be credible. And the credible leaders in the eyes of the clinicians and office staff tend to be those who have been around a while. You know they're not going to come and go in a couple of years as part of their career development.
>
> (Senior manager)

Leadership was dispersed rather than the preserve of senior figures, and opinion leaders at other levels contributed to improvements (Locock *et al.*, 2000; Berwick, 2003). Specialist nurses, for example, persuaded consultants (who saw them as credible) to change aspects of their clinical practice. Consultants could also be influenced by their secretaries, who could thus assist or block the sustainability and spread of changes such as booking. The redesign team, whose members could be regarded as change leaders, comprised internally recruited staff from a variety of backgrounds.

Good management–clinical relations

In discussing and implementing change, the inclusion of all relevant disciplines, at all levels, was seen as important. Clear communication and building effective relationships through a climate of honesty and trust appeared to contribute to receptiveness to change, and staff involvement in change was seen as essential:

> Basically, we've tried to make every cog in the wheel aware, to make it run smoothly, because it's no good setting up a premier service at this point, if everybody else is unaware of how it works, and the input that is needed.
>
> (Nurse)

It was also widely recognized that, without doctors 'on board', change was not going to happen, and the support of hospital consultants in particular was critical. Much attention has been devoted to the importance of processional support in implementing and sustaining change (Degeling *et al.*, 2003). However, many respondents indicated that practical guidance on how to engage clinicians in change required more clarification and higher prioritization.

Supportive organization culture

The culture at Parkside supported staff in their efforts to improve patient care, and this was linked to the hospital leadership style, clarity of vision, and good management–clinician relationships. The communication style was described as open, and lacking formal hierarchy. Managers listened to staff concerns, recognized effort, and rewarded achievements. There was an emphasis on participation, loyalty, and morale. A positive attitude towards change was evident in the departments involved in this study. Decentralized structures enabled staff to work autonomously, knowing that support was there when needed, an important influence on staff commitment (Sheaff *et al.*, 2003, p.90).

There was also a distinct sense of pride in the hospital's achievements. Many felt that Parkside was 'ahead of its time', as their change programme had been launched long before *The NHS Plan* was published in 2000. There was also a sense of competition and differentiation, as many staff were aware of how Parkside compared with other hospitals, and their relative success was a motivating factor.

Quality and coherence of policy

Parkside had a clear service improvement strategy, with ambitious aims, focusing on long-term issues, clinical excellence, patient involvement, and the recruitment, development, and motivation of staff. Front line staff were involved in and fully aware of the hospital's vision and strategy, and this reinforced the 'can do' culture. Parkside retained the 'three-star' rating in three consecutive years, making this one of the country's best-performing hospitals. An audit in 2002 recommended that several areas of good practice at Parkside should be shared widely across the health service, and in particular the work of the hospital redesign team.

Co-operative inter-organizational networks

Parkside had established strong links and good rapport with the local healthcare community over several years. This was also recognized in the 2002 audit, which concluded that 'the work of the trust in close partnership with other NHS and local authority organizations, as part of the local health investment plan, is notable. It is an extensive whole-health system capital investment and clinical change strategy.' Senior hospital managers persistently nurtured relationships between hospital consultants, general practitioners, and other key individuals in other relevant organizations, by providing new opportunities to meet:

> There are too few times when hospital doctors and general practitioners get together and discuss these issues, and actually discover that the problems are shared, the worries are shared, and they don't have to have those barriers.
>
> (General practitioner)

These networks and relationships were particularly important with regard to the development of booking, in which general practice has to be closely involved if both manual and electronic online systems are to function effectively.

Clear goals and priorities

Senior managers had made a compelling case for change. The redesign team ensured that changes were prioritized, and were manageable for clinical staff. Large-scale changes were 'modularized' in simpler steps, where possible. Most staff understood the principles behind booking, and supported the development of a better service for patients.

Fit between change agenda and organization

The government's modernization agenda was embraced at Parkside. The achievement of national targets reassured management that the hospital was performing well. Most staff had experienced recent successful changes, and attitudes were positive. When the National Booking Programme was launched in 1998, booking was not new at Parkside, because the practice was already in use, and the hospital had experience with the implementation and development of other major service improvements. It is more than likely that Parkside would have continued to develop booking regardless of the support of a national initiative (although receptiveness to these changes varied between clinical specialties).

The redesign team

A redesign team had been formed in 1996, to identify opportunities for service improvement, benefiting patients, and improving hospital performance. Led by the director of organization development, the redesign project was influenced by previous re-engineering programmes in other hospitals (McNulty and Ferlie, 2002). Initially, the team struggled to get under way, as the practical realities of influencing service improvement were not fully appreciated. Some hospital staff saw the team as 'an expensive luxury', but despite this initial scepticism, and with senior management support and perseverance, the team ultimately proved to be effective, justifying the cost. The team came to be regarded, externally and internally, as one of the hospital's strengths in implementing, supporting, and sustaining service improvements. A number of achievements, including a prestigious Prime Minister's Award, led to enquiries from other hospitals wishing to undertake similar work.

At the time of this study, four team members worked on booking, just one of the projects covered by the team. Each initiative, whether national or locally driven, had terms of reference, a project team (established in conjunction with operational staff as required), and a full-time lead, usually seconded internally. This approach combined staff from different professional backgrounds, with an appreciation of the skills of different groups. The team had no secretarial or administrative support; members were responsible for their own work. There was no management layer between team members and their board-level director.

The redesign team filled several change roles, such as motivator, facilitator, change agent, and provider of ongoing support (Senge *et al.*, 1999). They were examples to others, offering resources and expertise, facilitating the sharing of knowledge, holding an overview of the hospital's various modernization projects, and helping to co-ordinate those different strands of activity. The team was also a channel for communication with the national booking team and other stakeholders, including primary care trust, social services, and local council:

> Our business is patient care across boundaries. The project can only be successful by recognizing the value of staff and using their expertise.
>
> (Redesign team member)

No set approach to implementing and sustaining change was advocated, as the redesign team recognized that each type of change and specialty was different. The team worked with staff in a particular area to help with the design and implementation of new processes. One internal report concluded that: 'There is no magic answer. People need support, including financial support. However, most of the time it is about changing the culture and persuading people to do things differently without them feeling isolated or what they did previously was wrong.' The team constantly reviewed its actions with staff to ensure two-way communication.

Under sometimes difficult organizational conditions, facing internal and external pressures to 'deliver' to challenging deadlines, the team members worked together particularly well. When asked why this was so, they attributed their effectiveness to several factors:

● previous experience, in this hospital, across various clinical and administrative roles, but not in senior management positions;

- established prior relationships with key staff who would be involved in the development of booking systems;
- good understanding of the issues facing staff, and the potential impact of process changes on their roles;
- willingness to learn from (often unpleasant) experiences when trying to 'sell' ideas for service improvement;
- supportive team environment;
- board-level director sponsorship and guidance;
- chief executive commitment;
- lack of hierarchy, both in the team and in the hospital;
- the hospital's open communication style;
- team members who shared characteristics such as persistence and determination;
- sense of achievement;
- flexibility;
- central location of office on main hospital site.

Other organizations seeking to emulate this central team-based model would thus have to pay attention to a range of historical, social, experiential, organizational, structural, political, individual, interpersonal, emotional, and geographical issues.

The change process

The introduction of booking was facilitated by organizational receptiveness and by existing structures and processes, including the redesign team. As indicated, booking was not a new concept for Parkside when it joined the national programme. Several specialties had been giving patients a choice of appointment or admission date for some time, and a 'call and book' system had been established in 1998. A purpose-built centre was later opened in 2003, with extended opening hours, and out-of-hours voicemail and email. Participation in the national initiative gave Parkside an opportunity to build upon this earlier work, and the hospital continued to progress through to the fourth wave, meeting or exceeding most of its booking objectives. This research was conducted towards the end of the fourth wave, by which time Parkside was recording 85 per cent booking for daycase patients.

Implementation methods

The processes through which booking was introduced appeared to contribute to organization-wide spread and to long-term sustainability. This study highlighted the importance of involving staff as early as possible in the change process, and keeping everyone informed to encourage engagement and support, and to help sustain changes.

Most specialties decided to introduce booking by first piloting the approach, and allowing time to show results. This also provided an opportunity to test a new idea at minimum risk. Many initiatives began on a small scale, in particular specialties, or with specific staff, targeted because they were considered to be receptive, and because booking stood a reasonable chance of success in that area. The redesign team first targeted consultants who, along with their secretaries, were willing to consider new ways of booking patients. Pooled (instead of individual) waiting lists were introduced, and booking co-ordinators were employed, enabling secretaries to concentrate on other responsibilities.

Being able to observe booking in practice, and see positive results, both in Parkside and in other organizations, contributed to successful spread and encouraged sustainability:

> Most of their objections tend to fall by the wayside as they see it isn't as bad as it first appeared. The ones that were sceptical about it observed what we were doing. After it had been running for about a year or so, they said, 'we want to do this', so it was leading by example.
>
> (Consultant)

While demonstration and observation could be powerful influencing devices, this process could take a considerable time. A year was not atypical. Change in perceptions rarely happened rapidly. It was evident that, when a new practice was relatively straightforward, and 'felt right', it would be adopted quickly, and would probably work well. Implementation failures have been attributed in part to the rapid introduction of overly complex changes (Iles and Sutherland, 2001). McNulty and Ferlie (2002) argue that the more technically complex a working practice, the harder it is to redesign (or to re-engineer), and they highlight the complexity of booking. Booking procedures differ from one patient condition to another, and are unique to each organization. Staff moving from one hospital or general practice to another need to become familiar with the various local protocols, if the system as a whole is to operate effectively. This confirms that 'one size doesn't fit all', reinforcing the need to adapt new processes, tailoring them to the context rather than copying exactly.

Hard evidence and warm glow

Performance monitoring, evaluation, and feedback were an integral part of the change process. Kotter (1995; 1996) argues that behaviour changes must be anchored in the culture, and that this can be done by illustrating how new practices are linked to improved performance. Appleby (2005) similarly emphasizes the importance of information, analysis, forecasting, and monitoring in healthcare. At Parkside, service unit managers could access live waiting time lists on the hospital intranet. Having evidence to substantiate a case for booking was important, to persuade staff to adopt the practice, but also to sustain it. However, front line staff relied on the redesign team for the relevant performance figures, and knowledge of quantitative metrics (cancellations, DNAs, waiting lists) was patchy across the hospital. Many staff were content with 'the sense that services were improving':

> It's probably one of those untouchable things. It's just a feeling that something works in the NHS. You know, I pick up the phone, I book them an appointment in a week to ten days' time, and I tell them that, as long as everything is OK, you'll have your operation two or three weeks after that. And they're – 'oh, thank you doctor!' I think it's just one of those things where you actually think the system is working for the patient and for the doctors, and it just gives you a little bit of a warm glow.
>
> (General practitioner)

The role of 'hard evidence' in supporting changes in clinical and organizational practices has elsewhere been shown to be weak (Fitzgerald *et al.*, 2002), dependent on context and on individual perceptions and interpretations of that evidence.

Spread and integration

Changes were introduced in one part of the organization and shown to be successful. But it was interesting to note that this experience was typically not shared with other specialties, suggesting a degree of 'service isolation'. The redesign team was thus an important communication channel, or 'linking pin' between services. However, it is possible that this communications gap was intentional, with the team acting as 'knowledge brokers', spreading the principles behind new working practices, rather than facilitating direct copies.

Change in one area at Parkside, not surprisingly, often created a knock-on effect elsewhere. This was consistent with the suggestion from an early programme evaluation that booking should be viewed as an organization-wide change, and not as an isolated project (Ham *et al.*, 2002). One typical illustration concerned the use of process mapping in booking redesign, which variously led to the development of improved patient information and integrated care pathways, team-based protocols for treatments and processes, the formation of new teams, and collaborative working, among other innovations. Other studies (e.g. Sheaff *et al.*, 2003) have found that parallel interventions rather than isolated changes can be more successful.

Many respondents at Parkside had difficulty answering questions specifically about booking because these methods had been integrated with other process changes, and embedded in routine practice. Measures had been taken to ensure that new methods were both integrated and sustained, including staff training delivered locally, and the identification of responsibilities in clear job descriptions, protocols, and guidelines.

In some areas, having gained commitment from teams and individuals, a continued focus had to be maintained, and a sense of ownership and responsibility was important for long-term sustainability. Maintenance of booking became dependent on certain key individuals, who encouraged others, continued to develop the process, and took operational responsibility. One example of such a key role was the booking clerk. However, dependence on one or two key individuals was a potential problem, should they leave for any reason.

Change takes time

The significance of time was repeatedly emphasized, particularly in the planning stages, to allow staff time to build relationships, consider risks, make informed decisions, plan a controlled approach, and communicate and exchange information. Time was also required for implementation, and for staff to live with the changes, adapt to their needs, and evaluate the outcomes. In particular, sufficient time was needed for consolidation before introducing any further changes:

> There's been such an enormous amount of change. That's one of the things about sustainability; at times there is so much change that you never get time to consolidate one thing, before you're bringing in something else, and that can be a blocker, because people are saying, 'how much change am I going to have?'
>
> (Information specialist)

The redesign team advocated flexible target dates, putting ownership of projects before short timescales. With respect to the timing of implementation, the team recognized that, while small changes could occur quickly, radical changes take longer. Sustainable change cannot be rushed. Culture change and sustained improvements in this organization had previously taken many years. As Berwick (2003) noted, there are 'no shortcuts' in promoting improvements.

Specialties, teams, and teamwork

While Parkside could be described as an organization receptive to change, levels of receptivity varied across the hospital, affecting the sustainability and spread of booking. Booking was more compatible with some specialties than others. For example, it was easier to develop booking in areas which had a high proportion of outpatients, procedures that could be completed quickly, and where bed timing and use were predictable. But the support of staff for new working practices also had to be secured. Some teams were more enthusiastic than others. The call and book centre changed its shift patterns to match the times of greatest demand. Ophthalmology introduced telephone follow-ups to reduce the number of outpatient clinic visits. While many clinical teams were already established, booking encouraged the creation of new multi-professional teams. Effective working both within and across specialties was vital to the development and sustainability of booking (Sheaff *et al.*, 2003). The one binding value at Parkside was 'a willingness to improve'.

Considerable groundwork had been required to build relationships, as booking changed the roles of many staff members. For example, booking clerks and co-ordinators absorbed some of the responsibilities of medical secretaries. Hospital consultants had to collaborate with general practitioners to redesign patient-oriented processes, and relationships between these groups had to be forged before changes were considered. Teams were more effective where their relationships were well established. However, progress was slower than anticipated in some areas. Some specialties, teams, and individuals were less receptive to booking. Resistance from lead consultants presented one barrier which had a knock-on effect on other consultants and specialties. Some consultants were not prepared to work with consultant colleagues (a finding echoed in Chapter 10) because of differences in values, goals, and ways of working. Some consultants, for example, would not agree with referral and treatment protocols, or to pooled waiting lists. Some consultants also treated patients privately; a long hospital waiting list encouraged more people to choose the faster private route.

Perceptions were influenced by a range of other factors. For example, a small number claimed to have seen booking initiatives fail elsewhere. Some clinical staff saw booking as an administrative issue, not relevant to them. There was concern with implementing a standard process in different specialties. However, if one area was successful and another struggling to make booking work, the redesign team emphasized that each area faced different conditions, and that comparisons were unrealistic. However, evidence of success in the 'difficult' specialties was required in order to sway the sceptics.

Individual receptivity

The package of changes required to develop booking systems meant that many individuals had been faced with changes to their roles, behaviour, and ways of thinking. Individual differences in response to change conditioned the pattern of their decisions over time, in ways that could fundamentally reshape the change process. The importance of securing the support and commitment of those affected was repeatedly emphasized. Huy (1999) argues that individual receptivity first denotes a willingness to consider change. The redesign team in particular had met with a range of responses, from resistance to willingness, from resigned but passive acceptance to enthusiastic involvement, and those different reactions had been respected. Scepticism was felt to be a reasonable initial attitude, but by 'chipping away', it was potentially manageable. However, it was also acknowledged that some staff would always be resistant to change, described as 'stuck in their ways', and not wanting 'to move with the times'. Individual responses and decisions thus affect both the sustainability and spread of new working practices such as booking.

A typical initial reaction had been to question the need to change existing practice, especially if it appeared to be working well, and staff had been working hard in what they believed was the best interests of patients. Advocates of booking could thus be seen as criticizing current practice, leaving staff feeling undervalued. Resistance also arose where the modernization agenda was not perceived to be aligned with individual values, and where policies and targets were seen as being simply imposed. The redesign team recognized these responses, and sought in its approach to minimize their impact. However, to the extent that booking was seen to have advantages, the additional workload was more likely to be accepted:

> I like to improve what we are doing, make things easier for patients and staff as well. I mean, I like change, but I don't like change for the sake of change. If there is going to be a benefit from it, that's absolutely fine.
>
> (Nurse)

As Rogers (1995) and others predict, demonstrating evidence for the benefits of booking helped to encourage adoption and sustainability. Most respondents could describe the achievements of booking, mainly with respect to the effects on patients, and ways of working. The most important benefits were in providing a faster service in which the number of hospital visits was reduced, and patients knowing in advance what would happen to them.

Booking had disadvantages for staff, affecting adoption and sustainability. Initial scepticism was fuelled by concerns that booking meant more work, and indeed considerable effort was involved in data collection and reporting for the national booking team. Many staff questioned the consistency and accuracy of reporting, particularly as the definitions of 'fully booked' and 'partially booked' changed over the four waves of the programme, sowing confusion and jeopardizing sustainability. Perceived threats to job specifications and continuity also generated some resistance. The creation of new positions, such as booking co-ordinators and clerks, heightened these sensitivities, introducing concerns about status and grading, particularly among administrative and clerical staff. Booking required clinical specialists to relinquish control over some aspects of their work, including patient admissions, waiting lists, and surgical operation lists:

> If someone else is booking in for you, you don't have control. For some people, it's a problem. Someone's taking it out of your hands. You're not putting the list together any more. Surgeons generally like to be in control of things, like to be in charge.
>
> (Consultant)

Implications for policy and practice

The processes of sustainability and spread at Parkside were complex and interrelated, influenced by a number of factors at different levels of analysis, from attributes of the wider organizational context to individual perceptions, responses, and decisions. The impact of those factors appears to vary with time and context. In particular, the interactions between the substance of changes in booking, the implementation process (methods and timing), and context were critical. Consequently, there is no straightforward management checklist to guarantee the sustainability and spread of service improvements such as these.

The influence and stability of the organization's external context is a key factor jeopardizing sustainability and spread. Allocation of resources from a national programme with a 'wave' structure leads to short-term funding and temporary staff contracts. This has implications for recruitment and retention of key staff, the loss of knowledge when short-term contracts terminate, and subsequently the sustainability of the improvements which those staff have helped to develop and implement. Sustainability and staff security may be reinforced where resources can be supplemented at a local level, to reduce that external dependency.

The NHS Plan set out a series of structural and procedural reforms to achieve a number of performance targets, acknowledging that culture change would also be necessary to develop a more patient-centred service. However, the development of an organization culture receptive to such changes in the first place can take several years of persistent and determined effort. Preparation time was one resource for which national targets did not allow.

The recruitment, development, and retention of skilled change leaders is essential, as they can strengthen receptiveness to change, and encourage the sustainability of specific changes along with an improvement culture. Good management–clinician relationships, together with multi-professional teamworking, are an important factor contributing to receptivity. Relationships built on trust need to be established before change is introduced. However, those active in change implementation would welcome clearer practical guidelines on how to engage clinicians in service improvement, and to see this issue given a higher priority. Future developments in cross-professional education may reduce some of the common barriers and misunderstandings. The importance of stability and continuity of leadership has also been highlighted. One of the keys to the success of the Parkside redesign team concerned existing relationships, established over many years during work in other roles.

The development of a clear strategy and shared vision of the desired future state with a set of clear goals and priorities is also important. A health community perspective, involving co-operative inter-organizational networks, needs to be fostered. A supportive culture develops through shared priorities, a sense of loyalty, low staff turnover, and a lack of formal hierarchy. A sense of pride in the organization is enhanced when management recognizes and rewards effort and achievement. Communication strategies, to share information, experience, and knowledge, should be established prior to change implementation, and informal networks are one key component. Opinion leaders should be employed proactively to help understand how individuals and teams can be influenced to engage with change initiatives.

Parkside used a corporate redesign team to introduce, implement, and sustain change initiatives, consolidate resources, and share knowledge and experience. Before emulating this model, it would be prudent to revisit the list of the team's critical success factors, to ensure that all or most of those were in place in another setting. While the establishment of a dedicated team may appear costly (salaries and expenses, office space and equipment), Parkside management argued that the long-term qualitative and quantifiable benefits outweighed those costs. The redesign team is thus an innovation that other organizations would be advised to adapt appropriately to local conditions, rather than to 'copy exact'.

While the 'wave' structure of the National Booking Programme may have jeopardized sustainability (see Chapter 6), the small-scale development of simple pilot initiatives was effective at Parkside. This approach contributed to sustainability by making processes and improvements visible, and developing a sense of local ownership. In addition, each service is different, and it was more appropriate to spread the principles and thinking behind booking, rather than to identify an approach and ask all services to copy it. As observed, booking is easier to implement in some clinical specialties. Pilot studies which begin in receptive areas and demonstrate rapid gains are more likely to influence other areas to implement too. However, less receptive areas, and those with which booking is less compatible, should be supported with advice on how to address potential barriers. Sceptics in those areas need to be provided with evidence demonstrating that the initiative can work and is beneficial. Resistance in this context needs to be understood, not fought.

Continual monitoring and evaluation is necessary to demonstrate evidence of benefits. However, the value of evidence in spreading service improvements is not straightforward, and depends on the substance of the change, the context, and the manner in which evidence is communicated, received, and interpreted. Evidence is thus only one component in a strategy to influence sceptics and those who are blocking change. It appears that many healthcare staff may judge improvements on subjective measures such as 'gut feel', and a sense that something is working well. Many improvements in patient care are not quantifiable, and the collection of quantifiable data is often hampered by practical considerations, limited resources, and existing information infrastructures.

The Parkside experience highlights the problems with setting ambitious targets and short deadlines. Where targets and timescales are considered unrealistic, a 'quick fix' may be implemented to meet the target, without undertaking other process redesign. Once target dates have passed, and monitoring is discontinued, such changes are unlikely to be sustained. The focus in healthcare modernization has been, understandably, on implementation and results, but this overlooks the time required to develop and preplan the changes to be implemented, and subsequently to consolidate those changes before introducing further initiatives.

Implications for theory

The Parkside experience also lends support to a processual–contextual perspective on change. Change is not merely influenced by the presence or absence of particular conditions, but is also dependent on the wider context, and on the manner in which events unfold, including their timing, sequencing, and pacing. Context plays a significant role in sustaining and spreading service improvements, as context (such as service compatibility with particular changes) at all levels can influence the relative and perceived success of initiatives. The organizational context can also be seen as a stage on which other actors play significant parts; for example, the organization culture and the redesign team were established before Parkside joined the National Booking Programme. This event sequence suggests a path-dependency explanation (see Chapters 2 and 12) for the relative success with booking at Parkside, in which initial conditions are influential in shaping subsequent developments.

Change can also influence the organizational context through, for example, the development of new structures, roles, and processes, and individual attitudes and behaviours. And in this instance, at a national level, the modernization agenda was intended to change the organization culture, challenging traditional assumptions and routines, introducing new values. This suggests a more dynamic view of context, both influential and influenced, than the 'backdrop' perspective of context deployed in many processual perspectives (Dopson and Fitzgerald, 2005b).

While the organization may display the attributes of a context receptive to change, receptivity can vary across different levels. Receptivity at Parkside was thus combined with pockets of resistance. At the organizational level, leadership, culture, vision, strategy, and fit with the change agenda contribute positively. At the level of the clinical specialty, however, compatibility with the nature of the service and previous staff experiences may be more significant. Organizational and service receptivity may in turn influence individual responses.

In this study, organization culture and context appeared to have overriding influence. The National Booking Programme gave resources and measurement strategies to an initiative that was already well developed. An appropriate configuration of factors was already in place, enabling the booking initiative to be developed further. Parkside seized the opportunities presented by the national programme to promote existing objectives, and to help secure the sustainability and spread of this particular initiative.

What can be concluded from this single case study about the conditions that are necessary to encourage the sustainability and spread of major service improvements such as booking? In this case, adoption, sustainability, and spread were difficult to distinguish, as respondents clearly regarded the processes as linked, influenced by similar sets of conditions. Table 7.2 summarizes the conditions identified in this study, at different context levels, influencing these processes. Generalizing from a single case study, but to broadly similar hospital organizational settings, it may be that the implementation, sustainability, and spread of service improvement initiatives are more likely to be successful where those kinds of supporting conditions are in place, and more likely to fail where they are absent.

Table 7.2 *Conditions influencing adoption, sustainability, and spread*

Context level	Supporting	Jeopardizing
External	Long waiting times National targets and deadlines Demonstrated benefits Additional national resourcing Primary–secondary care links	Variation in clinical practice Multiple interpretations of goals 'Wave' implementation structure Non-negotiable deadlines, rapid implementation
Internal	Management vision, style, stability Organization culture and pride Shared strategy and vision Previous successful innovations Dedicated redesign team	Multiple site working Some consultants unwilling to co-operate with colleagues Changes to roles and responsibilities perceived as threatening
Clinical service	Effective teamworking Early engagement Fit with service goals and agendas High receptivity Service compatibility	Limited ability for change leaders to exert influence Lack of service compatibility
Individual	Redesign team's established relationships with key individuals Champions in clinical, managerial, and administrative positions Positive perceptions of booking	No evidence for improved clinical outcomes Sceptics in some areas Preferences of clinical teams Responses to frequent changes Perceptions of national programme
Change process	Adapt principles to fit Simple small-scale pilot schemes demonstrating observable benefits Data available Sufficient time	Fast pace to meet targets Lack of evidence in some specialties Inadequate time to plan and develop first Inadequate time for subsequent consolidation

Critical debates

1 If change, sustainability, and spread are influenced by such a wide range of factors, over time, at different levels of analysis, does this mean that these processes are inherently too complex to manage effectively, and why?

2 Those who genuinely believed that booking was not relevant to their clinical service, and that this system made no contribution to quality of patient care, were subjected to a range of overt and covert influence

tactics to persuade them to change their minds. To what extent are such tactics defensible in this organizational context?

3 Government ministers want it now, but you know that is not possible. What arguments make the best case that more time is required to implement, sustain, adapt, and spread service improvements effectively?

8 Layers of leadership: hidden influencers of healthcare

Annette Neath

Chapter aims

1 To demonstrate how leaders and change agents can be found at all levels of the organization.
2 To demonstrate how staff in non-traditional leadership roles influence the implementation, sustainability, and spread of changes in working practices.
3 To identify factors that contribute to the success of change influencers, agents, leaders.
4 To stimulate debate concerning how best to support and encourage staff in change leadership roles, to maximize their skills and expertise.

Key point summary

- Sustainable change requires leadership at all levels in the organization.
- Effective leadership and support from senior management, clinicians, and project managers is also necessary.
- Key individuals, not typically recognized as change leaders, can be the driving influence behind smaller-scale, cumulative, and sustainable change. Examples of such behaviours were found among administrative, secretarial, clerical, and nursing staff.
- Staff in non-traditional leadership roles can have several advantages when influencing others to engage with service improvements, based on their length of service, depth of organizational knowledge, well-established relationships with powerful colleagues, personal credibility, and political sensitivity.
- The more change agents and influencers there are dispersed across the organization, in positions not normally considered as leadership roles, the more likely are changes influenced by them to be sustained.
- Small-scale, incremental changes should not be discounted. Apparently minor step changes can be important in their own right, and can accumulate to generate more significant forms of service improvement.

- More encouragement, support, and skills development are required to develop leadership capabilities throughout the health service.

Leadership in demand

Stogdill (1950, p.3) defined leadership as 'the process of influencing the activities of an organized group in its efforts toward goal setting and goal achievement'. This identifies leadership as a social process in which goals are achieved through interpersonal influence. If the goals are not achieved, leadership has been ineffective. While most definitions of leadership share these contextual, processual, and evaluative components, there are a number of different perspectives on the nature of the phenomenon. Assuming that leaders are special individuals, researchers initially sought to identify the traits and other characteristics that leaders display. However, such attempts were unsuccessful, and attention switched to identifying contrasting leadership styles. While influential, that work overlooked the significance of context. A leader's style may be effective in one setting but not in another, and attention shifted to perspectives that tried to find a 'fit' between the leaders and the context in which they functioned. In the 1990s, it seemed that the role of the heroic, visionary, charismatic senior (typically male) leader was critical, triggering a fashion for what was variously described as 'transformational leaders', 'super-leaders', and a 'new leadership'. However, following a series of highly visible corporate disasters in the opening years of the twenty-first century, a number of commentators began to argue that those visionary, charismatic leaders were dangerous, as they can destabilize an organization and reduce rather than enhance performance. In other words, leadership theory has passed through a series of phases that have been described as trait spotting, style counselling, context fitting, the new leadership, and dangerous leaders (Buchanan and Huczynski, 2004).

Those perspectives overlook two other dimensions of leadership. One concerns the relationship between leadership and change agency. For most of the twentieth century, research and commentary on these topics proceeded independently. Research on leadership was stimulated by the need to recruit officers during two world wars, while change agency has its roots in the project management and organization development movements. Only in the 1990s does the term 'change leadership' come into popular usage, suggesting a link between these traditions. The second concerns the observation that leadership behaviours are displayed at all organizational levels; in other words, leadership is not the preserve of a senior management elite, but is a more widely dispersed phenomenon (Bryman, 1996). A number of commentators have also argued that change agency, traditionally the responsibility of senior managers and external consultants, has become a more widely dispersed responsibility (Buchanan, 2003; Caldwell, 2003; 2005).

Consequently, in this chapter, the term leadership is used in a broad sense, referring to staff behaviours, at all organizational levels, which have an impact, driving or blocking, on service improvement initiatives. With respect to the adoption, sustainability, and spread of new working practices in the pursuit of healthcare modernization, the ability to influence the decisions and behaviours of others can be regarded as critical to that agenda.

Effective leadership is widely recognized as critical to the success of service improvements in healthcare. Hackett and Spurgeon (1998), for example, argue that 'the demand for excellent leadership within the NHS has never been greater'. *The NHS Plan* explicitly addressed the need to develop leadership skills to ensure that objectives were met. From 2001, the NHS Leadership Centre was involved with trusts, health communities, and networks, developing leadership and organization change capability. One of the main tasks for the Agency's Redesign Team (subsequently the Innovation and Knowledge Group) was 'to build local capability and leadership improvement'. Leadership was thus a constant theme emerging from the Research into Practice studies (Neath, 2004a).

A traditional and popular view is that leaders are the few special people who have the capability for command and influence. Hackett and Spurgeon (1998) focus on the role of the chief executive. The 'leadership qualities framework' developed by the Leadership Centre (Department of Health, 2002a) identifies a series of competencies believed to be unique to healthcare chief executives and board-level directors. This view suggests that leadership, creating a vision and building commitment, is a senior management preserve.

A number of commentators have argued, however, that leadership should be vested in a wide cross-section of organizational membership, in informal as well as formal positions (Senge *et al.*, 1999; Kotter, 1996). Buchanan *et al.* (1999) found that over 90 per cent of managers surveyed agree that change agency knowledge and skills are relevant to all organizational levels. In healthcare, Shortell (2002) highlights the importance of developing leaders at all levels. Current practice in healthcare, however, does not fully reflect this perspective. Leadership programmes for non-clinical staff have focused on senior management, and on those who aspire to board-level and chief executive positions. Programmes for clinical staff have concentrated on training nurses in leadership skills, but clinical directors tend to rely on ad hoc short courses. The significance of dispersed leadership (Buchanan, 2003; Caldwell, 2003; 2005) has not been translated into appropriate training and development initiatives for other staff.

The findings presented here demonstrate how staff at all organizational levels have contributed to the implementation, development, sustainability, and spread of changes associated with the National Booking Programme. In addition, there are multiple forms of organizational leadership and influence, and each layer plays a significant role. For example, while senior managerial and clinical staff prioritize service improvements, influencing levels of support and commitment by example, staff in less senior positions, without formal decision-making authority, are vital to implementation and development through more subtle, covert, influence styles. This 'below the radar' approach (Meyerson, 2001) is particularly important when faced with scepticism and resistance from close colleagues and from potentially more powerful figures. The findings also demonstrate how apparently minor changes can combine to generate significant effects.

The evidence base

The significant role of dispersed leadership was just one theme emerging from our study of the National Booking Programme, which ran from 1998 until 2003, when responsibility for further development was devolved to strategic health authorities (see Chapters 6 and 7 for background on this programme). The overarching objective of the booking programme, based on a government imperative, was that all patients requiring either an outpatient appointment or an elective inpatient admission would be offered a choice of dates, instead of being sent home to wait for a letter giving them a date and time suitable to the hospital. This chapter draws on the findings of an in-depth case study of one acute hospital involved in the fourth wave of the booking programme (see Chapter 7), and on a national evaluation of that wave involving all NHS trusts and healthcare communities.

The aims of the fourth-wave evaluation were to identify factors contributing to the success of the programme, generating feedback to inform future development. A survey questionnaire, with 28 fixed-choice and a series of open-ended items, was distributed between July and October 2003 by email and through the national booking website to all NHS trusts involved in the fourth wave. The questionnaire was completed by local project team members, who were asked to include the views of all staff involved in booking at that site. Over 200 responses were received from 131 organizations; 42 responses did not answer the open-ended questions.

The case study, in contrast, was part of a wider, ongoing research project which focused on factors influencing sustainability and spread. The evaluation explored more broadly the progress of the booking programme, and was commissioned by the programme's senior managers, who wanted to know what was working well, what had to be changed, and what benefits were being derived for patients, staff, and organizations. As already indicated, the findings from both studies suggest how staff in a range of roles that would not normally be described as leadership positions were a key influence on the sustainability and spread of the changing working practices associated with booking. Given the consistency in results from these two studies, their findings are combined in the following discussion.

Beyond tradition

Most commentators seem to accept that large-scale organizational change needs to be driven by skilled and committed top management. However, can incremental step changes driven by staff who are not in formal leadership positions also accumulate to produce large-scale sustainable change in a clinical specialty, in an organization, or across a health community? The findings from these two studies reveal the possibilities, in relation to six main themes:

- essential leadership roles
- leaders and influencers at all levels
- is this really leadership?
- critical success factors
- supportive organization culture
- layers of leadership and influence.

Essential leadership roles

While emphasizing the significance of dispersed leadership, these studies do not contest the contribution of senior formal leadership roles in service improvement, which continues to be important. Echoing the argument of Denis *et al*. (2001), who describe the role of 'leadership constellations' in major change, involving small well-defined senior elites, our findings indicate that at least three interlocking contributions are involved: senior management (chief executives), clinicians (hospital consultants), and project managers:

> You need a damn good project manager, a strong chief executive and a strong lead clinician, and I think with those three key roles, you can really implement booking in a trust.
>
> (Regional booking manager)

Table 8.1 summarizes the typical contributions of those positions, highlighting the strategic role of the chief executive, the influencing role of the consultant, and the operational role of the project manager. While these roles in practice overlap, and there are differences across organizations, these

Table 8.1 *Leadership contributions*

Chief executive	Project Manager	Consultant
Provides strategic direction and ensures that booking has a high profile within the organization	Steers the project, provides operational support and expertise, and influences teams to take ownership of the change	Endorses the change, provides continuity, influences sceptical colleagues, and gives booking credibility with other staff groups

stereotypes seem to be broadly representative, and were frequently mentioned by respondents as critical interlocking leadership roles. Other research supports this perspective. For example, Locock (2001, p.49) argues that, while senior clinical staff play key roles as leaders and champions of change, top management support is still vital:

> Senior management commitment and involvement (as opposed to a passive backing) gives a psychological signal of the importance to the organization, and can unlock organizational barriers that individual departments cannot control.

Case study participants commented on the need for 'real support and commitment from the trust board', and 'for strong project management skills'. From the evaluation study, organizations meeting fourth-wave objectives attributed success in part to a strong leadership team including senior management, hospital consultants, and project managers. However, gaining support and commitment from managers and clinicians for booking, as for other service improvement initiatives, was not taken for granted, but appeared to be an ongoing challenge. There were problems in particular with engaging consultants:

> [This] should have been a specialty that lends itself to booking, yet the lead clinician didn't want to know, just basically said, 'Get stuffed. I am not even meeting with you.'
>
> (Senior project manager)

From the evaluation questionnaire, 43 responses referred to scepticism and resistance among clinical staff, and there were over 20 references to 'lack of ownership and commitment from senior and middle managers and the trust board'. In other words, senior management support for booking, while apparently critical, was not guaranteed. Lack of senior support naturally influenced the responses of other staff groups, discouraging junior colleagues who might otherwise have been willing to participate:

> [That consultant] is very powerful, so the others just chicken out and won't meet up with you, and won't take it any further.
>
> (Project manager)

> [Managers] are not keen, and so other staff are not given the opportunity.
>
> (Project manager)

Employed on short-term contracts, funded by the national programme, to implement booking in a specific hospital, project managers were rarely seen as resistant. However, commitment to the initiative may have weakened in some cases as those contracts came to an end.

Leaders and influencers at all levels

While not challenging directly the need for senior leadership for major change initiatives, little significant change can occur if it is only driven from the top (Senge *et al.*, 1999). Change that is simply forced, top down, may simply distract attention from real efforts to change. Research in other organization settings appears to support this dispersed view of change leadership, including the interlocking and complementary efforts of other levels of staff (Badaracco, 2001; Meyerson, 2001). Brooks (1996) found that the implementation and sustainability of change in a hospital depended on the chief executive, a cadre of middle managers, and a combination of formal and informal leadership, including a diagonal slice of a dozen staff. Meyerson (2001, p.93) discusses the impact of staff not traditionally seen as leaders or influencers. Referring to 'tempered radicals', she suggests that:

> They exercise a form of leadership within organizations that is more localized, more diffuse, more modest, and less visible than traditional forms – yet no less significant.

Our studies suggest that leaders are required throughout the organization structure, observing examples of leadership and influence among nursing, administrative, and clerical staff, and medical secretaries (confirming the findings of the first-wave evaluation of the booking programme; Kipping *et al.*, 2001). While some staff held relatively senior positions (e.g. nursing manager), their roles and job titles were far removed from those of the senior executive and management team and from more traditional formally designated leadership roles. One striking finding to emerge from both projects was the potential influence, positive and negative, that these groups were perceived to exert in implementing and sustaining booking. Examples of these, taken from interview quotes, are shown in Table 8.2. Interestingly, it was often hospital consultants who drew our attention to the role that administrative staff, medical secretaries, booking clerks and nurses can play, indicating that they would:

- adopt a leadership role in initiating and sustaining booking projects;
- influence sceptical consultants to offer patients a booked appointment;
- encourage booking to spread by influencing colleagues to adopt new ways of working.

Table 8.2 *Leadership and influence in non-traditional roles*

Positive influence	Negative influence
Leading change The leader doesn't have to be a clinical leader, but then if you get someone particularly strong in an admin role, they can pull it all together as well (Project manager) Quite often with this project, it's been my secretary who's come up with the best ideas (Lead consultant)	*Resisting change* We had some dreadful meetings. They kept banging their fists, and all the time they are quite obstructive (Nurse manager) The secretaries weren't keen, and they were being kind of obstructive, which meant booking didn't progress (Booking administrator)
Encouraging consultants You see, the secretary can then influence the decision of the consultant, because the consultant needs to actually keep the secretary sweet (Lead consultant) But when it comes to persuasion, it's best left to the nurses and secretaries (Senior project manager)	*Discouraging consultants* Two of my colleagues were quite willing, but their secretary wasn't and they were being kind of obstructive which meant that it didn't progress (Lead consultant) Booking had all fallen apart again because it was basically the secretaries pulling the strings of the consultants (Data quality/IT staff)
Encouraging spread When my secretary started doing it, Mr X's secretary started doing it. And then the secretaries are saying 'oh you know my pal over there is doing this now. I think you ought to give it a go', and another consultant will say yes (Lead consultant)	*Preventing spread* A couple of the secretaries in the department were keen to book, but two of them that had been here for a while put pressure on them not to change (Nurse manager)

As with some consultants and senior executives, a minority of medical secretaries exerted a negative influence over booking. Whereas leadership is traditionally regarded as behaviour that has a positive impact on change, a broader definition of the term encompassing influence in general admits consideration of influence attempts that prevent, delay, or divert change efforts. That negative influence can also be exerted across the organization hierarchy, disrupting the changes associated with booking by refusing to participate, and discouraging both immediate colleagues and more senior clinical staff. Some of the main reasons for this resistance included (see also Chapter 5):

- fear of losing control over the way work was managed;
- additional workload;

- the need to acquire new skills;
- inadequate IT systems;
- some managers;
- some doctors.

It is often assumed that efforts to overcome scepticism concerning service improvement should focus on clinicians. However, these findings suggest that those efforts should also encompass medical secretaries and administrative staff, who might subsequently be able to engage consultants. As one consultant suggested:

> I think the moral of the story is that it isn't necessarily influencing the medical person. You may have to influence their support staff, who in turn will influence the medical person, because without their support staff supporting it, it won't go ahead.
>
> (Lead consultant)

For example, in one acute hospital, the nurse manager and booking co-ordinator in one specialty worked together, first targeting one consultant at a time, persuading them to change the way in which patients were given appointments. They also persuaded doctors to introduce nurse-led follow-up appointments, which relieved consultants from some routine tasks. These examples, together with several other relatively small-scale changes, resulted in a reduction in waiting times for a minor routine operation from over 12 months to six weeks. In the same trust, a booking co-ordinator, promoted to supervisor of the newly established call centre, adopted the same strategy. She recognized that some doctors might be reluctant to let call centre staff schedule their patients' outpatient and elective surgery appointments. Rather than promoting the call centre across the entire hospital, she targeted the doctors she knew, who she thought might be willing to test the new service. In providing evidence of its success, gradually she changed the practices of more and more doctors and specialties. The influence of medical secretaries illustrates how changes can spread. As shown above, some medical secretaries were reluctant to change the way in which patients received their appointments. They enjoyed the responsibility of managing their consultants' diaries. Managers in the Transformation Team targeted enthusiastic secretaries to test the new booking system. Evidence of their own successful experience was more persuasive in influencing sceptical secretaries to change than the direct influence of the Transformation Team and its more senior staff. In turn, the 'newly converted', who benefited from the additional time the changes afforded them to allocate to other tasks, were able to persuade their consultants to try out the new booking system.

While these examples illustrate the persuasive powers of staff in 'non-traditional' leadership roles, they also reinforce the time and patience required to bring about sustainable change. The changes introduced by the nurse and booking co-ordinator took place over a 12-month period. Similarly the supervisor of the call centre anticipated a timescale of months rather than weeks, and it took almost a year for the medical secretaries to change their working practices and two of them still remained resistant to change. Staff in more senior positions may consider change in terms of shorter timescales, perhaps introducing the changes across an entire department. Our evidence shows that change that is hurried is more likely to be met with resistance and less likely to be sustained than when it is introduced over the longer timescales in these examples.

Is this really leadership?

But can changes influenced by administrative, clerical, and nursing staff have a significant impact, given the ambitious scale of the healthcare modernization agenda? Incremental changes may at first appear insignificant in this wider context, but the cumulative effects of minor changes can over time be substantial. Badaracco (2001) describes how a long series of small changes led by 'quiet leaders working behind the scenes' may appear to unfold slowly, but can often be the quickest way to address larger-scale organizational issues. Our own research suggests that changes are more likely to be sustained if they were implemented by those who took final responsibility, once one 'wave' of the programme comes to an end.

Critical success factors

The development of effective booking systems was attributed to a number of critical factors, including:

- adapting change through knowledge and experience;
- ability to develop relationships;
- small, continuous changes;
- personal characteristics.

Our findings also illustrated how staff in non-managerial roles could be more effective than senior and project managers in some situations, perhaps 'because of their ability to reach the parts that other leaders can't reach', as one interviewee observed. In other words, while some of that success influencing others was attributed to personal characteristics such as determination and persistence, their effectiveness also lay with, rather than in spite of, their positions in the organization.

Adapting change through knowledge and experience

As other chapters confirm, the organizational context of change plays a major role. Project managers from the case study and the evaluation said that, while they drew from previous knowledge and experience when introducing booking into new specialties, they also recognized that what worked well in one situation cannot always be replicated in another context, even in the same change initiative, in the same organization. Each implementation has to be adapted to suit local conditions. Most of those described as leaders and influencers had worked in the same hospital for a number of years. The case study site was the only acute hospital in the region, and so job opportunities in other hospitals were limited. Length of service was thus higher than average, although staff tended to move jobs frequently within the hospital. Consequently, they had considerable in-depth knowledge of the organization's systems, processes, and staff. As one project manager said, 'they know who's who and where to go for help, information and resources'. That context understanding contributed to their influence on change, enabling them to work around problems, and to adapt new practices to fit the particular situation. For example, a booking co-ordinator whose role in implementing and sustaining the system had been central had previously worked in the hospital as a receptionist for 10 years. With that background, she knew the department and its staff, what was likely to work well, and what should be avoided:

> I'd seen it before. I knew the background of the work here, I knew what had to be done, and the easiest and most efficient way of doing it.
>
> (Booking co-coordinator)

The hospital's director of modernization said that it was recognized at board level that administrative staff could assume leadership roles, stressing that this was partly because of their knowledge of the organization. Consultants tended to regard staff who 'had been around for a while' as credible and knowledgeable, while it was not uncommon for middle and senior managers to change jobs and hospitals every two to three years.

Ability to develop relationships

The success of staff perceived as leading and influencing change was also attributed to their ability to develop relationships with colleagues at every level, as a result of their tenure and their local knowledge. A nurse manager observed that she had good relationships with 'her' consultants because she communicated with them regularly, and she was good at networking. She was on first-name terms with most of them, and social events were held regularly with all staff in the department. Because of the length of time she had spent in the department, and the strength of these relationships, she knew who to approach with new ideas, contrasting her experience with the uncertainty of someone new to the organization. The modernization director felt that administrative staff were influential also because of the relationships they had developed with consultants over time; they were sympathetic towards the consultants, which enabled them to be more persuasive, and effect reorganizations.

Staff who were described as influential also claimed to have a good understanding of the 'in-house politics'. For example, one booking co-ordinator explained how she followed some of the 'battles' between consultants and other members of staff. When organizing meetings, she knew who could be seated together, who should be separated. Senior managers may not always be in this position, being too far removed from the local context to have an adequate depth of local knowledge concerning a particular specialty or department. Similarly, project managers appointed to specific programmes, such as booking, may have had a good understanding of the initiative, but be less knowledgeable about the organization:

> In truth, some of these poor devils [project managers] struggled. They didn't know enough people high up enough, or on the trust board, to be able to go to someone and say, 'I need your help'. A lot of the general managers just thought it was a fad, so they weren't supporting the project managers.
>
> (Modernization manager)

In terms of sustainability, project managers were typically assigned to the booking programme for one of the four waves, similar to many other modernization initiatives. As a result, they did not have the advantage of nursing and administrative staff, who had developed their understanding of the local setting and its characters through years of experience. Those project managers were encouraged regularly to move on, to progress their careers. However, one of the main reasons for initiative decay is that key individuals, such as project leads, leave. Because of their short-term appointments (18 months), there was little time to develop trust, credibility, and relationships with consultants, who often remain with the same hospital for many years. This was a source of tension between project managers and consultants, and one reason why many of the latter remained sceptical about this initiative.

It seems that administrative, secretarial, clerical, and nursing staff, who hold no formal managerial, leadership, or change agency positions, potentially exert more influence in the organization change process than either senior managers or project leaders, as they possess comparative advantage in the following respects:

- the small-scale, incremental changes which they progress may not even be noticed as changes at all, driven quietly 'behind the scenes' and 'below the radar', without the usual fuss and publicity of a major programme, project, or initiative;
- those minor adjustments were complementary and cumulative, contributing to major changes to working practices, systems, and behaviours;
- lengthy tenure equipped them with good local organizational knowledge, which more senior managers operating at a distance could not develop;
- they had enhanced credibility as it was expected they would stay with the organization, unlike project managers on temporary contracts and other managers who tended to move jobs regularly;
- their intimate local knowledge meant that they knew how to adapt new working practices to fit the conditions of a particular department or specialty;
- working daily with senior medical staff meant that good relationships were long established, so they had credibility with those colleagues, and knew who to approach, when, and how, combined with an understanding of the organization politics.

Small, continuous changes

Abrahamson (2000) argues that repeated, rapid revolutionary change can cause confusion and burnout, reducing organizational performance. He advocates 'painless change', implemented at a more measured and controlled pace. Furthermore, changes that are implemented too quickly may be difficult to sustain, as there is little time to understand new practices, to be involved in their development, or to adapt them effectively to the local context. Initiatives that are incremental, decentralized, and carefully paced may over time produce broader and more lasting changes in working practice, with less upheaval. Case study respondents stressed that developing a sustainable culture change takes time, especially to gain managerial and clinical support. As one interviewee observed, those wishing to progress change cannot assume that others are similarly enthusiastic, and should be realistic about implementation timescales. Another interviewee advocated a management strategy based on small step changes:

> It's about having a long term goal, with a manageable strategy that allows you to take small steps towards achieving that goal.
>
> (Booking co-coordinator)

Whilst those described as leaders in these studies remained focused on their longer-term goals, they shared the same approach to achieving them, by introducing small but continuous step changes. A nurse manager, for example, has introduced many changes over recent years.

Figure 8.1 illustrates her iterative approach to change implementation, and Table 8.3 describes this model with extracts from the interview.

This change process mirrors the PDSA approach (see Chapter 1). This was advocated widely by the Agency as a service redesign tool, based on the well-known total quality management technique developed by Walter Shewart, although he labelled it plan–do–check–act, or PDCA (Schaffer and Thomson, 1992). This begins with piloting the proposed change on a small scale (minimal risk, minimal cost) with those who are enthusiastic, gathering

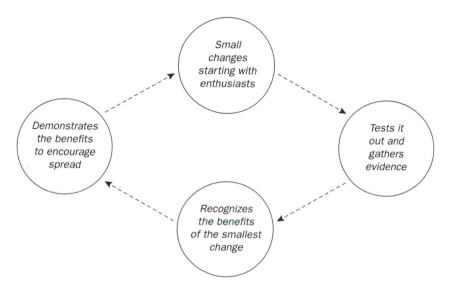

Figure 8.1 *An iterative small-scale change strategy*

Table 8.3 *A nurse manager's change strategy*

Small changes, starting with enthusiasts	Tests and gathers evidence	Recognizes the benefits of the smallest change	Demonstrates the benefits to encourage spread
You check on where you're going and you make small moves. I start it with one. One consultant was keen with the last project	We did a hundred patients, and then we did an audit	And even if I get just the one consultant that stays with me, and I save 10 appointment slots a week, that's 10 slots I've saved for something else. Imagine what that could add up to?	I presented it to the other doctors, and all of a sudden they were all on board. You've got to have evidence. I mean, I've always got one consultant here that's always very anti-everything

evidence with regard to the benefits, and then using that demonstration to persuade others to adopt the approach. Despite her reputation for effective service improvement at that hospital, our nurse said that she was never tempted to change her approach in an attempt to accelerate change; the process is repeated, for each new idea, until most of those to whom the new practices apply are on board.

The combined effect of such minor changes amounted to significant organizational changes, for which the hospital in question had received several awards. For example, in one department, most patients require the same routine procedure, for which they can be admitted as daycases, following direct referral to a consultant by a general practitioner. In this instance, the process from admission to discharge takes place in one day (assuming no complications). But the introduction of direct referrals to daycase treatment was resisted by all but one consultant. The nurse manager piloted the approach with that one enthusiast, gathered evidence demonstrating a significant reduction in patient waiting times, then repeated the process with the other consultants until the whole department worked in this manner. This process took almost 18 months to become embedded and for her to feel confident that it would last, before freeing her to introduce further changes. The nurse then applied the same approach to changes to pre-operative testing and post-operative follow-up appointments for this procedure. Traditionally, patients were required to attend the hospital for pre- and post-operative appointments. Under the new systems, a nurse conducted a telephone assessment, and if the nurse had any concerns, the patient would be asked to come to the hospital to see the consultant. This required a skilled nurse to carry out the assessments and additional training was given to nurses with the potential to take on additional responsibilities. While this required initial additional resources, the costs were outweighed by the reduction in clinic appointments. It also provided the opportunity for nurses to take on additional responsibility.

Personal characteristics

Meyerson (2001) describes the personal characteristics of change leaders and influencers who work quietly behind the scenes:

> Seeing things a bit differently from the norm – feeling at odds with the prevailing culture. They genuinely like their jobs and want to continue to succeed in them, to effectively use their differences as the impetus for constructive change. They believe that direct angry confrontation will get them nowhere, but they don't sit by and allow frustration to fester. Rather, they work quietly to challenge prevailing wisdom and gently provoke their organizational cultures to adapt.

What characteristics emerged from our case study and evaluation findings? Several interviewees and survey respondents referred to **determination and persistence**; influential staff displayed initiative and enthusiasm. Those who were influential in driving change used language such as 'getting stuck in' and 'having to sweat it out'. Another key attribute was **ambition for personal and organizational success**. One nurse manager said that she was motivated by and committed to a booking project because, if successful, this not only demonstrated the excellence of her department, but also contributed to the reputation of the hospital. Her view was that if she could continue to 'push herself that little bit harder', there would be gains for her and the trust, and she would 'get the trust's name in lights'.

Another characteristic shared by those exerting 'behind the scenes' influence was the **desire continuously to improve**, personally and organizationally. They proactively sought personal development opportunities, and set themselves goals to improve the performance of their specialty or department. In short, they were not satisfied with the status quo, and were seeking challenges and ways to implement further changes. Finally, it seems that those individuals were **resilient in the face of criticism** from sceptical colleagues. One respondent spoke of how she had been constantly criticized by colleagues for being over-enthusiastic:

> I still think they have voodoo dolls of me and stick pins in me. I mean, you know you dread going to the meetings. For me there is no release.
> (Booking co-ordinator)

She also commented on how a small group of secretaries had treated one of her colleagues (a booking co-coordinator), with whom she worked closely on several booking projects, commenting that 'they made her life hell, and in actual fact they still do'. It was not uncommon for the booking co-coordinator to be in tears because of the secretaries' comments. Furthermore, the group refused to help when her workload was excessive, and they also refused to cover for her when she was on holiday. Given an opportunity, they offered patients an appointment in the traditional way. Nevertheless, 'getting the job done' was seen as more important than approval from colleagues.

Some found other, more subtle, 'behind the scenes' ways to influence colleagues, and doctors in particular. Two respondents described how they brought sceptics and resistors together at meetings, in an attempt to shame them into participating. For example, they would discuss the short waiting lists of consultants participating in the booking programme, in the hope of influencing resistors who had longer waiting lists. They would also involve the enthusiasts in conversations, encouraging them to respond to the doubts and questions of the sceptics.

Supportive organization culture

These examples of change leadership from non-traditional leadership positions in the organization seem to be exceptional, rather than typical. Efforts to develop leadership capabilities at all levels are not common in the health service. As one senior management respondent observed:

> I think the NHS has lots of training, lots of guidance for middle-managers, and senior managers, and various similar people, but none of it is worth tuppence if you haven't got somebody on the ground floor trying to change this problem. You need good people, and you need to be supportive and encourage, and be protective.

One of the key attributes of the case study hospital on which this chapter is based was the degree of recognition, encouragement, support, and training offered to all staff, in the interests of service improvement. The director of modernization felt that it was necessary to have a persistent team that was willing 'to keep pushing change', despite the levels of resistance it might face. He also emphasized the need to support the team, and when necessary to protect it. In other words, a culture that encourages and supports change and innovation is necessary, to encourage change leadership and informally influence behaviours at all levels of the organization. Senior management support gives staff confidence to turn ideas into actions.

Consequently, in this hospital, all new staff, and those moving to new roles, were adequately trained. The hospital's redesign team (see Chapter 7) was trained in change management skills, which it then transferred to other staff involved in service improvement projects. While the team was often directly involved in change implementation, it saw its role primarily as a facilitative one, encouraging staff to take responsibility for implementing changes in their own department or specialty. However, many respondents contributing to the fourth-wave evaluation indicated that training in general, and the development of change management skills in particular, were not organizational priorities.

Layers of leadership and influence

These observations suggest a dispersed, collective, layered view of change leadership in healthcare with regard to sustained service improvement. Unlike the small senior elites who Denis et al. (2001) identify as 'leadership constellations', staff in non-managerial roles, in non-traditional leadership positions, can also be influential in driving change, through their own enthusiasm and persistence, and through the influence that they can bring to bear on significant others. Indeed, administrative, clerical, secretarial, and nursing staff may have comparative advantages over senior and middle managers, based on their length of service, depth of organizational knowledge, well-established relationships with powerful colleagues, personal credibility, and political sensitivity. Being 'closer to the action' than more senior managers, they are better placed to understand and address the caution and concerns of colleagues involved in change, and may also have a better understanding of how changes may have to be tailored to specific organizational conditions.

This perspective does not imply a shift of focus away from formally designated senior leadership figures; they play an essential role in driving and supporting improvement initiatives, providing encouragement and infrastructure, particularly with regard to training and recognition of achievement. But change leadership is not confined to the top of the hierarchy, nor is it concentrated in well-defined roles. Senge *et al.* (1999) suggest that an organization has many leaders, at all levels in the hierarchy, playing critical roles as elements in a leadership community.

These findings have two major implications for policy and management practice. First, there would be significant value in widening access to leadership and change management training and development. Provision has traditionally focused on senior and middle managers, and on doctors in 'hybrid' clinical–managerial roles (such as clinical directors and medical directors). Senior management support for and commitment to change is a necessary, but not sufficient, condition for implementing the large-scale and ambitious changes required by *The NHS Plan* and subsequent government extensions of those objectives (such as *The NHS Improvement Plan*, Department of Health, 2004a). Other layers of staff, and more significantly other layers of influence, need to be deployed to those ends. Second, in a climate of expectation that puts a premium on rapid and radical performance improvement, there may be temptation to overlook the small-scale changes that do not appear to promise significant impact, and to concentrate on major 'top-down' initiatives. Meyerson (2001, p.95) offers a more balanced perspective on small, incremental changes that are:

> [G]ently and continually pushing against the prevailing norms, making a difference in small but steady ways and setting examples from which others can learn. The changes they inspire are so incremental that they barely merit notice – which is exactly why they work so well. Like drops of water, these approaches are innocuous enough in themselves. But over time and in accumulation, they can erode granite.

Critical debates

1 Provide leadership and change management skills training for staff at all levels, and not just for senior managers: what are the arguments for and against such a policy?
2 To what extent is the development of change leadership capability an individual or an organizational responsibility?
3 In what ways does the profile of skills and attributes of the 'quiet' change leader operating 'below the radar' differ from traditional stereotypes of organizational leaders?

9 Sustaining and spreading change: the cancer collaborative case experience

Elaine Whitby and Rose Gollop

Chapter aims

1 To explore the experience of one hospital with the sustainability and spread of new working practices associated with the Cancer Services Collaborative modernization initiative.
2 To highlight the implications of the findings from this study and identify critical issues for debate.

Key point summary

- The context in which improvements in cancer care are sustained and spread is organizationally complex. Inter-organizational processes and relationships involve individuals, teams, hospital, and cancer networks.
- The collaborative approach involves the simultaneous promotion of numerous improvements *and* improvement methodologies. Findings in this case indicate that a comprehensive understanding of methodologies is at least as, if not more, important as the adoption of new practices for continuous improvement to be sustained.
- Continuity of strategic direction and good manager–clinician relationships supported sustainability and spread.
- There was little evidence of hospital consultants sharing new working practices and associated information with each other. Managers play a role in transferring knowledge across professional and specialty boundaries, but their role is often covert.
- Effective teamworking influences sustainability and spread, particularly clarity of team leadership, widespread involvement of team members, and shared decision making.
- Hospital and network staff identified the collection of performance data as time consuming and difficult. However, local service-specific data were instrumental in this case in sustaining the focus on continuous improvement.

Increasing complexity

Previous chapters have focused on the National Booking Programme, which was designed to give patients a choice of appointment or admission dates. The Cancer Services Collaborative Programme, however, was more complex, for two main reasons. First, it sought to sustain and spread multiple changes to organizational and clinical practice through novel (to the service) improvement methodologies. Second, rather than focusing on change in the individual hospital, or clinical specialty, the collaborative programme involved the development of complex inter-organizational relationships and processes, across a health community network of organizations involved in different types and stages of cancer care.

Since the mid-1990s, there have been a series of national initiatives to improve cancer services in England, culminating in the development of managed clinical networks which involve primary care, cancer units (often district general hospitals), and specialist cancer centres. Care pathways for many cancer patients are complex, involving primary, secondary, and tertiary providers. For care to be effective, linkages and partnership working between these different levels were required. This network model was derived from an influential review (Calman and Hine, 1995), which advocated a restructuring of services to achieve equality of access to high levels of expertise.

As with booking, the cancer collaborative was implemented in waves, or phases. Phase 1 was launched by the National Patients Access Team (which in 2001 became the NHS Modernisation Agency) in November 1999, in nine pilot network sites. The focus of this phase lay with five cancer tumour sites considered high priority: breast, bowel, lung, ovarian, and prostate. The aim of the collaborative was:

> To improve the experience and outcomes for patients with suspected or diagnosed cancer by optimizing care delivery systems across the whole pathway of care.

Although first advocated in 1995, cancer networks were still in the early stages of development when the collaborative's initiative was launched. The term 'collaborative' reflects the anticipated benefits from sharing experience and mutual learning. Derived from the 'breakthrough' model developed by the American Institute for Healthcare Improvement (Kilo, 1998; Kerr *et al.*, 2002), collaboratives are designed to bring together multi-professional teams to share ideas and progress through applying quality improvement techniques. One of the main methods advocated (see Chapter 1) was the 'plan–do–study–act', or PDSA, cycle (Langley *et al.*, 1996). This involves designing small-scale changes that can be introduced and evaluated quickly and with no risk.

In 2000, *The NHS Plan* was published, setting standards and targets for the development of all cancer services, and committing additional funding to cancer care. Cancer networks now had a formal responsibility to deliver the separately published National Cancer Plan (Department of Health, 2000a; 2000b). Phase 2 was launched in April 2001, extending the pilot programme to 34 cancer networks, and involving a comprehensive programme to 'roll out' improvements to all cancer services, including radiography and palliative care.

Phase 3 began in 2003, as the networks developed a stronger role and developed greater independence from national direction and support. At this stage, the initiative was renamed, and became the Cancer Services Collaborative Improvement Partnership (or CSC-IP). The study on which this chapter draws was carried out around the transition between phases 2 and 3.

The Walkerville context

This study was carried out at Walkerville NHS Trust, an acute hospital, and its associated cancer network, which included 12 acute hospital trusts and 15 primary care trusts. The Walkerville network was one of the nine pilot sites in phase 1 of the collaborative initiative; the colorectal team was identified as the network pilot for colorectal cancer services. In phase 2, the Walkerville lung and urology teams joined the programme. Data collection focused on the colorectal and lung teams, including consultants, nurses, managers, administrative staff, and allied health professionals. Walkerville was established in 1991. A large district general hospital, it provided acute services to a population of 340,000 and employed 5,000 staff. The cancer network included 15 primary care and 12 acute trusts. During phase 2, the network used its own and health action zone (HAZ) funding to develop one of the largest collaborative programmes in Britain, involving 10 out of the 12 acute trusts. Nationally, the transfer of responsibility for the collaborative to local networks occurred during phase 3. However, at Walkerville, the regional team was disbanded in 2002, and the collaborative's work became a fully integrated network role.

The aim of the study at Walkerville was to identify factors influencing the sustainability and spread of new working practices, based on the experiences of staff working with the cancer collaborative. Qualitative case study methods were thus appropriate, particularly with respect to locating that experience in its organizational context. However, establishing the unit of analysis in this instance was challenging. A 'case' can be defined as any single unit (individual, family, team, department, organization, healthcare system) that can be studied in depth (Stake, 1995; 2000). Faced with a network of almost 30 different and geographically dispersed organizations, determining the research focus was problematic. In negotiation with the cancer collaborative national team which sponsored this study, no clear agreement was reached on what would constitute a useful 'case study site' in this context; nominations included whole networks, individual provider organizations, cancer specialties, cancer care pathways, individuals and teams, and 'consultant x' and 'radiography in network y'. This range of choice demonstrated the potential complexity of the processes and communication patterns that could influence sustainability and spread in a collaborative network. The logistical problems for a research team faced with studying a network of organizations on this scale clearly echoed the complexities facing those working in that network.

Consequently, a 'nested' case study design was agreed with the national team, and the focus of the study lay with two clinical services dealing with lung and colorectal cancers respectively, at one of the acute hospitals, including their multi-professional teams and the wider hospital and network organization context in which they were embedded. One of those teams had joined the collaborative in phase 1 and the other in phase 2. Like most other hospitals in Britain, Walkerville had a relatively conventional clinical directorate structure.

Case study data were collected in 2002–2003 from several sources:

- semi-structured interviews with 21 hospital, network, and primary care trust staff, including managers, doctors, nurses, allied health professionals, and clerical staff;
- focus groups with 17 cancer collaborative project managers from across the network;
- researcher general observations, recorded in field notes;
- researcher observation of multi-professional team, hospital, and network meetings;
- extensive collection and analysis of relevant hospital and network documentation.

Data were subjected to content analysis to identify recurrent themes, with regard to the changes that had been implemented at Walkerville, and particularly with respect to factors influencing the sustainability and spread of those changes.

The service improvements that had been implemented were numerous and varied, including the introduction of novel (to Walkerville) service improvement methods as well as new working practices. Those methods included process mapping, capacity and demand analysis, and PDSA cycles (see Chapter 1). Substantive changes included:

- the use of coloured markers to flag the notes of patients with suspected cancer;

- establishing a team rather than individual referral system, resulting in the even distribution of work across consultants;
- reviewing and modifying the process map for barium enemas, thus reducing waiting times from 13 weeks to 2 weeks;
- streamlining of outpatient procedures, reducing non-attendance rates to less than 1 per cent.

Establishing the timeline for service improvements was difficult, as these changes were introduced gradually, involving large numbers of staff, at different times. A referral proforma piloted in early 2000 had not been widely adopted two and a half years later; by November 2002, the hospital team was still accepting faxed letters from general practitioners as well as proforma referrals. As other experience reported elsewhere in this book confirms, apparently simple changes can take considerable time to implement where several professional groups, and organizations from different parts of the health service, are involved. In addition, although practices that have been in place for several years may appear 'normal', that perception can often disguise how radical they were considered when first implemented.

With regard to factors influencing the sustainability and spread of new working practices, four major themes, and several sub-themes, were identified, suggesting a 'cumulative effects' perspective with regard to the outcomes of these processes:

1 Management roles and relationships:

- stability, continuity, and commitment to a clear agenda;
- management–clinician relationships;
- change facilitators.

2 Receptivity to new practices:

- who is spreading the message;
- perceived similarities between services;
- degree of importance of new practice;
- communication mechanisms.

3 Teamwork dynamics:

- leadership;
- team involvement;
- joint decision making and support.

4 Data management and reporting:

- the value of data;
- data management capability and resources;
- data reporting volume and complexity;
- quality of information.

Management roles and relationships

Under this heading, three sets of issues appeared to be critical in terms of sustaining and spreading new working practice at trust and network levels. These included the continuity of the modernization agenda, the quality of relationships between management and doctors, and the role of managers as change agents and facilitators.

Stability, continuity, and commitment to a clear agenda

Walkerville had a stable senior management team, many of whom had been in post for many years. The chief executive related this stability to the hospital's success in leading culture change, observing that culture change had 'a long lead-in time', and that only an established team could accomplish this. Sheaff *et al.* (2003) argue that the experience and tenure of senior management and healthcare professionals contribute to organizational adaptability. Walkerville had adopted an incremental approach to change. One executive director described how the spread of improvements in the trust was 'nicely low key, gently working something into our day-to-day systems', echoing the 'behind the scenes', 'below the radar' methods used in spreading the new working practices involved in patient booking; see Chapter 8.

Senior management at Walkerville regarded this measured approach as one of the hospital's strengths, acknowledging that it may not always be 'ahead of the pack'. However, senior management did adopt many new practices, and perhaps more importantly, it appeared to sustain these. The incremental approach was deemed essential to allow time for the 'hearts and minds work that is an absolute fundamental prerequisite to success' with organizational change. In addition, the corporate agenda displayed a clear commitment to modernization, including the personal involvement and commitment of the chief executive to the collaborative approach. This support was demonstrated by the appointment of a permanent cancer manager and collaborative lead, instead of appointing a temporary project manager, a common approach especially with phased modernization initiatives like the collaboratives and booking.

In sharp contrast, the network had four directors during the first three years of its existence, the director being the most senior manager in the network's executive management team. As one other manager observed, 'To have four network directors has been problematic in terms of delivering a vision, and the coherence to that.' But despite those management changes, the national collaborative programme was described as having a strong and successful presence in the local network from the beginning, both evolving together:

> The Cancer Services Collaborative is very much part of our network
> team, whereas in other networks, you'll find that the CSC teams are
> managed separately. Phase 3 is all about them being part of the network
> team, but in our network, that's already the case.
>
> (Manager)

Inspection of network documents indicated that it was on target to achieve 100 per cent coverage for the five main tumour site teams involved by the end of phase 2. Few other networks were expected to achieve this outcome so quickly.

The instability created by the succession of network directors appears to have had little impact on phase 2 of the programme. This contradicts findings from an evaluation which argued that stability in cancer network management was central to providing leadership; networks with unstable management were criticized as lacking vision and purpose (Ferlie and Addicott, 2004). One possible explanation for this inconsistency lies with the degree of integration between the national collaborative programme agenda and the local network. Continuity of vision and purpose may have been provided, through the collaborative improvement agenda, despite the change in leadership. The aims and objectives of the collaborative were clear. There were regular meetings between network and collaborative staff, and the collaborative also monitored the progress of the networks in meeting targets, which could have further influenced the network to adopt and sustain the collaborative agenda.

Management–clinician relationships

Contradicting the conventional stereotype of tension between grey suits and white coats, most of those interviewed at Walkerville said that relationships between managers and doctors were good. One manager described the role of his colleagues as 'that extra piece in the jigsaw, to make the whole picture move forward'. A nurse saw managers as 'being there to champion the clinical team' at corporate level. A consultant described the role of managers as 'completing the cycle' of implementing solutions to problems such as waiting times; he described relationships with management as 'really good; probably better than a lot of other places'. Another doctor described receiving 'a lot of backup from management'. Continuing dedicated management support for clinical teams engaged in service improvement was widely regarded as critical.

Change facilitators

Many interviewees referred to the significance of peer-to-peer influence in supporting service improvement, a process that has been recognized elsewhere (Locock, 2001). However, at Walkerville, the management role in supporting change was also associated with information sharing and the transfer of learning between services, managers acting in a liaison role to promote the spread of new working practices. One manager described this as 'matchmaking really, putting people together', and 'introducing new ideas to people that have got set ideas'. Another way in which to describe these roles draws on the concept of 'boundary spanners' (Davenport *et al.*, 2003; Dopson *et al.*, 2002), individuals who occupy a neutral middle ground between individuals, teams, and organizations, and who co-ordinate, facilitate, and help to build consensus. Project managers in the cancer network in this study thus had boundary-spanning roles that were key in promoting the adoption, sustainability, and spread of novel working arrangements and practices. For the purposes of this study, access to several hospital and network groups was facilitated by managers who, in two instances, controlled the meeting agendas, providing them with opportunities to influence attendance and topics for discussion. Mintzberg (2003) argues that managing expert groups with strong professional identities requires an 'indirect' or unobtrusive approach, understanding interpersonal concerns, and deploying covert rather than overt power and influence. In other words, and consistent with the observations in Chapter 8 concerning dispersed and layered change leadership that operates 'below the radar', middle and project managers in particular may play a significant, but not always visible, role in spreading new working practices.

Receptivity to new practices

While the teams and organizations on which this study was based had been recommended as 'good examples' of the implementation of new ways of working, the degree of internal spread of new practices at hospital and network level was surprisingly limited. For example, although one consultant often shared examples of service improvements with colleagues from other specialties, there was no evidence that those ideas had been adopted elsewhere. The reverse seemed to be the case: 'Nobody catches the ball and runs with it. Nobody says, what a fantastic idea; let's do it.' The findings from this study indicate that, in the professional organization of healthcare, the transfer of new working methods is influenced in particular by the way in which the receiver perceives the information; this perception outweighs considerations of 'evidence' when making adoption decisions (Fitzgerald *et al.*, 2002). Furthermore, three issues appear to be critical to the influence process:

- the people spreading the message;
- perceived similarities between the messengers' and the receivers' services;
- degree of importance the receiver places on the new practice.

Any or all of these sets of conditions can influence the manner in which a message is received and perceived, and the impact that has on the receiver's response.

The people spreading the message

The appeal of strong leaders with drive and determination, and discussions with motivational enthusiasts, can be attractive, but do not engage everyone. Enthusiasts can make a significant impact in their own service, but may have limited effects on colleagues in their own or other areas. In other words, to promote the spread of new working practices, enthusiasm alone is not always sufficient. One doctor, for example, while admiring the work of a colleague who was 'pro-change', commented that, 'I don't think I could do that', as those new ways of working were not consistent with his own preferred approach. In addition, perceived over-enthusiasm, overselling, and evangelism also tended to be counter-productive, and for some a more understated approach was more effective:

> There's another clinician from [that area], very quiet in his manner, very methodical. He came and presented the successes he's had. You could see others engaging.
>
> (Manager)

Many commentators distinguish innovators from opinion leaders (e.g. Rogers, 1995; Berwick, 2003); the role of innovators in diffusion or spread is likely to be limited, as they move on quickly to the next new idea. (Berwick argues that physician innovators are 'mavericks'.) Opinion leadership is described by Rogers as the degree to which an individual is able to influence others' attitudes and behaviours in a desired way with relative frequency. Locock et al. (2000) identify different types of opinion leaders, some experts and some peers, suggesting that a spectrum of involvement at different stages in the process of change spread may be appropriate. In other words, different interpersonal influence styles may influence perceptions and engagement, and consequently have an impact particularly on adoption; there is no single 'correct' approach.

Perceived similarities between services

Rogers (1995) argues that *homophily*, where individuals share beliefs, education, values, and meanings, assists the communication of new ideas. The clinical specialty or healthcare context in which service improvements are introduced can thus influence perceptions of whether or not a new practice (or practices) can be transferred to other areas. Fitzgerald and Dopson (2005a) discuss the numerous boundaries, social and professional, that inhibit the diffusion of clinical innovations. In the development of the cancer collaborative networks, boundaries between clinical specialties were particularly noticeable. New practices and methods that, at face value, were applicable across specialties were not readily transferred. One doctor described sharing 'good practice' in meetings with colleagues who typically replied that, 'We could not possibly do that in our specialty, because we have more patients.' Recipients focused on differences in working patterns rather than considering ways in which new practices could in principle be applied more broadly to their own areas, commenting: 'We're different, therefore we can't use your approach.' Locock (2001) argues that individual clinical departments may not have a view of relationships across the organization, and project managers in this study described their role as prompting teams to ask, 'How will it work for us, and how will it benefit us?', reinforcing that narrow focus. This highlights the bridging or 'linking pin' role of managers in helping to transfer new practices across organizational and professional boundaries.

Another factor compounding the difficulties in spreading new practices was the apparent existence of unspoken codes of behaviour, preventing one specialty team from approaching another with ideas for improvement. For example, one doctor was happy to volunteer to speak to colleagues at events organized by managers, but was not comfortable approaching other doctors directly. Another consultant said that he had no plans to share his new practices with other specialists in the hospital; this was not something that he had considered doing. However, there was evidence to suggest that the transfer of ideas across professional boundaries did occur. One manager, for example, had contacted another clinical service in the hospital to learn about tape recording patient consultations, illustrating a 'pull' model of spread, where staff identify an area for service improvement, then actively seek information about the possibilities and methods. However, it is not clear what factors trigger individuals and teams proactively to seek information beyond their traditional boundaries.

As well as boundaries between clinical specialisms, there was considerable variability among staff involved with the cancer collaborative in the extent to which they spread improvement principles and new practices to all aspects of their services. One clinical team applied improvement methods to multiple aspects of its service, for patients with cancer and with other conditions. However, in the other clinical team, there was limited transfer, exemplified by one doctor who observed that, 'I just wish the same process could apply to many of the other conditions; I would like more of that sort of system'. Applications across the service require a thorough understanding of improvement methodologies, and this too was variable. One doctor described how, in phase 1, clinicians and managers received in-depth training in improvement methods, giving them a comprehensive common understanding. But in phase 2, the training had been 'broad brush', for clinicians only, and was seen as less effective. Joint education facilitated spread by contributing to mutual understanding. In addition, an evaluation of collaborative methods (Øvretveit et al., 2002) showed that didactic presentations were of limited value, and that staff needed opportunities to learn for themselves how to apply quality methods, so that teams could then sustain a focus on service improvement at the end of the formal programme, and help spread the approach to other areas.

Degree of importance of new practice

The perceived degree of importance attached by the receiver to information about new working practices also affects whether and how those practices spread. One doctor described a system in his service area as 'a bit haphazard'. However, while acknowledging that a new system might be beneficial, he did not feel strongly about this, as long as the situation was being handled effectively by the multidisciplinary team, and patient care was not compromised. In other words, information about new ways of working was not in this instance seen as important, and was consequently not acted upon.

The degree of importance attached to an issue is never an isolated decision, but is influenced by the wider context. Timing is one influencing factor, which Rogers (1995) discusses in relation to the relative earliness or lateness of adoption of the innovation, and the elapsed time occurring between individuals first hearing of an innovation and its adoption or rejection. Our findings indicate that there is a degree of serendipity about this. For example, one respondent heard about a new initiative at a neighbouring trust at a time when her own service was experiencing a problem. Had these events not coincided, it is possible that she might not have seen the relevance and significance of the issue, and the new practice would not have been adopted. The impact of timing and changes in context on the adoption of new practices should not be underestimated.

Communication mechanisms

If messages and information are to be transmitted and received effectively, appropriate communication mechanisms are required. Group meetings provided one such mechanism for the sharing of ideas between colleagues. Of the formal group meetings observed by the researchers, and described by respondents, most appeared to offer limited opportunities for in-depth exploration of new working principles and practices. Generally, although new practices were outlined briefly in those settings, there was little discussion. One exception was a network project management meeting where both the 'what' and the 'how' of service improvement were discussed; new practices were outlined, and implementation problems and solutions were also discussed. Newell *et al.* (2003) argue that sharing process knowledge is more useful than exchanging the details of new working practices. Process knowledge includes how the implementing team achieved the change, who was involved and their respective contributions, and how decisions were made.

There was little evidence of information and ideas being exchanged by the two clinical teams at Walkerville involved in the cancer collaborative. The success of the first team to join the collaborative encouraged the second team to join. A nurse explained how she had 'seen and heard things that had happened in [the colorectal] team', and a manager described hearing about their success 'on the grapevine'. However, this influence did not appear to continue, and there were few opportunities created for the two teams to collaborate with each other. A nurse from one team was active in spreading its learning beyond, but not within, the hospital, and had no knowledge of how services for other tumour sites in the hospital were progressing: 'I'm not involved with them', she commented. The cancer manager was the only link between the two teams, illustrating again the potential opportunities for managers to assist with spread by acting as 'linking pins'.

Teamwork dynamics

Success in introducing, implementing, and sustaining new clinical practices is influenced by interdisciplinary team members' roles and relationships, which can combine to result in effective teamwork.

Numerous respondents identified one of the clinical teams involved in this study as exemplifying a highly effective team. The team members themselves concurred with this view, and identified teamwork as one of the most important components of achieving and sustaining new practice. Team members talked about their team in positive ways, describing it as 'close knit' and 'an exceptionally good team'. One doctor said, 'We do believe in the concept of a team, rather than the nominal notion of a team and the individuals pulling in opposite directions.'

Leadership, widespread involvement within the team, and joint decision making and support were all identified as contributing to effectiveness, and this particular team displayed those characteristics. The team had introduced numerous service improvements, and had achieved a team culture of continuous improvement. Examples from both teams illustrate this.

Leadership

The lead cancer clinician in the close-knit team was described by one senior manager as typifying 'enthusiasm and commitment and progressiveness in relation to clinical care of patients', and was described by colleagues as 'a driving force'. That particular clinician held clear leadership responsibility in the team for cancer developments, including the collaborative, and acknowledged that the momentum generated by the cancer collaborative was probably only maintained by the team's own continued presence.

In this team, other members had clearly designated and defined leadership roles for clinical issues outside cancer. In the other team, medical and nursing staff were identified as taking the lead for the collaborative on different occasions. One respondent proposed that their team should identify a single person responsible for developing the collaborative programme agenda, observing that this person would need both 'the time and the drive' to do this. West *et al.* (2003) also found, in their work with health service teams, that clarity of team leadership roles was associated with clarity of objectives, high levels of team member participation, commitment to excellence, and support for innovation.

Widespread involvement

Both of the clinical teams studied tried to include staff from all disciplines and grades of seniority in cancer collaborative projects, including senior consultants, managers, nurses, allied health professionals, and administrative and clerical staff. The inclusive nature of team relationships was valued, and was identified as helping to create an atmosphere where all members felt able to contribute:

> I'm not scared of going to the top bods and saying, 'Look, you know you could do this differently'. They always listen.
>
> (Allied health professional)

Widespread involvement extends further than just attending team meetings. Achieving a feeling of ownership within the team is an essential factor in aiding sustainability because it distributes responsibility for ensuring that improvements are maintained.

Joint decision making and ongoing support

Although both clinical teams tried to involve all team members in meetings, differences were observed in the degree of joint decision making. For example, one of the clinical teams met weekly. Individuals brought ideas that were discussed, and joint decisions were made: to implement, not to implement, or to explore an issue further. If changes were introduced, they were almost always implemented across the whole team. The team made the decision, and nothing was forced on anyone. A degree of compromise in the decision-making process was described. If most colleagues were in agreement, the new practice was adopted. It may not be the preferred option for all team members, but as long as they had no strong views to the contrary, the change was tried. This did not mean that disagreement did not occur. On the contrary, 'heated debate' was reported on one occasion, with one team member proposing:

> Sitting down, communicating, and thrashing it out. Even if you have a big row between you all, it means you are talking, and that's good.
>
> (Clerical assistant)

The same level of debate and shared agreement was neither described nor observed in the other team. One particularly complex service improvement that the team was trying to progress had been discussed on a number of occasions. The team then met with another department which it was trying to influence. That meeting proved very difficult. A nurse member of the team said, 'I felt I'd had no backing from anybody in that meeting'. She described how important it was to gain consensus and support in such circumstances, indicating that this was not always achieved: 'I think when you are looking at big changes like this, it has got to be your whole team'.

In this study, teamworking was identified as a factor supporting implementation of new practices and sustaining a focus on service improvement, potentially leading to improved patient care, treatment, and experience. For example, other recent research has identified a link between teamworking and patient mortality (West and Johnson, 2002).

Data management and reporting

There was considerable variability in data management procedures across the cancer network, with Walkerville being atypical in this respect. The hospital had a history of commitment to good data systems, the chief executive having been involved in developing the national information management and technology strategy. One manager described Walkerville as 'far ahead in IT'. However, despite long-term executive commitment, there were still data management limitations. There were also considerable challenges associated with data collection and reporting across the network, relating to the value of data, data management capability and resources, data reporting volume and complexity, and quality of information.

The value of data

Monitoring the timing of the patient journey from referral to treatment was described by one doctor as 'the biggest chore of the cancer collaborative'. However, information obtained from these data kept staff focused on their improvement goals, by providing evidence of progression and the success of specific changes. Evidence of success was central to sustaining interest in service improvement.

Use and appreciation of data were not exclusive to medical staff. One administrator described how the figures had elicited a response of 'Wow, haven't we improved!' Project managers agreed that monitoring was important for sustainability, one proposing that this was more important than sustaining enthusiasm alone, as it provided early warning of slippage.

Data management capability and resources

While the need to continue monitoring performance data was acknowledged, clinical team resources were limited. One team funded a data analyst. However, data collection was rarely funded, and often fell to a team member such as the specialist nurse, who did this in addition to clinical work. Competing priorities and responsibilities for staff in relation to data, service improvement, and clinical commitments were thus identified as detrimental to sustainability.

Human resource issues were thus also impediments to the spread of new practices. For example, one clinical team successfully established a database to meet its needs. However, when other teams tried to implement similar systems, they experienced difficulties, because they increased demand for scarce IT department resources. The development of other initiatives was also impeded because of IT capacity problems. The national team and the local cancer network were aware of data management and reporting issues. Consideration of the provision of data support to all tumour groups in the network was ongoing during this research. However, there were differing views as to whether support should be funded by the network or by the acute and primary trusts. This demonstrated a potential tension that may arise between the network and trusts regarding funding decisions and resource allocation, with decisions by the network having significant implications for trusts.

Data reporting volume and complexity

Data collection at Walkerville was highly varied in nature and scale, with different systems operating for lung, colorectal, and urology cancer services. These systems were developed in response to the differing needs of clinical teams, and to accommodate the requirements of associated professional bodies, which had database requirements that did not always match the hospital's needs. Another factor contributing to the complexity of reporting was that the datasets required by different bodies were constantly changing. Data collection for the cancer collaborative was described by one manager as particularly time consuming. The volume of data collection and reporting at network level was also significant. Notes from a project managers' workshop indicated that they could each have to complete up to six reports every month, raising questions concerning the priorities of the collaborative programme; the burden of data collection could take priority over service improvement. However, a number of ways of addressing the volume of reporting were being explored. This involved, for example, moving from monthly to quarterly reporting, and seeking support from a member of staff skilled in information management to review current methods of collating and presenting information and to develop alternative approaches.

Quality of information

Quality of information also varied across the network. A doctor at a clinical specialty network meeting reviewed data presented from his own hospital, and noted that they were inaccurate saying, 'We might as well get a random numbers machine.' At the same meeting, for one topic, only four of 12 trusts involved provided the information required, because of difficulties with data collection. Other variability related to the timing of data capture. For colorectal services at one hospital, this occurred more or less in real time. However, another hospital in the network used a paper-based system where data were only logged at the end of treatment, resulting in a long delay before data were available for analysis. Nevertheless, one doctor observed that, while problems remained, information quality had improved significantly over the life of the network.

There were clearly challenges concerning both data capture and use in supporting service improvement at Walkerville and across the network.

While clinical teams said that data were crucial to evaluating improvements and sustaining interest, there was little evidence of the impact of data reporting across the network. On a positive note, information was shared between trusts in a constructive and non-judgemental manner. However, when comparing information, there was little evidence of exploration of differences and similarities, and the factors that might be influencing this.

Discussion

What does the Walkerville experience reveal about the sustainability and spread of new working practices? We will discuss the answer under three headings:

1 new practices, new methodologies
2 cross-boundary knowledge transfer: opinion leaders and influencers
3 data and information.

New practices, new methodologies

Research on diffusion of innovation in healthcare had tended to focus on clinical interventions. In addition, the focus is often on a single clinical change, often in a single speciality, such as the transfer of best practice in cataract diagnosis and treatment (Newell *et al.*, 2003). Some studies have encompassed more broadly based innovations, incorporating organizational and clinical components, such as the 'changing childbirth' initiative in maternity care (Fitzgerald *et al.*, 2002). Evidence suggests that changing practice, even on a single issue, can be complex, involves a range of factors, and takes considerable time. The cancer collaborative had an extremely wide focus, trying to spread multiple new practices across all cancer specialties and pathways. This study showed that the spreading of new practices across specialty boundaries was limited. In addition, the collaborative was promoting the spread of new improvement tools or methodologies, as well as new working practices. The Walkerville experience indicates that a good understanding of improvement methodologies is at least, if not more, important than spread of new practices for continuous improvement to be sustained. Where should efforts to promote healthcare improvement be channelled? Should the promotion of new working practices be emphasized, or would investment in spreading knowledge of improvement methods generate a higher return?

Cross-boundary knowledge transfer: opinion leaders and influencers

Although the significance of peer-to-peer influence in spreading new practices has been widely recognized, there was little evidence at Walkerville of consultants sharing information about working methods. One consultant was visibly successful in introducing several key improvements to her clinical service, but this had little influence on her colleagues. Chapter 10 reports similar findings in the context of spreading 'rapid access' methods in the diagnosis and treatment of prostate cancer. Ferlie (2005) concludes that clinical opinion leaders must retain credibility with their colleagues if they are to be effective in exerting influence. Consequently, if they step too far beyond current norms, they may lose credibility and influence, and need to balance innovation with peer group acceptance. Difficulties in engaging the 'right' opinion leaders have also been noted by Locock et al. (2000), who suggest that the definition of opinion leaders is problematic, and has been oversimplified.

The practice of using existing forums and meetings to appraise new practices and share processes for implementation could be expanded. This would widen exposure of staff to a range of views including those of innovators, enable opinion leaders to emerge, and opinions to be heard by a wider audience. Interestingly, although both clinical teams studied at Walkerville were participants in the cancer collaborative, a founding principle of which was to share and learn, both teams did this within their respective collaborative phases, and predominantly within their clinical specialisms, through the specialty groups established by the network. There was little or no evidence of the collaborate concepts of sharing and learning from each other being applied more widely. Arguably, as research evidence suggests that new practices transfer effectively through established peer networks, the network approach of organizing clinical specialty groups would appear to be an appropriate one. However, such an approach also potentially reinforces the closed clinical group, and minimizes the cross-fertilization of ideas and practices between areas.

In their study of the social networks of clinical directors and directors of nursing, West et al. (1999) found that the networks of senior doctors exhibited a degree of homophily, characterized by links to professional organizations, and a tendency to discuss professional matters with peers rather than junior staff. They labelled this type of social network a 'clique', suggesting that these networks do lend themselves to the transfer of knowledge. However, the lack of external ties limits the introduction of innovations arising outside the clique. In addition, as autonomous professionals, any individual has little power to endorse change across the social network. Consideration should thus perhaps be given to widening participation in clinical network groups, which at Walkerville were mostly populated by doctors, with minimal nursing or managerial representation. Such a move could be challenging. The basis of professional medical power lies in part in control over specialist knowledge, and there may be resistance to sharing this with other disciplines and professions.

Managers at Walkerville appeared to be influential in brokering the transmission of new practices across professional boundaries, but this was managed covertly. However, if the management role is covert, how can this contribution be identified? Currently, the roles and functions of managers are viewed as less critical to the health service, illustrated by national targets to increase the numbers of doctors, nurses, and other clinical staff (but not managerial staff). On the contrary, there have been targets to reduce management numbers. For example, *Commissioning a Patient-Led NHS* (Department of Health, 2005c) identified further restructuring, advocating the engagement of clinicians in designing and commissioning services, while requiring a 15 per cent reduction in managerial and administrative costs. How clinicians will develop commissioning skills, and find time to implement these, and share best practice with colleagues, receives scant attention.

Data and information

A significant body of literature on diffusion of innovation in healthcare relates to evidence-based medicine, and discusses the nature of research evidence and practical implications (Dopson *et al.*, 2003; Fitzgerald and Dopson, 2005b). However, this study suggests a different emphasis, highlighting the use of a particular kind of evidence: local, experiential data and their impact on sustainability and spread. Cited as key to sustainability, effective data management is nevertheless extremely difficult, but unless addressed, these difficulties may limit ongoing improvement. In this case, demands for performance data, from numerous organizations, including the national programme, undoubtedly stretched organizational and team resources. However, local data on performance enhanced sustainability. Many changes introduced by the teams were not clinical innovations based on randomized controlled trials or systematic reviews, but changes to systems and processes resulting in benefits to patients, including reduced waiting times. The evidence collated on these times enabled demonstrable improvements to be achieved and then sustained, and local service-specific information was key to this.

Inadequate information systems thus inhibit information transfer and service improvements, as demonstrated at Walkerville and elsewhere (Ferlie and Shortell, 2001). However, the largest investment in information technology within the health service was launched in 2004, 'Connecting for Health', and a Department of Health agency was tasked with integrating information systems across the service. Engaging clinicians in the development and implementation of this national programme will be a key facet of its development. However, if the full benefits of this involvement are to be realized, the different needs of national bodies, local management, and clinicians must be addressed. There has to be greater understanding of the needs of these different groups and the complementarities between their requirements in order for effective information systems to be developed.

Finally, using clinical staff to collect and analyse performance data is not necessarily the most effective use of their time and expertise. It may be more appropriate to invest in specialist administrative support staff and information departments who can support clinical teams, enabling them to access information as required.

Critical debates

1 *Managing complex changes*: When implementing large-scale, strategic change involving multiple local improvements, where should change leaders invest time and energy? Should they focus on promoting new working practices, or on developing understanding of improvement methodologies? And how should this dilemma be managed?

2 *Knowledge transfer*: The spread of ideas from one doctor to another in this study was minimal. Managers can play a role in transferring knowledge across professional and specialty boundaries, but that role is often covert. How can the transfer of knowledge across boundaries be more effectively promoted?

3 *Data and information*: The findings show that local performance data were particularly important in sustaining improvements. However, that may be specific to this hospital, and other chapters show how performance data are not always used, as staff intuitively determine that improvements have taken place rather than relying on tangible evidence. Why should the role of performance data differ from one context to another?

10 High impact: key changes in cancer care

Rose Gollop and Sharon Saint Lamont

Chapter aims

1 To explain the concept of 'high-impact changes' in cancer care.
2 To explore how one of these changes was implemented, through a study of prostate cancer assessment in England.
3 To discuss the significance of the findings from this study with respect to evidence-based practice.
4 To explore implications for the sustainability and spread of clinically focused service improvements.

Key point summary

- The Cancer Services Collaborative 'Improvement Partnership' advocated that men with suspected prostate cancer should be offered a 'rapid access assessment' process, in order to speed diagnosis and reduce the number of hospital visits.
- In order to gauge the spread of such services, the programme commissioned a study of practice in a sample of urology departments across England.
- Urology services in this study were strongly consultant led in terms of choice of assessment procedures.
- Autonomous decision making among consultants led to procedural differences not only between hospitals, but also within individual urology departments, affecting the spread of this particular innovation.
- Some clinical staff prioritized clinical evidence above patient preferences, and in the absence of proof of improved outcomes from faster assessment, generally opted not to offer patients a choice.
- Clinical staff who preferred traditional assessment processes argued that disease complexity and lack of evidence for improved outcomes made rapid access assessment inappropriate for prostate cancer patients.
- While the cancer collaborative supported clinical teams wishing to make changes to their assessment procedures, its impact did not extend to influencing clinicians to adopt access assessment methods.

● Adoption and spread of rapid access assessment methods were not influenced through the mechanism of communities of practice.

Introduction

Prostate cancer is now the most common cancer in men in the United Kingdom. It has been described as 'the most mysterious of all cancers' because of its natural history, and the uncertainties that surround its detection and management. During the 1990s, waiting times for referral to treatment were longer than for other cancers. The average waiting time from general practitioner referral to first definitive treatment for 90 per cent of all new prostate cancers was 143 days for men referred as urgent, and 292 days for others. In contrast, average waits for women with suspected breast cancer were 62 days (urgent) and 90 days (non-urgent) (Spurgeon et al., 2000). As a result of the considerable investment in cancer services made by government in the late 1990s, and in line with national targets for cancer, some anomalies between tumour types regarding waiting times had been eliminated by 2004–2005. Specifically, the target that all patients referred urgently by their general practitioner should receive a hospital appointment within a period of two weeks ('the two-week wait') was largely being met. By the first quarter of 2004, 98.7 per cent of urgent referrals for all urological cancers (including prostate cancer) were being seen by a consultant urologist within two weeks (Department of Health, 2004b). A further target, to be achieved by 2005, was that all patients referred as urgent should wait no longer than 62 days between general practitioner referral and first definitive treatment ('the 62-day wait'). If this were achieved, it would banish the variation in waiting times across different cancers, but this was known to be more difficult to achieve with respect to prostate cancer without fundamental changes to assessment processes.

As the Cancer Services Collaborative 'Improvement Partnership' rolled out its programme of service improvement, it began to accumulate a wealth of practice-based evidence concerning successful change. In 2001–2003 (phase 2) the programme identified a number of high-impact change principles designed to accelerate evidence-based improvements and meet the NHS Cancer Plan targets (Department of Health, 2000a). The identification of those high-impact changes was the culmination of months of collaboration between clinical teams and programme leaders and facilitators. The collaborative structure is shown in Figure 10.1.

Many changes to care processes had been extensively tested using the 'plan–do–study–act' (PDSA) methodology (see Chapter 1), by many clinical teams. Despite the variations in procedures between teams working in

Prostate cancer: diagnosis and treatment

PSA: prostate-specific antigen	PSA is a protein produced by the prostate gland. The level of PSA in the blood can be raised for several reasons, including the presence of cancerous tissue. Up to a third of men with prostate cancer, however, have normal PSA levels, making the test controversial as a mass screening tool
TRUS: trans-rectal ultrasound-guided biopsy	TRUS biopsy involves an internal examination of the prostate gland to measure its size and density, and also to extract tissue from which a definitive diagnosis can be made. This procedure is performed rectally, with a local anaesthetic, and carries a degree of risk of infection (in rare cases death), minimized by the use of antibiotic cover
Management	Treatment options include surgery, radiotherapy, hormone treatment, and active surveillance or 'watchful waiting'. The management of locally advanced prostate cancer is controversial, due to difficulties in accurate staging, and because of the potential side effects of some treatments

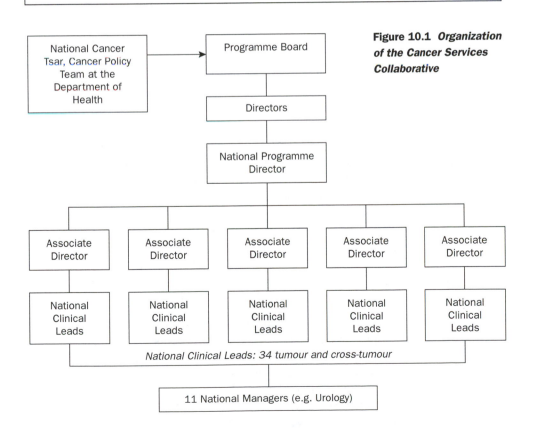

Figure 10.1 *Organization of the Cancer Services Collaborative*

different specialty areas, consistently successful approaches to service redesign were identified for each of the major tumour service pathways – approaches that demonstrated significant, quantified, and sustained improvements. In specific ways implementing these changes was seen as helping to:

- eradicate unnecessary delays for patients;
- contribute towards the delivery of the cancer waiting times targets;
- enhance the patient's experience of care;
- improve the working lives of staff.

The high-impact change principles focused on four significant stages in the patient pathway, namely referral, diagnosis, treatment planning, and follow-up. At each stage, examples of steps that could be taken to help achieve improvements were identified:

Referral: replacement of 'urgent', 'soon', and 'routine' categories with a single queue for all patients, reducing overall waiting times, and ensuring that all patients were treated within an appropriate time frame.

Diagnosis: introduction of 'one-stop' clinics, where all diagnostic tests were performed at one visit, reducing the number of appointments and speeding diagnosis.

Treatment planning: extension of the system of multidisciplinary team review of individual patients' treatment needs, streamlining care plans, and reducing duplication of processes.

Follow-up: introduction of nurse-led clinics, which reduced waiting times for new patients by freeing up consultants' time.

For diagnosis, one of the main changes thus involved combining tests and visits to reduce and co-ordinate the number of appointments for patients, and speed their passage through the system. This could streamline services and increase capacity, reduce waiting times, and enable treatment to start more quickly. The reduction and co-ordination of visits also reduced the period of uncertainty experienced by patients waiting for a diagnosis, an effect not always measured, but one that can have a significant effect on morbidity. Research into the experiences of women with breast cancer, for example, has shown that the time between discovery of symptoms and diagnosis is frequently characterized by high levels of anxiety and distress (Woodward and Webb, 2001; Cornford *et al.*, 2004).

By 2004, the collaborative had collated the change principles and was beginning to promote these and their potential benefits more widely. The accompanying document (NHS Modernisation Agency, 2005), endorsed by the NHS chief executive, included case studies of how high-impact change principles had been implemented in a number of different tumour areas. The collaborative's intent was to define 'high-level' principles, such as extending the nursing role, leaving local teams to decide on the details of implementation; the consequent changes thus differed from one location to another. During the development of these principles, the national steering group for urology, a multidisciplinary team of managers and clinicians, identified ways in which urology departments had been able to reduce waits and delays for patients with symptoms of prostate cancer. Central to this was the introduction of access assessment clinics which combine diagnostic tests, reducing the number of hospital visits patients make prior to receiving a diagnosis, to just one or two. One of the case studies outlined the introduction of this type of system.

Case illustration: introducing rapid access assessment to prostate cancer services

What changed?

● Through developing a standardized service, with all patients being treated in the same manner, ultrasound waiting times decreased from over 20 weeks to four weeks.

Why was the change undertaken?

● Waiting times were previously over 20 weeks, with poor patient flow across healthcare boundaries, resulting in patients having to visit the hospital several times.

How was change achieved?

● Development of rapid access prostate cancer assessment clinic.
● Appointment of specially trained nurse to run the clinic.
● Training of a sonographer to perform TRUS-guided biopsies.
● Use of standardized protocols for examination.
● Introduction of a patient booking system.

What was the impact?

● Decreased waits from over 20 weeks to four weeks.
● Direct booking system maximized patient choice of appointment time.
● Reduced number of patient visits to the hospital.
● Reduced waiting times from referral to diagnosis and treatment.
● Radiologists' time for other procedures increased.
● Role development opportunity for clinical nurse specialist and sonographer.

Prostate cancer was one of the first five tumour areas on which the cancer collaborative had focused during its pilot phase. However, it was proving to be one of the most difficult in which to make significant improvements. The case example outlined above was by no means representative of prostate cancer assessment processes nationally.

Traditional methods versus rapid access assessment

Traditionally, if you were male, and your local doctor suspected that you had prostate cancer, you would typically experience the following process of assessment:

Step 1: You visit your general practitioner with a urinary problem. Following examination and the result of a PSA test, you are referred to a specialist hospital consultant. You may or may not receive information to help you to prepare for the diagnostic methods that the hospital consultant will use.

Step 2: You attend your first hospital appointment for a digital rectal examination, second PSA blood test, information giving, and counselling regarding treatment options. Where appropriate, you are given an appointment to attend at a later date for TRUS examination. (These two steps could take several months to complete.)

Step 3: If your results at step 2 were abnormal, you visit the hospital again for the TRUS examination. This could take one week, but could take ten weeks or more.

Step 4: You return to the hospital to discuss test results if there is a positive diagnosis of prostate cancer; you may be telephoned at home by a member of the clinical team if your results are negative, and you may be given an appointment for further investigations. This takes between one and two weeks.

Faster access, to diagnosis and subsequent treatment, appears to be an obvious goal. Not only are patient anxiety and suffering curtailed, but for a progressive disease such as cancer, treatment that is delayed can be ineffective. Rapid access assessment as a process of speeding diagnosis and treatment has thus been used for the management of many conditions and symptoms, including lower back pain, chest pain, jaundice, and heart failure, and also in accident and emergency departments, and specialized outpatient clinics. Procedures for referral and patient-initiated presentation vary considerably. Evaluations of such services usually focus on their impact on resource outcomes such as hospital admission and waiting times, as well as clinical outcomes in terms of mortality and morbidity.

In cancer care, rapid access to assessment forms part of the process that starts in primary care, in the surgery of the general practitioner, with an urgent referral to hospital services for appropriate cases. The differences for patients who experience rapid access assessment, compared with those who do not, lie with the number of hospital visits, and the overall time taken to confirm diagnosis. The rapid access assessment process typically unfolds like this:

Step 1: You visit your general practitioner with urinary problems. Following examination and the result of a PSA test, you are referred to a specialist hospital consultant, and given an information leaflet describing what to expect on your first visit to the hospital. This takes up to two weeks.

Step 2: You attend your first hospital appointment for a suite of tests and interventions that include: digital rectal examination, PSA blood test, information giving, and counselling regarding choices. If the results suggest an abnormality, a TRUS examination is performed that day. You return home with a date for the next appointment to discuss the results.

Step 3: You return to hospital for test results if there is a positive diagnosis of prostate cancer, or you may instead be telephoned at home by a member of the hospital team if the results are negative for cancer. You may be given an appointment for further investigations. This takes between one and two weeks.

By cutting the number of hospital visits, and reducing time to diagnosis, the rapid access assessment approach meant that the sequence of steps that once took 10 weeks or more to work through could now be completed in around 10 days. Rapid access assessment did not necessarily influence subsequent treatment, because prostate cancer is usually a slowly progressive disease. However, in addition to reducing the period of uncertainty and anxiety for patients, access assessment led to more efficient use of hospital resources.

The sustainability and spread of rapid access assessment

Although the collaborative programme promoted high-impact changes vigorously, the organization and delivery of prostate cancer assessment services were known to vary considerably. The reasons why some changes were widely adopted, while others were not, were not fully understood by the national team, but it was clear that the ability of the national improvement programme to influence clinical staff was limited. Consequently, in 2003, the national team commissioned the Research into Practice team to explore current practice in prostate assessment in a sample of urology departments. This chapter presents the main findings from that work, and explores the implications for sustainability and spread.

The study used semi-structured telephone interviews to obtain the views of staff working in 10 urology departments. Departments were sampled purposively and in discussion with members of the national collaborative urology team, to obtain a mix of assessment procedures, with some using rapid access methods and some not. In each department, the lead clinician (a consultant urologist), a clinical nurse specialist for urology, and a department manager were interviewed. The service improvement lead in each cancer network represented in the sample was also approached, as were representatives from two national prostate cancer charities. None declined to take part and a total of 38 interviews were conducted during the early part of 2004. Data were analysed iteratively using thematic analysis (Holloway, 1997), resulting in themes derived from both the interview guide and issues arising spontaneously.

Structures, processes, roles

Significant differences in practice were identified. For example, patients attending one unit could expect to receive a diagnosis within seven days and with two visits, whereas those living in a different part of the country waited between seven and 11 weeks, and attended four appointments during this time. Some of these differences related to the availability of equipment, but many were due to the way in which clinics were organized and to staffing capacity. Although most TRUS investigations were undertaken by consultant urologists, radiologists also performed these in some cases, and in two units clinical nurse specialists were trained in the technique. Having more staff qualified to undertake investigations helped to reduce waits. There were other examples of the way in which nurses' roles had expanded, particularly in relation to their responsibility for co-ordinating urology clinics and to their pivotal role in providing information, and counselling patients.

Differences in staff roles and responsibilities were significant because they illustrated some of the underlying tensions in clinical teams with regard to the redesign of clinical services. Role redesign is a core element of service redesign, yet this frequently engenders strong feelings among those involved (Kneebone and Darzi, 2005). In this study, some consultants expressed concern about nurses performing invasive procedures such as the TRUS examination, and some suggested that where radiologists perform them, the assessment process could be delayed. Nurses also held differing views about whether they should perform these procedures, most expressing the opinion that this constituted an inappropriate and unnecessary extension of their traditional role.

A willingness to expand the responsibilities of nurses and radiologists to include prostate cancer diagnostic assessments could thus contribute to the sustainability and spread of rapid access methods. In contrast, both the sustainability and spread of this approach were jeopardized by the reluctance of doctors to delegate those responsibilities, and by the reluctance of other staff to expand their roles accordingly.

Interface with primary care

A theme that arose spontaneously during interviews concerned the interface between primary and secondary care, particularly in relation to communication between professionals, and the preparation of patients by general practitioners for the hospital assessment process. Many respondents criticized general practices for not always giving patients sufficient information. This lack of preparation slowed the pace of the assessment process, as patients arrived in clinic not understanding what would happen to them, or why, and hospital staff had to spend time explaining, and then dealing with anxieties. Respondents held differing views as to whether general practitioners were sufficiently informed about the technicalities of prostate cancer assessment, and about how much they should be expected to know. Referral practices were also criticized, some respondents expressing the view that too many men were referred for investigation by their local doctors simply on the basis of one abnormal PSA test, and prompted also by pressure from patients themselves:

> You've only got to look at the number of people turning up for PSAs who feel well, but just want a PSA by the GP. When it's abnormal, they are going to get referred on for a biopsy. Certainly the biggest group of people having prostate biopsies these days are the worried well.
>
> (Consultant urologist)

No general practitioners were interviewed for this study, and it is worth noting that the views expressed by hospital staff could not be challenged by their primary care colleagues. However, many respondents raised these concerns, suggesting that communication between primary and secondary care could be improved.

Attitudes and preferences

Attitudes and preferences were the dominant themes of this study, and are discussed in more depth because of what they reveal about individual responses to change, and the implications for sustaining and spreading new working practices.

Interpretations of 'rapid access assessment'

One of the findings emerging from interviews was that there was no common understanding of the term 'rapid access assessment'. In some urology units, the term described a 'one-stop' service, where all diagnostic investigations for urgently referred patients were performed during one appointment. In one unit, however, the term described a system of linked, booked diagnostic appointments arranged within a relatively rapid time frame. Other units did not explicitly use the term 'rapid access assessment' to describe their services, but still achieved comparably short throughput times. Pathways and processes varied not only across the 10 units, but also within them, by consultant, and in some multi-site units, the site at which the patient was seen. There was variation in the number of appointments leading to diagnosis (between two and four), and in the time from first visit to diagnosis (between five days and 11 weeks). However, irrespective of the approach used, none of the departments in the sample exhibited waiting times as long as those described by Spurgeon *et al.* (2000). In this respect, all departments were offering a form of rapid access to hospital investigations for patients referred urgently, in comparison with much of the previous decade.

The principal difference in process lay in the timing of the TRUS investigation, and specifically whether this was performed at the same appointment as all other tests or on a separate occasion. Patients offered all investigations at the same time could expect to attend hospital only twice before receiving their diagnosis, once for the tests and once for the results. Patients whose consultants performed the TRUS biopsy separately needed to attend three, or possibly four, times, and they also waited longer to hear their diagnosis. The issue of the timing of the TRUS biopsy proved to be particularly controversial, especially among urologists and nurses, and it soon became clear that this was the most important factor for urologists in deciding what type of service to offer. For simplicity, rapid access assessment in which all investigations are performed at the same appointment will be described as 'one-stop' services from this point, although it must be made clear that this is our interpretation of the term and not necessarily that of all participants in this study.

Although resources, in terms of the availability of ultrasound machines and appropriately trained staff, influenced consultants' ability to offer a 'one-stop' service, this was not the major factor in determining whether such a service was favoured. Most of the participants cited clinical autonomy (in this case, that of consultant urologists) as the principle that underpinned their decision. Consultant urologists were the principal decision makers in their teams, and there was little evidence that nurses or managers were influential in choosing assessment pathways, although they were involved in debating the issues. Doctors argued that they based their decisions on a number of factors including the nature of the disease, the evidence relating to speed and outcomes, and the needs of their patients.

The evidence base

Respondents who chose not to operate a one-stop service cited the lack of evidence for improved clinical outcomes (specifically mortality and physical morbidity) as an important reason. Obtaining a speedy diagnosis would not necessarily change the course of this disease, and therefore was interpreted as not being in patients' long-term interests:

> In my opinion, there is absolutely no clinical reason to rush making the diagnosis because it's not going to affect the survival at all, and there is no proof anywhere on the planet that [it] is, so I think you're doing the patient a disservice by that.
>
> (Consultant urologist)

Those who argued against shortening the assessment process because of a lack of evidence did not acknowledge that patients may experience anxiety as a result of waiting longer to receive a diagnosis. Only one participant from a trust not operating a one-stop service reflected on the potential difference between disease outcomes and psychological outcomes from a patient perspective:

> Testicular cancer – that needs to be operated on as quick as possible, whereas prostate cancer, on the whole – waiting for the results to come back is not a real problem. Psychologically, for the patient, it's a major problem.
>
> (Clinical nurse specialist)

Extending the argument that speeding the assessment process does not improve disease outcomes, some respondents said that too rapid a process could increase physical morbidity because it can lead to treatment (which could prove to be inappropriate) starting too soon. Conversely, respondents who did operate one-stop services argued for speed in reaching a diagnosis, although not in relation to disease outcomes. They emphasized issues such as reducing psychological morbidity, improving organizational efficiency, and improving access for patients, irrespective of the final diagnosis.

Patient readiness

Participants stressed the need to be prepared, physically and psychologically, for diagnostic examinations. Preparation for the TRUS biopsy examination was particularly important, because of its invasive nature and associated risks. Virtually all clinical participants mentioned this issue, and for those who did not run one-stop services, it was a major reason in choosing not to do so.

With regard to TRUS biopsy, respondents' main reservations concerned the risks of performing the investigation on patients who had not been adequately prepared physically for this intervention. There were concerns about the risks, although small, of potentially very serious complications, especially septicaemia, and in rare cases death. Thorough patient preparation to minimize such risks was therefore particularly important. Processes for initiating antibiotic regimes, and identification of patients taking anticoagulants, were the two most commonly cited examples of this. However, respondents expressed differing views about safe medication protocols, as these comments indicate:

> We like the antibiotics to be in the circulation, because it has been shown that if you get the antibiotics into the patient prior to biopsy, you reduce the complication rate significantly. We know that you're going to increase the complication rate of your prostate biopsy if you do it on a one-stop basis.
>
> (Consultant urologist)

> We have in the past started antibiotics twelve hours beforehand, and we did that simply by prescribing antibiotics from outpatients, so that was not an issue. In fact our policy has changed on microbiological advice, and we now give it one hour before, so that again is not an issue.
>
> (Consultant urologist)

The need for patients to be psychologically prepared was highlighted more frequently than were the physical aspects. It was recognized that patients must be informed of the purpose and risks of the investigation and its implications for treatment. Among those who were against a one-stop approach, the age profile of men with suspected prostate cancer was of concern, the implication being that older men need more time to absorb information. Indeed the importance of having time to reach a decision was mentioned frequently:

> I think it's a good idea for them to have a cooling off period. They have the information about the biopsy, and they might change their mind.
>
> (Clinical nurse specialist)

Flexibility

Among those who did not run one-stop clinics, there was a perception that 'one stop' equates to 'one opportunity' for patients in terms of choice. One consultant said that if ultrasound machines were turned on and ready for use, everyone attending the clinic would be biopsied, irrespective of need. The feeling was that patients arriving at a one-stop clinic entered into a process from which they could not escape. Respondents used terms such as 'conveyor belt' and 'escape', and described how biopsies were performed 'automatically':

> If you come for one-stop access, you're on the conveyor belt, and you don't have time to reflect on whether you really want to have your biopsy carried out.
>
> (Consultant urologist)

However, those offering one-stop services emphasized both the flexibility and quality of their processes. They described ways in which services were run with an awareness of individual patient needs:

> [The consultant] will actually sit down and talk to the patient about why they are here, what the choices are for them, would they like us to go ahead and biopsy them, or would they like a bit of breathing space? So just because they are booked onto the clinic . . . there's a huge amount of get-out clauses for them. If it's too much for them we can delay; not a problem.
>
> (Clinical nurse specialist)

Irrespective of what type of access pathway they personally preferred, some respondents felt that the most important issue was to offer choice and flexibility to meet all patients' needs.

Complexity of the disease

A fourth issue in the clinical autonomy debate was that of the complexity of prostate cancer in comparison with some other cancers, and its impact on assessment and management. The difficulties associated with screening, the inaccuracy of PSA testing (and to a lesser extent, of the TRUS biopsy) as a diagnostic tool, and the perceived overuse of radical treatments were all raised to support this argument. None of those who raised complexity as an issue operated one-stop clinics, and they generally referred to it as a reason against introducing them. This was because of the perceived need to spend longer with patients discussing options on an individual basis, allowing them time to reflect before making a decision as to whether to proceed with invasive investigations. It was seen by these respondents as being incompatible with the speed with which patients pass through a one-stop service:

> It isn't straightforward like other cancers, so although it would be an excellent idea, I feel that in practice, and for the sake of the patients, I don't know that pushing them to have biopsies on the same day might be the right way forward.
>
> (Consultant urologist)

Patients' influence

There was little evidence of the influence of patients or voluntary organizations on the type of assessment service offered. Most departments did, however, seek the views of patients, through satisfaction surveys and focus groups. Respondents also referred frequently to feedback obtained informally from patients during consultations, citing this as evidence that they were aware of patients' preferences. However, only one department appeared to have involved a local support group in the development of a new patient pathway, and it was not clear whether this had included asking patients if they would like the option of being assessed at a one-stop clinic. In this respect, it was evident that clinicians were not generally apprising patients of the different assessment pathways, even in those departments that operated several systems to cater for the preferences of different consultant urologists.

The views of those arguing against a one-stop service were in marked contrast to those of the representative of one of the national patients' charities. Although these remarks cannot be interpreted as a proxy measure of patients' views, they are based on this respondent's own experience as a patient, and of his long experience of listening to other men's concerns through the medium of a telephone helpline. They are therefore of interest, and point to the need for more widespread and robust methods of obtaining the views of those who are on the receiving end of prostate assessment investigations:

> Of major concern to patients is the delay between intervening tests, waiting for results; they're the things that really do potential harm in raising levels of anxiety and concern. On the helpline, the majority who've been diagnosed, potentially with a late cancer, all say that, 'The time interval between all the appointments and tests has been really devastating.' Countless patients say it. Knowledge is the enemy of disease, and so if you have an understanding of where you are, the far better you are able to cope with it. What better than going to a one-stop clinic and be told everything's fine?
>
> (National charity, patients' representative)

That particular charity had been involved with national and European research and policy-setting groups, yet had been unable to influence what happened to patients at the level of local service delivery.

Other influences

What factors influenced some consultants to support one-stop assessment methods? Several cited the need to meet performance targets as having been a spur to re-examine their services. Others chose rapid access assessment because they had experienced it in other hospitals, for example during training, or because they had actively sought information from peers in other parts of the country. Most were already offering one-stop clinics for patients with haematuria, a symptom of bladder cancer, and some had seen the benefits of this approach in terms of streamlining services, influencing them to extend it to prostate cancer assessment. One consultant compared the choices available to patients in the private sector, making the point that patients expect, and receive, speed when they are paying for their care, and that NHS patients should be treated no differently. He also added that consultants operating in private clinics are generally the same ones who are prepared to let their NHS patients wait longer.

The role of the cancer collaborative programme appears to have been to provide support, resources, and advice to teams wishing to change their services, but not to influence clinicians in their decision making. Indeed, the collaborative's endorsement of particular assessment pathways was challenged by some urologists:

> The collaborative can make their views felt, but it doesn't necessarily mean it's clinically the right thing. And I think this is a good example.
>
> (Consultant urologist)

There were several other examples of consultants expressing irritation with centralized attempts to direct clinical practice for the purpose of meeting government targets. With regard to the influence of cancer networks, nursing staff referred to the importance of sharing learning, but urologists were more likely to focus on individual choice before network-wide agreement on clinical issues such as assessment procedures.

Implications for theory and practice

Table 10.1 summarizes the factors in this study which were identified as either supporting or jeopardizing the sustainability and spread of rapid access assessment methods for prostate cancer patients.

The use of differing assessment pathways, not only across cancer networks, but also in the same hospital, raises some interesting questions about the spread of innovations within professional groups. One set of studies into the spread of healthcare innovations observed the disputed interpretation of evidence across two neighbouring surgical specialties, and between hospital and family doctors (Ferlie et al., 2005). However, this research concluded that, where clinicians belong to teams based on a single specialty, one doctor cannot adopt significantly changed practices without discussion and consent from colleagues from the same specialty. This was not the case in the

Table 10.1 *Factors supporting and jeopardizing sustainability and spread of rapid access assessment*

	Supporting	Jeopardizing
Adoption and spread	Excessive waiting times, 1990s	A 'complex' cancer to diagnose and manage
	Cancer Plan targets, 2000	Wide variation in clinical practice
	National evidence base (high-impact changes), 2003	Need for close primary–secondary care liaison
	Experience of rapid access assessment for other urological conditions	Multiple interpretations of the term 'rapid access assessment'
	National collaborative programme clinical leads as champions	Strong local, individual clinical autonomy
	Promotion by the cancer collaborative and the Agency	Limited ability for change leaders, nurses, or managers to influence
	Significant gains in terms of speed	Lack of evidence for improved clinical outcomes
	Preference of clinical teams operating the system	Concerns about negative impact on morbidity
		Lack of meaningful patient involvement
		Reluctance of medical and nursing staff to extend the nurse role to perform TRUS biopsies
		Lack of resources
Sustainability	National targets and deadlines, 2005	Strong clinical autonomy
	Pressure from national collaborative and local network	Lack of meaningful patient involvement
	Communities of practice	Lack of resources
	Demonstrated benefits	
	Patient feedback	
	More doctors exposed to rapid access assessment methods in training	
	More nurses and sonographers trained to perform TRUS biopsy	

urology community in this study. Indeed, one consultant urologist working in a unit where he was the only surgeon offering a one-stop service for his patients said that he and his colleagues operated in a situation where they agreed to disagree about almost everything. The overall impression was one of clinicians sharing facilities and staff support, but making individual autonomous decisions about how they treated their patients, based on their own interpretation of evidence, and largely independent of the methods endorsed by their peers, the national collaborative programme, or the local cancer network.

If the practices demonstrated by staff in this study are representative of the urology community as a whole, the implications for sustainability and spread are significant. Rapid access assessment for prostate cancer was not spreading among the professional group that held the power to adopt and promote it – consultant urologists. Limited spread, in turn, jeopardized long-term sustainability where new practices were not 'normalized'. The influence of the collaborative and the cancer networks appeared to be limited, and they seemed not to be regarded as trusted sources of evidence in terms of challenging this particular area of clinical practice, in contrast to sources such as the guidance produced by national professional bodies.

This role of the Cancer Services Collaborative as an agent of government health policy was highlighted in some respondents' views regarding the appropriateness of applying general targets to patients with suspected prostate cancer. Blanket targets, in effect, categorize cancer as a single entity instead of a loose collection of diseases with disparate natural histories, diagnosis and treatment needs, and prognoses. The argument that prostate cancer is different from, say, breast cancer, in terms of how quickly it needs to be diagnosed and treated, was evident among clinicians who were resisting the adoption of rapid access assessment pathways. In other words, they would not be forced by government policy on access and waiting times into adopting practices that were not supported by evidence of effectiveness.

One way of spreading and sustaining innovations is through strong communities of practice. Ferlie *et al.* (2005) argue that single professional groups provide powerful communities of practice for the exchange of learning and information about day-to-day working methods. Yet the evidence from this study disputes that. Although learning was undoubtedly shared within the urology community, it did not appear to influence working practices in relation to the adoption of rapid access prostate assessment. Brown and Duguid (1998) suggest that communities of practice sometimes block change as they can fail to acknowledge the limitations of their own world view. Perhaps this explains the limited spread of this particular practice; when urologists meet to discuss clinical issues, the power of the dominant view against rapid access assessment outweighs that of those arguing for it.

Perhaps unsurprisingly, nursing and managerial staff felt that they were unable to influence consultants in their choice of patient pathway. The clinical nurse specialists interviewed generally agreed with the urologists, although they did discuss the issue of rapid access assessment in their own networks, and there was some evidence that these discussions helped form or confirm opinions among them. Managers might have wished to have been able to influence medical colleagues, since this could have helped them achieve some of their performance targets. Possibly the looming deadline of another *Cancer Plan* target (that no patient should wait longer than 62 days from urgent general practitioner referral to first treatment by 2005) was exerting pressure on managers and consultants to find new ways of speeding up the assessment process. By the end of 2004, the collaborative programme had become focused on leading a drive to ensure that targets were met through a much more widespread adoption of redesigned working practices than had been achieved previously.

This study also revealed the lack of influence on clinical processes exerted by patients and patient advocacy groups. Strengthening the role of patients and the public in healthcare has been a central aim of the modernization agenda, encouraging patients to take an active role in decisions about their own care, and creating opportunities for wider public participation in service development. In this respect, the choice of rapid access assessment at local levels fails on both counts. While advocacy groups are familiar with alternative assessment pathways, they have been unable to penetrate the professionally dominated structures that determine what is available locally. Individual patients are less likely to be aware of the differing pathways that they could follow, and are therefore disempowered through lack of information. One study of user involvement in cancer care showed the concept to be unclear to many patients, indicating a need for increased awareness and understanding of what user involvement is and how it can work (Evans *et al.*, 2003). Whether informed patients are able to exert influence where peer pressure has failed remains to be seen, but the growth of the patient choice agenda coupled with the increasing availability of high-quality patient information may at least strengthen this possibility.

Ultimately, changes such as the introduction of rapid access methods of assessing patients for prostate cancer will only have 'high impact' if they are widely spread and sustained over significant periods of time. However, it may be that changes such as this which are clinically focused are particularly difficult to spread, given the overriding influence of medical staff with regard to the adoption, or rejection, of new practices. This particular change, clearly dependent on its acceptance by doctors, was controversial, in spite of its endorsement by the cancer collaborative programme and by individual clinical champions.

Critical debates

1 How can decision making based on clinical autonomy be modified to promote the spread of innovative practice, while maintaining a system that upholds professional independence?
2 How can organizations such as the collaborative programme and local cancer networks increase their influence on the sustainability and spread of changes to working practice that they have identified as having high impact on service delivery and outcomes?
3 What are the barriers preventing patients and advocacy groups from exerting stronger influence on the spread of new working practices to improve quality of care, and how could those barriers be addressed?

11 Spreading is easy: the 'see and treat' experiment

Sharon Saint Lamont

Chapter aims

1 To identify factors influencing the extraordinarily rapid spread of an initiative known as 'see and treat', which was designed to reduce waiting times for patients with minor injuries in hospital accident and emergency departments. The focus of this chapter thus lies with spread, and not with sustainability.
2 To consider whether one or two particular factors were important in this regard, or whether a particular combination of issues, arising around the same time, were influential in promoting the spread of this new approach.
3 To consider whether this conjuncture of issues and events was idiosyncratic, and unique to this particular case, or whether similar configurations could be proactively managed in future to encourage the spread of further new working practices.

Key point summary

- Most hospital accident and emergency departments used a system known as 'triage' (from the French *trier* – to sort) to prioritize patients in terms of how urgently they required attention and treatment.
- Triage meant that those patients with the greatest clinical need were seen and treated before those with minor complaints and injuries. When the emergency department was busy, with larger numbers of more seriously ill and injured patients, long queues of 'minors' would build up, and some patients would wait for many hours.
- Long waiting times in emergency departments had become a nationally recognized problem, reinforced by its highly visible nature in the form of long queues of patients. However, little was being done to find and implement solutions.
- The Emergency Services Collaborative piloted a new method of handling emergency patients called 'see and treat'. A relatively simple approach, patients were seen immediately, regardless of their condition, and treated (if

necessary) either by a senior doctor or by an emergency nurse practitioner. While this approach relied on the availability of suitably qualified and experienced doctors and nurses, 'see and treat' quickly and significantly reduced waiting times and queues.

- Most new working practices tended to be contained in the units where they were first implemented, and were not adopted readily by others. However, 'see and treat' was different, spreading to most emergency departments within a year.
- Two factors in particular seem to have contributed to the rapid spread of 'see and treat': the high visibility of the problem, and national targets for reducing waiting times. However, while apparently necessary, those factors alone were not sufficient.
- A combination of other factors helped the spread of 'see and treat', including individual, peer group, leadership, organizational support, communication, and wider social issues, along with certain properties of the innovation itself. No one factor seems to have been particularly influential in this respect.
- This conjunctural explanation of the rapid spread of 'see and treat' raises the question of whether this configuration could in future be managed to facilitate the spread of similarly innovative working practices in other settings.

Waiting, waiting, waiting

This initiative has undoubtedly been amongst the most successful in the Agency's short history. Not only has it transformed patient experience by gaining much faster access to care, but it has also transformed the working lives of A&E staff by bringing order to what at some times have been chaotic working environments. Remarkable as this change has been, an equally interesting aspect of this phenomenon has been its rapid spread and adoption across the country. The vast majority of departments (now rated at over 80%) adopted this change within 12 months of its conception.

(Michael Scott, Director of Service Improvement,
NHS Modernisation Agency, speaking to accident and
emergency departments in 2003)

Improving the quality of emergency care, and reducing waiting times in hospital accident and emergency departments, has long been a government priority. This was recognized by the introduction of challenging new targets as part of *The NHS Plan* for *Reforming Emergency Care* (Department of Health, 2001c). The aim was that, by the end of 2004, no patient would spend more than four hours from arrival in an accident and emergency department to admission, transfer, or discharge. The strategy for reform proposed ways in which targets could be met by adopting a 'whole systems' approach. The modernization programme for accident and emergency that started in 1999 had attracted investment (across England) of £115 million, and this new reform agenda was allocated a further £100 million.

There were many reasons for introducing a waiting time target. It was recognized that many patients could often be dealt with more appropriately in other environments, or through new ways of working (Browne *et al.*, 2000; Grouse and Bishop, 2001; Lindley-Jones and Finlayson, 2000). Some studies suggested that reducing waits in accident and emergency departments would improve patient satisfaction (Trout *et al.*, 2000), and result in better clinical outcomes and better use of resources (Derlet and Richards, 2000). Waiting time in an accident and emergency department has several components: total time spent in the department, waiting to see a doctor, waiting for test results, waiting for admission to a hospital bed, sometimes waiting on a trolley in a corridor (known as a 'trolley wait'). Combinations could cause long delays and lead to excess waiting times. An Audit Commission (2001) report indicated that waiting times to see a doctor and for admission appeared to be lengthening.

Accident and emergency departments

Type 1   Full resuscitation facilities, able to receive and accommodate accident and emergency patients, led by a hospital consultant.
Type 2   A single specialty department, such as paediatrics, ophthalmology, or dental.
Type 3   Departments able to handle minor injuries only.

The process of managing emergency care has been increasingly scrutinized, and practice has been shown to vary considerably from department to department (Byrne *et al.*, 2000; Cooke *et al.*, 2000; 2002). Initiatives have been suggested to reduce waiting times, including a separate stream of care for minor injuries (Cooke *et al.*, 2000). This is not a new concept; experiments with systems for fast-tracking minor injuries were carried out in 1999, and a consultant in Staffordshire developed a version of 'see and treat' in the early 1990s (Wardrope and Driscoll, 2003). It has also been suggested that 'fast-tracking' was the norm at busy periods in many emergency departments before the triage system was introduced (Windle and Mackway-Jones, 2003). Before the reform strategy was launched, work was already under way to speed up the investigation and assessment process for patients; for example, some departments established dedicated clinical decision units or medical assessment units. However, the effectiveness of these units lacked systematic evaluation, and there was also a need to disseminate more widely good practices once identified.

The Emergency Services Collaborative

The Emergency Services Collaborative was a national programme designed to help reduce waiting times in accident and emergency departments, and to improve the experience of patients and carers. Part of the Agency, this programme focused on the whole system of emergency care, helping emergency departments to meet the national maximum patient waiting time target of four hours from arrival to hospital admission, transfer, or discharge. The collaborative method (see Chapter 1) allows staff from different organizations to learn from each other and to share good practice. All 24-hour emergency departments in England were involved in a series of implementation waves over a two-year period from October 2002 to August 2004. Local teams were expected to implement improvements by analysing and sharing their current practices.

The triage system

Traditionally, patients arriving in hospital emergency departments have been managed using a system of triage, from the French *trier*, meaning to sort. This system derived originally from the need to prioritize the treatment of soldiers wounded in battle. Triage was introduced to hospitals from the battlefield in the 1900s, but was not in widespread use until the second half of the twentieth century. This system means that, following a first brief clinical assessment, usually by a trained emergency or triage nurse, the most seriously injured or seriously ill patients are treated first, rather than being dealt with in the order in which they arrived in the department. This approach can lead to improved outcomes for patients, and also ensures that, when demand is high, limited resources are directed to those patients in greatest need.

Triage systems typically allocate patients to three or four categories, from category 1 obvious emergency (cardiac arrest, massive blood loss), to category 4 non-urgent (medication refill, 'lumps and bumps'). British and Canadian hospitals typically use a more sensitive five-level triage system, based on standardized guidelines, and considered to reduce the chance of categorizing patients incorrectly.

The triage system is not without drawbacks. Triage is a high-risk activity, as decisions are often made quickly. When staff are under pressure in a busy department, subtle indicators of more serious illness or injury may be missed, and patients can be inappropriately allocated to a low-priority category. While initially not threatening, some conditions can become more serious if a patient is kept waiting long enough, and the increased degree of urgency may be overlooked unless patients are reassessed. Triage inevitably means that patients with conditions that are considered not to be urgent will always have to wait until the more urgent cases have been dealt with first. Triage systems were not designed to reduce waiting times, but have the effect of increasing waiting times for patients with minor injuries or ailments.

One solution was 'see and treat'. This is a relatively simple approach that involves both assessing and treating patients as they arrive in the emergency department, and was endorsed by the British Association for Accident and Emergency Medicine and the Royal College of Nurses (RCN). From 2001 onwards, 'see and treat' was presented at regional roadshows by the Agency, and was featured on a national television documentary that subsequently formed the basis of an interactive CD (NHS Modernisation Agency, 2002b). Several hospitals adopted 'see and treat' methods in the summer of 2002, and the technique was subsequently disseminated further by the Emergency Services Collaborative.

One of the puzzles that triggered the research work in this book concerned the lack of wider spread of 'best practice'. 'See and treat', however, starting with only a few hospitals, soon spread to over 160 of the 202 'type 1' emergency departments in England within 12 months (NHS Modernisation Agency, 2004a). Departments implemented the approach in different ways, however, and the high number of adopters disguises wide variations.

The 'see and treat' system

On arrival in the emergency department, patients with less serious injuries and illnesses are seen immediately by a doctor or an emergency nurse practitioner, treated, and then either referred or discharged, instead of being seen briefly and categorized in terms of urgency by a triage nurse. Patients who are seriously ill, or who require more detailed assessment and treatment, are typically moved to and dealt with in a separate area. Consequently, patients with minor complaints are not moved to the back of a queue. Emergency departments need to have enough staff to handle the patient flow without a queue developing. For an arrival rate of up to 10 walk-in patients an hour, one doctor and one nurse have been shown to be effective.

As with triage, 'see and treat' also has problems. At certain times of the day and week, the hourly flow of patients can greatly exceed 10, and more doctors and nurse practitioners are thus required to prevent long queues from forming. Some hospitals created nearby assessment units where emergency patients with even minor complaints could be sent for further investigations; patients who were seen quickly and then sent to that unit would be regarded as having been dealt with inside national guidelines, but could then wait hours for further assessment and treatment. Behind the simplicity of 'see and treat', it was also necessary to find ways to 'fast-track' diagnostic testing to support the approach, leading to new working practices in areas such as phlebotomy (blood testing) and radiology (for X-rays). Doctors specializing in accident and emergency medicine quickly tired of dealing with 'bruises and toenails', jeopardizing the sustainability of the approach. One way to address some of these issues was to apply 'see and treat' only at particularly crucial times of the week.

Criticism of 'see and treat' quickly emerged. Some commentators (Windle and Mackway-Jones, 2003; Leaman, 2003) suggested that the system was pressed into service before proper assessment because it impressed managers and politicians. Wardrope and Driscoll (2003) called for evidence that the diversion of staff to deal with minor injuries did not compromise the care of serious cases. Ellis (2003) argued that 'see and treat is great – if you're a general practitioner', suggesting that many patients who would have waited to see their family doctor would now head for the nearest emergency department knowing that they would not have to wait, with negative consequences for primary care, which could see fewer patients. Others continued to argue that 'see and treat' was the better option, providing a basis for continuing to improve patient care (Castille and Cooke, 2003). Why then did this particular initiative spread so widely? Based on previous work (Gollop, 2002; Whitby, 2002; Jones, 2003), the Research into Practice team was commissioned to identify the factors contributing to this exceptional initiative.

Exploring 'see and treat'

The aim of this study was to explore the experience and views of 'see and treat' of a range of healthcare professionals, focusing in particular on why this approach had been so quickly implemented and spread. The fieldwork was carried out in 2003–2004, through semi-structured interviews with five hospital chief executives, six managers, and 10 medical and nursing staff, including two lead clinicians and five hospital consultants; interview transcripts were content analysed to identify recurring themes. The Emergency Services Collaborative provided details of all hospitals using some form of 'see and treat', and a sample of 10 'type 1' emergency departments was identified, including departments in large inner-city hospitals and smaller hospitals in rural areas. Hospitals which had not adopted 'see and treat' were not included in the study. Interviewees were asked about their attitudes to the approach, how it had been implemented, what factors influenced adoption, what effect it had on patients and staff, and about wider lessons from the experience. This section introduces the main themes emerging from the study, summarized in Table 11.1 (see also Lamont, 2004; 2005).

What's the problem?

The themes that arose in answer to this question included a number of patient and staff issues.

Table 11.1 *'See and treat' opinions*

What's the problem?	*Patient issues*: Waiting times Complaints	*Staff issues*: Anxiety Inefficient working
Why now?		Targets Visibility
What facilitated adoption?	Roadshows Networks Media Near peer groups Leadership Enthusiasm Ownership Professional development	Homophily Type of decision It matters It's adaptable It's simple It's testable It's observable
How was support organized?		NHS Modernisation Agency Emergency Services Collaborative Existing networks Near peer groups Strategic Health Authority reporting
What inhibited adoption?	Interpretation Inexperience Roles and resistance Quality and safety	Accident and emergency mindset Demand Resources Existing performance

Patient issues: waiting times, complaints

Patient issues related to waiting times and complaints. Waiting times
in accident and emergency departments were an established problem.
All respondents spoke about the inefficiency of existing systems and
practices, the rise in the number of patient complaints, and the consequent
need to reduce queues and waiting times:

> A lot of our systems and processes are geared to putting people into
> queues. It doesn't do anything for the people that you put into the queue.
>
> (Chief executive)

Staff were aware of long queues and increased anxiety levels in the
department, as patients waited long hours before being seen by a doctor.
When asked why action had not already been taken to address these issues,
several respondents replied that their department had been the focus of
redesign for several years. As departments developed and changed,

modifications had been made to the use of rooms, to staff development, and to streaming categories of patients. It was perhaps not surprising to find that no two accident and emergency departments were the same. However, the degree of variation in staffing and practice was striking. Some departments relied heavily on emergency nurse practitioners. Others were more consultant led, and some had embraced a more collaborative teamworking approach.

Staff issues: anxiety, inefficient working

Queues and long waiting times were issues for staff as well as for patients. Staff talked about the anxiety they felt when faced with a full room of anxious patients, and the pressure they found themselves under. The following comment highlights the need for change, as a colleague suggested that the waiting room be enlarged to handle more waiting patients:

> We were finding we were under increasing pressure. It came to a head for me one day when accident and emergency said that they needed to carry out a building scheme to expand the waiting room. It's like accepting you can't cope and making provision to not cope even more.
>
> (Chief executive)

While respondents in this study were aware of the waiting times problem, not all agreed that the solution lay in reducing waiting times for patients with minor injuries. Several respondents believed that 'minors' were just one part of a larger system that had to be addressed in order to relieve the overall pressure in emergency departments.

Why now?

If long waiting times were seen as a problem, but not as a priority, why was 'see and treat' adopted so readily and so rapidly by emergency departments? The factors that moved waiting times higher up the political agenda, enabling 'see and treat' to be viewed as a solution, included the issues of targets and visibility.

Targets

While most respondents maintained that there was a constant drive to improve the quality of patient care, and reduce waiting times for all patients, most also mentioned the importance of targets as 'a way of making change happen now'. Implementation of the four-hour maximum waiting time target thus became a catalyst for change, and 'see and treat' was identified as a key initiative to help achieve that goal.

Visibility

Visibility also affected problem identification in this instance and the search for an appropriate solution. Emergency departments tend to be structured around the waiting system, and everyone – patients and hospital staff – could see the queues. In addition, nothing actually happens in the waiting room: just patients waiting to be seen, treated, referred, or discharged. As one respondent said, 'it was in your face':

> Accident and emergency is a fine example of a process that involves lots of players and you see it there and then on the day. It's very visible to staff where the shortfalls are, much more in your face.
>
> (Chief executive)

> I am very passionate about waiting times in accident and emergency, not just because it is a government target, but because it is not good quality care.
>
> (Chief executive)

> It can be seen as the politically correct thing to do. There is a lot of pressure on managers to implement this in some form or other.
>
> (Emergency consultant)

> Targets were not the key driving force for the implementation of 'see and treat', but we recognized it had an impact on targets.
>
> (Modern matron)

Waiting times in hospital emergency departments had attracted persistent media attention and publicity. The expectation that people attending accident and emergency departments should be seen and treated promptly was linked to the historical and cultural expectation that they might have to wait, perhaps for a long time. The combination of problem visibility, public pressure, and non-negotiable national targets promoted the need for a solution to the problem.

What facilitated adoption?

It is significant that no one factor, or small group of key factors, appears to have been responsible for the rapid and widespread adoption of 'see and treat' methods; the same range of factors also contributed to the decision to reject this approach, in some instances. However, one set of issues contributing significantly concerned the communication channels that were used to generate and to share information about the approach. In particular, four broad features of those communications were:

- getting the message across;
- social processes;
- characteristics of the innovation;
- timing.

Getting the message across: roadshows, networks, media

The 'see and treat' approach originated in one hospital, and a subsequent report of the success of the approach, produced by the Emergency Services Collaborative, was covered by a television documentary called *The Service*. While government ministers then wanted to enforce the practice on all hospitals, the collaborative wanted it to be adopted voluntarily. The Agency then hosted a series of regional roadshows to help spread the method. An open invitation was sent to all trust chief executives and health authorities, asking them to come to these roadshows, informing them of the potential to reduce waiting times in emergency departments, and offering a free copy of the television programme. Many respondents mentioned that these roadshows, combined with the support and assistance provided by staff from the collaborative, had the desired effect. This combination of publicity, information, and support allowed emergency departments to think of other ways to solve the waiting times problem, by abandoning traditional triage.

Social processes: near peer groups, leadership, enthusiasm, ownership, professional development, homophily, type of decision

Most of us do not evaluate potential innovations scientifically: face-to-face, interpersonal communication is critical (Rogers, 1995). In other words, while we may pay attention to the evidence, we also rely on subjective evaluations conveyed to us by colleagues, by our peers. The essence of the social component of the spread process was captured by one respondent who said:

> Word sort of gets around within the small community of accident and emergency departments.
>
> (Senior emergency department nurse)

Consequently, social processes, including leadership, enthusiasm, ownership, and professional development, help to produce a more rounded picture of the various factors that influenced the spread of 'see and treat' methods.

All respondents identified one individual who initiated the practice in their organization. This was often the accident and emergency consultant, or in one case the department's lead nurse manager. It seems that concern about the problem of waiting times, and the search for a solution, was the responsibility of those members of staff whose job it then was to convince colleagues that the principles of 'see and treat' would work.

The concept of 'ownership' was particularly significant. Many respondents indicated that the role of the Department of Health was to provide information on principles, on good practice, and to advise on and support initiatives such as 'see and treat'. However, it was also argued that individual hospitals and emergency departments should be responsible for the local development, modification, and implementation of the approach:

> It has to be very much driven by the staff who are running the services, as opposed to managers telling them to go and do it. It has to come from the bottom up, so that staff have ownership, and they can implement it how they like. Where people are told they must do things, they won't.
>
> (Chief executive)

The autonomy to develop the approach to fit local needs encouraged a degree of ownership and professional development, particularly for emergency nurse practitioners who had been introduced to the method during their training. In addition, several respondents mentioned the importance of single-discipline meetings, bringing together emergency department consultants, nurse practitioners, and managers, as well as multidisciplinary meetings. Where disparate individuals share common meanings, perhaps because they all work in the same discipline, a shared language develops, and communication is likely to have a greater impact in terms of knowledge transfer and attitude change.

People share common meanings, perhaps because they work in the same discipline, a shared subcultural language develops, and communication is likely to have greater effects in terms of knowledge gain, attitude formation, and change. The spread of a method such as 'see and treat' is thus facilitated by shared language, understanding, and attitudes, or in other words, by *homophily*:

> It's much easier for groups of consultants to talk to other groups of consultants about the same issue.
>
> (Manager)

Interview responses clearly indicated that peer discussions, between 'like-minded people', had a positive influence on the spread of 'see and treat'. Adoption was thus influenced by sharing ideas with professional colleagues of similar status. However, the rejection of 'see and treat' was influenced by similar conversations.

Decisions to implement organizational initiatives can take one of three forms:

- optional
- collective
- authority

Decisions can be regarded as ranging on a continuum from optional, where the individual has responsibility for the choice, through collective, where the individual has a say but the group makes the decision, to authority, where individuals have no influence, but are instructed what to do. Broadly speaking, authority decisions can lead to faster adoption rates, and optional choices can be made more rapidly than collective decisions. Although most respondents said that decisions in accident and emergency departments were typically team based, involving all staff, decisions affecting 'see and treat' appear to have been mainly individual and optional ones. The decision to adopt or to reject 'see and treat' was typically made, in each hospital, by one or two key individuals who had the status and the expertise to implement their decision without challenge. This may reflect the observation that 'see and treat' was informally introduced, without evaluation or planning before the approach 'went live'. The method was comparatively simple, and the principles could be readily observed in practice in the few trusts that initially adopted the approach. To test the approach, the co-operation of only one senior doctor was required. However, as the use of the approach became more widespread, and appeared to work effectively, the subsequent decision-making style in 'late adopting' hospitals may have been closer to authority than to optional, particularly when health authority monthly reporting requirements made it clear that department waiting times were being closely monitored.

Characteristics of the innovation

Features of the innovation itself were also key facilitating factors. Rogers' (1995) framework of innovation characteristics was used to categorize perceptions of 'see and treat', and Table 11.2 summarizes the interview comments. The approach seems to meet all of Rogers' criteria, although some staff questioned the relative advantage of 'see and treat' compared with traditional triage methods, which were still regarded as useful, to some degree. While those five criteria appear to have contributed to the attractiveness and consequently the rapid spread of see and treat, it is important to recognize the role of the many other factors identified in this analysis. No single factor appears to have been critical; what mattered was this particular combination of factors which developed over time.

Table 11.2 *Characteristics of 'see and treat'*

Relative advantage	Some respondents observed that triage did not work in the best interests of patients
	Others argued that 'see and treat' was just another method of queueing, causing delays and promoting ineffective working practices
	Some respondents insisted that a form of triage was still needed
Compatibility	'See and treat' was seen as compatible with the needs of patients and staff, and was claimed to reduce excessive waiting times
Complexity	'See and treat' was simple to communicate and operate
	Potential adopters did not need specialist equipment or expert knowledge
Trialability	'See and treat' could be tested over a short period with little preplanning
	The lead consultant in the emergency department often adopted the approach with the help of a senior nurse
	The results were rapid as the waiting room typically cleared quickly
Observability	'See and treat' was particularly easy to observe, and the results are immediate
	Positive observations included a less crowded waiting room, shorter waiting times, and improved staff morale

How was support organized?

The Agency, and especially the staff of the Emergency Services Collaborative, continued to support 'see and treat' through the various waves of its implementation across the country. Communication with existing networks enabled ease of access to various social and professional groups beyond individual accident and emergency departments. These included emergency nurse practitioner training groups and accident and emergency networks across the regions. The collaborative work also encouraged the development of local teams, and enthused managers and clinicians alike:

> Consultants made it clear from the beginning that they wanted it to be successful.
>
> (Manager)

> It's a 'feel-good' team down here too. They were all very close and enthusiastic, a good team spirit.
>
> (Chief executive)

> Overall we started the process well, as we had an enthusiastic manager who employed a G grade nurse from a minor injury unit who was very

experienced and pro 'see and treat'. This set the scene for staff
development and support.

(Nurse)

Despite the importance of support groups, the evidence suggests that an
equally important factor contributing to the spread of 'see and treat' was
the effect of the strategic health authority feedback reports. The four-hour
waiting time target for patients in emergency departments was a key feature
of those monthly reports:

There is a definite message to trusts to operate some form of 'see and
treat'. We have to report 'see and treat' figures on a monthly basis.
Previously, the health authority asked you to tick a box on whether you
had an emergency nurse practitioner. Now, they want to know what our
plans are for 'see and treat'. The inference is, we're expected to do it.

(Manager)

The monthly reporting form used by health authorities thus asked whether
the hospital was practising 'see and treat'. If the answer was 'no', the next
question requiring a response concerned what was being done in its place.
As mentioned earlier, this may have transformed early 'optional' choices
to adopt 'see and treat' into subsequent 'authority' decisions.

What inhibited adoption?

The implementation and further spread of 'see and treat' was inhibited by
several factors, in two main categories:

personal and professional   interpretation
inexperience
roles and resistance
quality and safety
accident and emergency 'mindset'

organizational   demand
resources
existing performance

Personal and professional

The ways in which healthcare staff interpreted the idea of 'see and treat'
influenced the adoption of the approach, as it required changes in both
thinking and practice in emergency departments. Some respondents were
concerned that, as 'see and treat' methods had not been subject to a
systematic evaluation of their benefits and wider impact on quality of care,

triage should not be abandoned. The speed with which patients were seen, for example, involved an element of risk; some nurses were concerned that not enough time was devoted to giving patients a thorough examination:

> Nursing staff were sceptical at first. They were concerned about the quality of care. Were we pushing patients through the system too quickly, and not doing proper examinations? Would we get more returners because of this? What are the risks of not having triage and people having to wait 20 minutes to be seen?
>
> (Nurse)

Respondents recognized that 'see and treat' required experienced front line staff who were able to make critical decisions quickly, and that the system could not be led by junior medical staff or by nurses. Lack of adequate numbers of appropriately qualified staff thus meant that the approach could not be implemented. Nevertheless, there were examples of 'see and treat' being operated by staff with different levels of skill and experience.

Some staff simply resisted the method. A number of doctors, for example, were unwilling to be involved in treating minor injuries. Doctors often choose to work in accident and emergency departments because of the crisis element, which is more interesting than dealing with cuts, sprains, and bruises:

> One of the behaviours they had to overcome was that emergency medicine clinicians think too often that they're only about the emergencies, the two per cent. We're looking at the margins rather than the bulk.
>
> (Chief executive)

> If you do psychological profiling on emergency medical staff, they're what's called sensation seekers. 'See and treat' is the most dull form of what we do.
>
> (Accident and emergency department consultant)

Organizational

Following the implementation of 'see and treat', respondents reported an increase in demand for accident and emergency services. Patients who would normally have left the department when they became tired of waiting ('Did Not Waits' or DNWs) now stayed. Almost all respondents agreed that, although this was a relatively straightforward change in department practice, additional resources (particularly, qualified staff) were required to operate 'see and treat' effectively. Lack of resources typically meant that 'see and treat' could not function at weekends or during the night, times where there could be a high volume of minor injuries to deal with. Consequently, this affected staff stress levels. Physical space could also be a problem; while all accident and emergency departments had triage rooms, most of those were not appropriate to 'see and treat' methods, for which there was often no dedicated space.

Paradoxically, perceptions of existing performance levels in accident and emergency departments could also inhibit the introduction of 'see and treat'. Where this approach was seen simply as a way to reduce waiting times for patients with minor injuries, and a department was considered to be performing well in that regard, 'see and treat' was seen as unnecessary – of real benefit only to departments that were 'under-performing in minors'.

Visibility, targets, timing

Why did 'see and treat' become so popular when it did, and then spread so rapidly? The problem of long waits for patients in accident and emergency departments had been widely acknowledged for some time, and traditional triage was considered by many to be inefficient. However, several respondents did not see waiting times as the only issue to be addressed in emergency departments, and also felt that, if current waiting times were acceptable, staff would have no need to find a 'solution'.

The two factors critical to the spread of this approach appear to have related not merely to characteristics of the innovation (Rogers, 1995) but to the visibility of both the problem and the consequences of the solution, and to performance targets. Hospital accident and emergency departments are busy places, visited by patients accompanied by relatives and friends, and long queues are a highly visible feature. The waiting times targets in *The NHS Plan* also promoted the spread of this new approach, encouraging the search for new ways to achieve those performance measures. In other words, the visibility and scale of the problem alone were not sufficient to prompt widespread change; the visibility of the problem heightened awareness, but targets increased the urgency. The two cut-off dates set by the Department of Health hastened decisions. First, the target for 90 per cent of patients attending an emergency department to be seen within four hours was to be met, and maintained, by March 2003. Second, all hospitals in England were expected to meet the four-hour target for 98 per cent of patients by December 2004. For the year to April 2003, 23 per cent of patients spent more than four hours in emergency departments, but that had fallen to just over 5 per cent for the three months from April to June 2004. However, 24 per cent of patients who were in emergency departments for longer than four hours were waiting for a bed, while a further 24 per cent waited because it was difficult to obtain a specialist opinion in time (Eaton, 2004). Once implemented, the potential benefits of 'see and treat' were also visible, in the absence of queues in emergency department waiting areas. In addition, those performance measures were monitored routinely by strategic health authorities, encouraging hospitals to consider and to sustain the new approach, and perhaps giving them limited choice with regard to adoption.

The findings from this study thus suggest that the imposition of new performance goals to address a known problem was not alone adequate to prompt the spread of new methods. Further facilitation and support were instrumental. Consequently, regional roadshows and television reporting were powerful vehicles for communicating the 'see and treat message' to a wider audience. The effective marketing of, and support for, this approach provided through the Emergency Services Collaborative programme added to the momentum. A range of personal and professional factors, and the attributes of the innovation itself, also supported adoption. A critical mass of people became involved in piloting and assessing a relatively simple technique that made a visible difference to patient experiences and staff morale. While 'see and treat' was encouraged by internal and external, processual and contextual factors, timing was also optimal. This combination of factors came together to encourage, to support, and widely to communicate the adoption of a fresh solution to a known and long-standing problem. It is not possible to identify one factor, or a small number of issues, contributing to this success story; the explanation lies with the conjuncture of events and issues. However, if such a pattern of factors is required to encourage the rapid spread of new working practices, is it possible to recreate such a configuration with regard to further healthcare initiatives?

Critical debates

1 Given what we know about the many factors contributing to the rapid spread of 'see and treat', what predictions can we make concerning the probability that this new approach will be sustained? Would this approach to spread support or jeopardize sustainability? And would the factors contributing to the sustainability of new working practices such as these be the same as the factors that contributed to the adoption and spread of the methods in the first place?

2 Could a similar configuration of factors be proactively managed to promote the spread of future innovations in working practice in healthcare? Or is the combination of issues contributing to rapid spread in this instance unique, and difficult if not impossible to recreate?

3 The role and impact of measurable performance targets in healthcare have been controversial. How does the 'see and treat' experience contribute to this debate, by highlighting the benefits and drawbacks of a 'targets-driven' change strategy?

Part III
Implications

12 The sustainability and spread story: theoretical developments

Louise Fitzgerald and David A. Buchanan

Chapter aims

1 To develop, from a processual perspective, explanations for the improvement evaporation problem: why are new working practices sustained in some settings, while they decay in others?
2 To develop, from a processual perspective, explanations for the best practices puzzle: through what processes are working practices in one setting redesigned, adopted, and spread to other units?
3 To develop a perspective that explains these two processes and the links between them and their mutual influence.

Key point summary

- Sustainability can mean to anchor, embed, maintain, perpetuate, normalize, routinize, integrate, or institutionalize change. Sustained change is resilient, has resisted erosion and decay, has withstood challenge, has become durable, has become irreversible.
- Sustainability can also mean ongoing improvement, retaining the principles while developing the details of practice to accommodate changing conditions, to achieve even higher performance standards. Paradoxically, the survival of new working practice may require adaptation.
- Sustainability is a convenient label for a category of problems concerning 'improvement evaporation', which happens for various reasons. This concept cannot be given one universal definition, as that depends on the organizational context.
- Sustaining working practices can be damaging, and it is beneficial for some initiatives to decay, necessitated by external circumstances, to allow further improvements to be developed, to give staff opportunities to develop new competencies.
- The spread of new working practices is also known as diffusion, adoption, transfer, dissemination, assimilation, 'innofusion'. Change that has spread has moved into other organizational areas or units, and has not been contained where first implemented.

- Spread is a convenient label for a category of problems concerning 'the best practices puzzle', where apparently good ideas are not adopted by others who could benefit. This precise definition of this term also depends on the specific organizational context.
- While some changes can be relatively straightforward, many operational innovations involve multi-faceted and interrelated changes to practices, structures, systems, and facilities, which take more time and resources to implement, sustain, and spread.
- The substance of change is often intimately related to a performance target. While some targets appear straightforward, the changes required to meet them are complex.
- The time frames of sustainability and spread are dependent on local factors and developments in the wider environment. The subsequent conditions necessary to sustain organizational changes and encourage further spread may be different from the conditions that encourage initial implementation.
- While sustainability and spread for analytical purposes may be considered discrete phases in a protracted event sequence, whether changes are routinized or decay, spread or are contained, is influenced by other stages in that event sequence.
- The interlinked processes of sustainability and spread can unfold over protracted timescales, with no clear start and end points, influenced by some of the same factors.
- Where particular combinations of factors are present (conjunctural causality), new working practices may spread rapidly. However, those factors do not necessarily contribute to the longer-term sustainability of those changes.
- Organizational changes can decay through a combination of path dependency (initial conditions, critical junctures) and cumulative effects, through which the set of initial supports for those changes are gradually eroded.

A tale of two problems

Table 12.1 summarizes the main conclusions from the preceding chapters, including the context and literature reviews (Chapters 1 to 3) and the empirical research (Chapters 4 to 11). How do these conclusions contribute to our understanding of organizational change and of the sustainability and spread of new working practices? In particular:

- Why do some service improvements evaporate, following apparently successful change programmes and initiatives, and how can decay be managed?
- Why are apparently effective approaches to service improvement often 'contained' where they are implemented, and are not then adopted by other parts of the service, and how can spread be facilitated?

Table 12.1 Contribution to theory: summary of findings

Chapter	Key issues
1 Introduction	The changes studied derived from an ambitious, policy-driven, target-based, national modernization plan, supported by a central organization development agency whose role evolved as the agenda progressed, from leading and implementing national initiatives to facilitating and supporting local changes
2 Sustainability	Traditionally, 'keeping things the way they are' has been a problem, not an objective. However, the sustainability of new working practices is now critical in healthcare, where there has been little previous research. This is a broad concept that can only be defined precisely in relation to a particular setting. The sustainability of new practices is vulnerable, influenced by multiple factors at different levels of analysis over time. It may be beneficial for some changes to decay when obsolete, or to make way for further innovations
3 Spread	This research studied changes to working practices, not new products. New ideas are more attractive when they are: advantageous, compatible, understandable, observable, trialable, and adaptable. The nature and credibility of the source of information can be as important as the quality of evidence. Individual behaviour change can be protracted. Organizational change relies on adopters, the exchange of information through networks, and organization culture. The processes of sustainability and spread are closely linked
4 View from the top	The use of the terms 'sustainability' and 'spread' varies from one individual to another. However, these are linked processes which are influenced by many of the same kinds of factors: change substance, organizational context, processes of individual engagement, the significance of key roles and influential relationships, the effective exercise of collective leadership, the timing and sequencing of events. The time required effectively to implement change has implications for national policy and local management practice
5 Shades of resistance	Healthcare modernization met with significant resistance and scepticism from staff. This is explained partly by the history and culture of the NHS and the dominance of powerful groups, and partly by a complex mix of current issues including the substance of the changes, individual reactions, and aspects of timing and context. Sceptics can become supporters for many reasons, but mainly through understanding the resulting benefits. Skilled change agents can influence this 'conversion' process by using tailored influence tactics. Support, however, is fragile and may require continuous reinforcement
6 Tracking sustainability	Giving patients a choice of appointment dates, booking reduced waiting times and anxiety. The goal of booking was simple, but the changes affected roles, administrative procedures, clinical practice, information systems, physical facilities, and inter-organizational collaboration. Spread was supported by a process in which subsequent 'waves' learned from early adopters, but it was inhibited by medical scepticism, confusion around objectives, diversion of resources, and the complexity and costs of the process changes. Sustainability was reinforced by benefits to staff and patients, but was jeopardized by shifts in priorities and by the short-term nature of the implementation waves

continued

Table 12.1 continued

Chapter	Key issues
7 Booking case study	The sustainability and spread of booking depended on many factors, including change substance, process, and timing, and aspects of the organizational context. Changes were required at several levels: individual, team, clinical service, organization. A receptive context had key people in leadership roles, good clinical–managerial relations, a long-established supportive culture, good external relationships, and 'fit' with organization strategy. Sustainability was supported by changes in policies, procedures, and job descriptions which contributed to staff continuity and security. Sustainability and spread were also influenced by evidence from pilot studies, by teams sharing information, and by the support of a dedicated redesign team which may be a model for other settings
8 Layers of influence	While senior managers, clinicians, and project leaders are critical, sustainable change also depends on leadership at all organizational levels. Key individuals, not typically seen as occupying leadership roles, can drive small-scale but cumulative and sustainable changes. These leaders include administrative, secretarial, clerical, and nursing staff, who often combine the advantages of long service, depth of organizational knowledge, established relationships with power brokers, personal credibility, and political sensitivity. The more change agents are dispersed across the organization, the more likely are their changes to be sustained. Wider support for developing these leaders is appropriate
9 Cancer collaborative case study	The context of cancer services is complex, with inter-organizational processes involving individuals, clinical teams, hospitals, and other network organizations. Understanding improvement methods is as important as understanding new working practices for improvements to be adopted and sustained. Doctors did not always share working practices and information, and managers played a covert role in transferring knowledge across professional boundaries. Sustainability and spread were supported by teamwork that involved clear leadership, widespread involvement, and shared decision making. While collating performance data was time consuming, local service-specific data were vital in sustaining a focus on continuous improvement
10 High impact	Introduction of rapid access assessment methods aimed to reduce time for diagnosis and cut the number of hospital visits for patients with suspected prostate cancer. Urology services were led by hospital consultants whose autonomous decisions determined whether this innovation was adopted. Clinical staff gave clinical evidence a higher priority than patient preferences in these decisions, and patients were not given this option where it was felt that there was little proof that rapid access assessment would lead to better outcomes. Some argued that lack of evidence and the complexity of the disease made rapid assessment inappropriate, and sustained their traditional methods

Table 12.1 continued

Chapter	Key issues
11 Spreading is easy	The 'see and treat' initiative was designed to replace conventional triage methods in accident and emergency departments, in order to cut the typically long queues of patients and waiting times by, literally, seeing and treating patients as they came into the department. Dependent on the availability of qualified and experienced doctors and nurses, 'see and treat' quickly and visibly achieved its objectives, and the approach spread to the majority of hospitals within a year. This rapid spread was supported by high problem visibility and national performance targets, but the conjuncture of other factors also proved influential, including individual, peer group, and wider social issues, organizational support, communication and leadership issues, and properties of the change substance itself, with no single factor dominant

The answers lie with the ways in which sustainability and spread processes unfold over time in specific organizational contexts. In this chapter, we focus on developing theoretical understanding, using the processual–contextual perspective outlined in Chapter 2. It is important to recognize that the kinds of multi-faceted changes that we are concerned with raise issues different from those related to the product innovations with which much of the 'diffusion' literature in particular is concerned. These operational innovations relate to non-standardized and flexible personal health services, provided by a complex professional organization in which several powerful and competing stakeholder groups can complicate the management problem of implementing even minor changes to working practices. However, these characteristics are shared by many other complex organizations in other sectors, and are by no means unique to healthcare. The findings and implications of this research may thus have a much broader relevance to other organizational settings and changes. The wider implications for change implementation practice are discussed in Chapter 13.

Our working definitions of these twin problems for healthcare modernization were:

sustainability   The process through which new working methods, performance enhancements, and continuous improvements are maintained for a period appropriate to a given context. The opposite of sustainability, where change is not maintained and benefits are lost, is *decay*

spread
The process through which new working methods developed in one setting are adopted, perhaps with appropriate modifications, in other organizational contexts. The opposite of spread, where changes at one site are not adapted and adopted by others, is *containment*

Neither of these concepts is amenable to more precise definition. While the issues may be similar, this will always depend on the organizational setting, or settings, under consideration. With regard to sustainability, that setting could concern an individual, a ward, a clinical service, an outpatient clinic, an acute trust, a regional collaborative network, or a local health community. Spread may also involve individuals, clinical teams, and services in the same or different trusts, or perhaps different organizations. The setting in each case is likely to open opportunities, generate constraints, and present other conditions and challenges that may influence the sustainability and spread of the changes, initiatives, or working practices of interest. The temporal and spatial issues are also highly dependent on context. Sustain for how long? Spread over what groups, services, units, and organizations? This is why we described sustainability and spread as labels for categories of organizational problems.

Another key question is always 'sustain or spread what?' While Fraser (2002) identifies different types of spread, our evidence suggests that properties of the change substance are more significant. Generally recognized as one of the components of a processual perspective, change substance is often covered in a descriptive passage of an account which focuses in more depth on issues of process and context. However, there are a number of characteristics of the substance of changes in healthcare that influence the change process as a whole, and affect sustainability and spread. The properties of substance that appear to be significant are:

• Most of these changes have been what Hammer (2004, p.86) calls operational innovations, or 'the invention and deployment of new ways of doing work . . . coming up with entirely new ways of filling orders, developing products, providing customer service'. His examples relate to novel ways of performing steps in a commercial organization's value chain, and there are direct parallels with changes in patient flows, journeys, or pathways in healthcare. Operational innovations are thus concerned with the way in which products are developed and services provided. The main changes are organizational and are often (but not always) multi-faceted, involving structures, systems, and procedures, for example.
• Operational innovations in healthcare thus often involve 'complementary changes' (Pettigrew and Fenton, 2000) straddling a number of previously

discrete stages, rather than adjustments to single steps or processes. In the treatment of cancer, for example, delivery of care involves a number of different components of the service: people, departments, and organizations; an individual's treatment is not always confined to a single doctor, group of doctors, hospital ward, or clinical service. Even small changes in one area can have knock-on effects for other areas and services, and these kinds of changes can be more difficult to implement. Thus, in order to meet patient booking targets, changes to organization policy, structures, roles, links with primary care, computing and information systems, clinical practice, and physical facilities were often necessary. Some operational innovations can be more straightforward, and may be more rapidly implemented; for example, a single consultant urologist may decide to implement a one-stop 'rapid access assessment' diagnostic service for patients, regardless of the views of colleagues in the same department.

- With multi-faceted operational innovations, it is highly unlikely that a set of new working practices can simply be codified and copied from one site to another without any adaptation to suit local circumstances. The term 'substance' typically refers not to a predefined set of activities, but to an approach, a general style, broad guidelines, a set of principles, a way of approaching and dealing with a particular set of issues or problems. While most of the literature on diffusion concerns the adoption of new products, we are concerned with the customization of fluid organizational arrangements. In the process of adapting ideas and ways of working to fit new settings, some elements may be abandoned as inappropriate, and other elements may be developed further.

- The substance of many of the changes we have considered was shaped by performance goals or targets that were disarmingly simple to articulate, such as the 'two-week wait' for patients diagnosed with suspected cancer. In many cases, multi-dimensional packages of operational innovation had to be implemented in order to achieve those simple goals. But as many of the targets were straightforward, expectations of the timescales for implementation, sustainability, and spread were ambitious, perhaps naive. The apparent simplicity often disguised the complexity of implementation, and more significantly for the processes of sustainability and spread, the protracted timescale of the changes required to meet those targets.

- Some changes relied on targets that were regarded by medical staff in particular as politically expedient and without a firm clinical basis. Developing rapid access assessment for prostate cancer patients was one example. This reduced the credibility of the changes, diverted attention away from what were regarded as more significant priorities, and encouraged a sceptical if not hostile response. However, if the target could be dismissed as inappropriate, this would jeopardize the implementation, sustainability, and spread of the whole interlinked change package.

- The complex operational innovations studied here often required, as with the booking and collaborative initiatives, the establishment of new arrangements for ongoing intra- and inter-organizational collaboration. This increased the number of organizations and stakeholders implicated in the changes, consequently extending the timescales for consultation, persuasion, design, and implementation.

- While the core substance of 'rapid access assessment' methods (Chapter 10) was clinical, the patient booking initiative was primarily organizational or administrative. But even with booking, significant changes to clinical practice were also required. Those changes were often inconsistent with traditional, trained behaviours, and were not surprisingly often met with scepticism and resistance, particularly where they were regarded as clinically unproven, were seen as thinly disguised criticisms of current practice, and especially where they could be seen as potential threats to professional boundaries and autonomy. It is thus difficult to draw a clear distinction between clinical and organizational change.

- Perhaps most significantly, operational innovations are often at a disadvantage with regard to two of the attributes claimed to contribute to diffusion (Rogers, 1995): advantageous when compared with current practice, and observable in demonstration sites. The demonstration of benefits can be problematic where multi-dimensional changes affect a range of qualitative and quantitative outcomes. Some quantifiable measures can have awkward definitions, and can be difficult to operationalize, different stakeholders can hold different views of what counts as beneficial, and the 'hard evidence' is invariably contestable (Fitzgerald et al., 2002). While the observability of a new product may be a simple matter to arrange, the observability of an operational innovation extends to both process (working methods) and outcomes. Thus, while the outcomes which flow from implementing a 'see and treat' approach in an accident and emergency department (Chapter 11) are often immediately apparent (no queues of waiting patients), the underlying processes are not so readily visible, and in that case may be more easily observed than the processes that underpin patient booking or cancer collaborative network arrangements. Complex operational innovations are only visible in action, which could involve observing significant numbers of people and their interactions over time across a number of different locations. Consequently, the substance of these kinds of changes makes it difficult unambiguously to demonstrate the benefits to all those who are implicated, and makes it difficult for those doing the persuading to show others how it all works. However, where benefits can be quantified and demonstrated, that contributes to a sustained focus on continued improvement (see Chapter 9).

Some operational innovations thus appear to be more straightforward than others. It may be presumed, for example, that the issues raised by attempts to sustain and spread relatively straightforward changes to nurse and patient behaviour on a ward, say to prevent cross-infections, would generate issues different from those raised by attempts to introduce system-wide initiatives such as patient booking. However, this 'simple, complex' distinction often breaks down in practice, as apparently straightforward changes can on close inspection reveal other dimensions, often dependent in part on the nature of the change and in part on aspects of the local context. Those simple changes develop and evolve, and can in that process become multi-faceted and complex.

Many healthcare service improvements thus involve operational innovations that are target driven and multi-dimensional; that are not predefined ways of working but approaches that are constantly adapted to new settings; which combine organizational and clinical changes; which can involve new forms of inter- and intra-organizational collaboration; which can sometimes be seen as potential threats to key professional groups; which are difficult to observe and demonstrate in practice; and which can sometimes be difficult to support with unequivocal evidence. Consequently, studies of the redesign of bounded organizational processes, and research into the diffusion of single new products, may not be wholly relevant to service improvement in healthcare, which is a dynamic and rapidly changing organizational context.

We know, broadly, what conditions influence whether changes are more likely to be sustained or to decay, whether new working practices are more likely to spread to other units or to be contained. Chapter 2 concluded that sustainability was influenced by 11 sets of factors: substantial, individual, managerial, leadership, organizational, financial, cultural, political, processual, contextual, and temporal. Chapter 3 argued that similar factors influence spread, particularly aspects of the change substance (attractive, adaptable), individual response (stage in change process, perceptions of benefit), social factors (such as the role of networks, opinion leaders, and communication strategies), and aspects of the organization context (readiness for change, absorptive capacity). However, we cannot weight or prioritize those factors, claiming that leadership is more important to sustainability than organizational policies, or that networks are more significant in spreading new working practices than communication strategies. Those claims may be accurate on occasion – but in relation to specific settings at particular times, and not as universal truths. We also need to take all of those factors and their interactions into account, as their independent effects cannot be isolated. The same leadership behaviours may have different consequences in different organization cultures at different times, given different financial conditions, and so on.

In June 2002, about a year into the research behind this book, a team member presented interim findings to a group of regional directors for one of the initiatives being studied. One member of this group asked questions about 'the critical variables' and 'cause and effect' concerning sustainability and spread. It is important to remember that, in healthcare, 'scientific' tends to mean the experimental double-blind randomized control trial, which is regarded as the 'gold standard' with regard to generating credible proof. Small-n studies are suspect, especially where qualitative data are involved. We are considering two processes, sustainability and spread, that are difficult to define precisely, and that involve multivariate packages of changes involving several individuals, groups, organizations, and localities.

We cannot answer the regional director's questions. Are these settings too complex to permit the confident development of generalizable explanations? Sustainability and spread are context-dependent issues, and critical variables are difficult to identify and define precisely. In multivariate processes that unfold over time, it is difficult, if not impossible, to isolate which variable led to what outcome, due to the nature of the phenomena under investigation and not to the research methodology. To answer questions about sustainability and spread, we must turn to other modes of reasoning, and in particular to processual perspectives on organizational change. This entails new ways of conceptualizing change processes, involving considerations of causality that are more fluid and circular, and less rigid and linear. This reconceptualization regards traditional 'cause and effect' analyses as less interesting and relevant than conjunctural forms of causation, where outcomes derive from the shifting configurations of a range of factors interacting in particular contexts over time. While such a 'new mode of thinking' is a relatively intangible outcome from a study of this kind, it encourages new ways of approaching the management of organizational change, sustainability, and spread processes that may have profound practical implications.

Processes, narratives, and paths

In most studies of change, the focus has been with the 'front end', with initiation, resistance, and implementation. The aim of this project has been to explore the full story, considering subsequent events, concerning the fate of change over time, and the adoption of new working practices by other parts of the organization. As indicated in Chapters 2 and 3, diffusion has attracted considerable research attention, while sustainability has been relatively ignored, and there are few analyses of the links between these processes. There is a further limitation of 'front end' analysis, which sometimes assumes that the factors contributing to effective implementation are the same as those required for sustainability: for example, Ham *et al.*'s (2003) discussion of factors affecting the adoption and sustainability of booking. While there may well be significant overlap, there is no guarantee that the mix of local and national contextual conditions and management actions contributing to first implementation are those that will also support long-term sustainability. Indeed, from a study of patient waiting times, Appleby (2005) argues that short-term actions, which may be highly effective, do not lead to sustainable improvements without the development of other long-term actions and policies, and that 'Successful trusts found that different strategies and tactics were needed to reduce waiting times compared with sustaining reductions' (p.3). He finds that:

> Strategies needed to reduce waiting times are not always the same (or of the same importance or scale) as those needed to sustain reductions. For example, the need to protect resources used for elective activity, or to manage demand – through, say, referral protocols – is less relevant once waiting times are so low that all referrals can be processed quickly.
>
> (Appleby, 2005, p.5)

We therefore need to look beyond the 'front end' and consider the process of change over a longer time frame. What is process theory, and why does this perspective help to explain sustainability and spread? A process theory is simply an explanation for why a sequence of events unfolds over time in a particular way (Van de Ven and Poole, 2002). The explanation is usually qualitative, and written in the form of a theoretical narrative, which in our context describes why a change process was sustained over time or decayed, and why some changes spread elsewhere in the organization or stuck where they were first implemented.

The regional director in the previous section was expecting to hear about a variance theory of sustainability and spread. Variance theories explore causal links between independent and dependent variables, assuming that independent variables can be operationalized and measured with some precision, and that their individual effects can be identified. Process theories rest on different assumptions. Explaining this distinction, Mohr (1982) argues that organizational phenomena are rarely amenable to variance-based explanation. The variables of interest mean different things in different contexts, they are typically vague and difficult to measure (organization culture, leadership style), and outcomes are often generated by combinations and interactions of factors whose independent effects are indeterminate.

To study the effects of one variable (salt consumption) on another (blood pressure), a variance approach is appropriate. To explore poorly defined organizational processes that have no clear start and end points, that are influenced over time by shifting patterns of conditions, leading to a range of potentially interesting outcomes that are also difficult to measure, a variance approach is not only inappropriate but misleading. Process theories generally state that, to understand change, it is necessary to understand the interaction of change context (inner and outer), substance, and process. Process perspectives also emphasize the iterative, non-linear, and politicized properties of most organizational change (Dawson, 2003a; 2003b). There are at least four other properties of process perspectives relevant to our field of interest. These concern probabilistic explanations, cumulative effects, conjunctural causality, and path dependency.

Probabilistic explanations

Variance methods develop explanations in which causes and outcomes, or independent and dependent variables, are related in unchanging ways in a defined population. The values of the explanatory variables predict values of the outcome variables. The absence of a causal factor is thus associated with the absence of the outcome in question. Process theories offer probabilistic explanations in which explanatory factors, or combinations of factors, are likely to generate the outcome or outcomes of interest, but not in every case. Dark clouds, for example, suggest that it will probably rain, but precipitation does not always occur.

This means that outcomes may be observed when some of those factors are absent, and the consequences of interest may not in some settings be observed even when all of the specified factors are present. Summarizing findings from the Minnesota Innovation Studies, Van de Ven *et al.* (1999) emphasize the role of chance in 'the innovation journey', which is inherently unpredictable. However, they conclude that, while they cannot make accurate predictions, they can explain broad categories of sequences and processes, and suggest interventions to strengthen the odds in favour of the desired outcomes.

Cumulative effects

Outcomes sometimes depend on an accumulation of factors or pressures, such that no single factor may be responsible for the observed outcomes (Pierson, 2003). However, 10 per cent of the factors do not necessarily generate 10 per cent of the outcome, an assumption of variance explanations. Variance theories in search of universal covariation tend to overlook cumulative and temporal factors. Process theories are more concerned with event sequences which unfold over periods of time, the appropriate time frame of analysis depending on the issues being studied. The accumulation of factors leading to a particular outcome in one setting may not necessarily be the same as that which brings about those consequences elsewhere. Outcomes of interest may be achieved through the weight of pressures moving events in a particular direction over time or through a particular kind of combination of factors.

Conjunctural causality

While cumulative effects involve the gradual build-up of pressures, conjunctural causality occurs when a combination of factors, at different levels of analysis, together generate the consequences of interest. Once again, no single factor may be responsible, and more than one combination of factors may lead to similar outcomes. Goldstone (2003) uses this line of argument to explain the occurrence of political revolutions, identifying a series of contributory events and conditions which can be compared from case to case, country to country, to establish recurring patterns from which a theory can be constructed. The presence or absence of a particular combination of factors or conditions, therefore, can help to explain the likely occurrence or non-occurrence of the outcomes of interest.

Path dependency

Path dependency relates to a class of explanations, rather than to one model. Comparative historians and institutional theorists use these analytical approaches to explain the pattern of revolutions (Mahoney, 2001) and institutional persistence (Thelen, 2003). Similar modes of theorizing can be applied to processes of organizational change (Poole *et al.*, 2000). The flow of events and outcomes are influenced, in this perspective, by initial conditions and critical junctures. The subsequent event sequence is not necessarily 'locked in' by triggering circumstances, influenced by the decisions and actions of key stakeholders, and the responses of those implicated in the changes. One mechanism which can sustain a sequence of events, at least for a time, concerns increasing returns. If the consequences of change for stakeholders, power brokers, decision makers, and the organization are beneficial, this positive feedback loop helps to ensure ongoing action to sustain the new arrangements, at least while those stakeholders can resist pressures from those with contradictory views. If similar event sequences are observed in different settings, then inferences can be drawn concerning how these conditions, in this kind of context, can trigger this event sequence, producing those outcomes. A path-dependency explanation also invites us to consider that the conditions which sustain new working practices and contribute to their further diffusion may be different from the conditions that initially encouraged the development of those practices.

Table 12.2 *Process theory concepts, and the questions they raise*

Concept	Key questions
Processual perspective	How are sustainability and spread influenced by the untidy, iterative, politicized nature of organizational change, which is shaped by the interaction of context, substance, and process?
Probabilistic explanations	What organizational and contextual conditions are almost always necessary for sustainability and spread to occur?
Cumulative effects	Are sustainability and spread affected by the build-up of pressures which eventually determine whether an initiative is sustained or decays, and whether new practices spread widely or not, and what are those pressures?
Conjunctural explanations	Can we identify particular combinations of factors which, when present at approximately the same time, tend to lead to sustainability and spread, or to decay and lack of spread?
Path dependency	Do the processes of sustainability and spread display similar event sequences, paying attention to initial conditions, critical junctures, decisions of key actors, and feedback mechanisms?
Theoretical narrative	Is it possible to identify recurring stories of successful and unsuccessful sustainability and spread, illustrating the typical kinds of sequences of events, in different contexts, and informing practice with regard to managing those narratives?

This conceptual framework is summarized in Table 12.2, which identifies the components of a processual perspective, and the kinds of questions which they raise for a study of change, sustainability, and spread. It is important to recognize that we need to be able to explain both sustainability and decay, both spread and containment. Sustaining some working practices can be damaging, and it may be appropriate for some particularly context-specific innovations not to spread to other units where they could be less effective or unworkable.

This approach raises concerns about generalizability. Surely the cause and effect sequence relates to one specific setting? This criticism overlooks two important issues. First, the findings from even a single case can inform theory, either to challenge or to support current thinking, and can also inform practice in broadly similar settings. Second, even a small number of narratives can reveal similar sequences or recurring patterns, leading to the derivation of plausible inferences concerning a defined set of circumstances (say, kinds and sizes of organizational unit and types of change in working practices).

Sustainability and spread stories

The distinction between sustainability and spread is of value for analytical purposes. However, the mechanisms through which new practices are developed, implemented, sustained, and adopted (and adapted) by other units are part of the same interlinked process, influenced by many of the same factors. New working practices cannot confidently be regarded as adopted or spread if their use is transient and has not been, or is unlikely to be, sustained. Similarly, new working practices that have been sustained at one or a small number of units are of little consequence in terms of the performance of the health service as a whole unless their methods and benefits spread to many other sites. These processes are mutually influential. The way in which new practices are spread (rapid or slow; compulsory or choice; with or without adaptation) can have implications for their durability. Change that decays rapidly, for whatever reason, may damage the further spread of beneficial methods, while attempts to maintain working practices for prolonged periods may well interfere with attempts to spread other new and perhaps even more effective forms of working arrangements. The separate treatment of these interlocked processes is thus somewhat artificial, and this has to be taken into consideration in the following discussion.

Sustainability

Any organizational process dependent on the continuing presence of multiple factors or conditions is potentially fragile. From a theoretical perspective, therefore, it may be more instructive to consider how to prevent (or delay) decay than to support sustainability.

To illustrate this viewpoint, consider the case of Rapid Bay Jetty on the Fleurieu Peninsula in South Australia, 100 kilometres south of Adelaide. The jetty was built in 1940 to service a local limestone and dolomite mine. When the company abandoned the jetty in 1990, it became a popular spot for anglers and divers. By 2004, due to winds, waves, and boating accidents, the outermost 'T' section was closed because it had become dangerous. Then, in 2005, for similar reasons, the whole jetty was closed, causing a public outcry at the potential loss of tourist revenue. However, nobody would assume responsibility for its upkeep.

Path dependency and cumulative effects provide both a framework for explaining these events and the basis for predicting outcomes in similar situations. Initial conditions present us with a sturdy, well-built structure. While the owners' abandonment of this structure was a critical juncture, that action had no immediate effect on the jetty, which continued in use for many years, but it set the conditions for the event sequence that followed.

The context in which the jetty operated was hostile; although the jetty was constantly 'under attack' from the weather and accidental encounters with boats, there was no malicious threat to its existence. But, as the jetty was not maintained, it is not difficult to predict the outcome. We cannot be sure of the precise timing of that outcome; the jetty could last for years, or be wrecked by a storm tomorrow. In addition, we cannot predict which supports will fail first, which later, and which critical failures in parts of the structure will bring about the final collapse. However, the final collapse is something that we can predict with confidence.

A similar argument can be applied to the sustainability of organizational changes. Let us begin with a successful set of changes, proved to be effective; initial conditions thus present us with a sturdy structure. Critical junctures might include the departure of project leads, the termination of special funding, or the distraction of senior managers by other priorities. The professional organization context of healthcare does not have to be actively hostile to our changes, but may do damage simply by diverting attention and other resources to other issues. If those involved in the changes do not actively maintain them, as with the jetty at Rapid Bay, we can predict the probable outcome. We may not be able to predict the precise timing of that outcome. We may not be able to predict which key person, or which part of the budget, or which other factors will deal the fatal blow. But, by taking cumulative effects into account, we can still predict probable eventual decay. In summary, a path-dependency explanation of improvement evaporation based on cumulative effects suggests the following narrative:

- initial conditions, a sturdy structure;
- critical juncture, removal of staff, management support, resources;
- hostile environment, making other demands on time and resources;
- lack of attention from those whose actions could make a difference;
- eventual decay, predictable, although not timing or precise causes.

However, many practices in healthcare persist; they appear to stick 'for ever' and may be seen as problems because they do *not* decay. The counter-narrative, in which improvements do not evaporate, is not difficult to construct, and may unfold in the following manner:

- initial conditions, a sturdy structure;
- no relevant critical junctures, but events that support the new practices;
- a benign environment, resources are not diverted to other issues;
- ongoing support from those responsible for operating the practices;
- persistence of the changed practices, predictable, for an indeterminate period.

In other words, where the conditions in this counter-narrative apply, we can predict with a high degree of confidence that the changed practices will be sustained, at least until other events and conditions interrupt and reshape the narrative. These predictions will always be probabilistic, not deterministic, as unforeseen events and combinations of circumstances can intervene (meteor strikes jetty; affluent patient donates funds). While critical junctures and environmental conditions may not be directly manageable, many of these factors can be anticipated, an appropriate degree of attention to 'maintenance' activities can be put in place, and the timing of decay can also be anticipated and planned accordingly. The practical implications of this argument are explored in the following chapter.

Spread

We know from previous research (Rogers, 1995) that diffusion is likely to be more rapid where the new product or practice is:

1 advantageous when compared with existing practice;
2 compatible with existing practices;
3 easy to understand;
4 observable in demonstration sites;
5 testable;
6 adaptable to fit local needs.

However, several other recent studies of organizational change and innovation have suggested that Rogers' perspective is oversimplified, by highlighting the multivariate properties of the processes involved (e.g. Van de Ven *et al.*, 1999; Locock *et al.*, 2000; McNulty and Ferlie, 2002; Dopson and Fitzgerald, 2005a). The findings reported here thus suggest that, while the spread of new working practices in healthcare can be influenced by those six attributes, they are also influenced by other considerations. An illustrative (and doubtless incomplete) list of those other factors is thus likely to include:

- perceived impact on professional autonomy;
- perceived impact on other organizational groups, occupations, and power brokers;
- quality of relationships between managers and clinicians;
- presence of multiple change agents in appropriate roles;
- organizational positioning of 'lead' staff;
- timing and duration of those 'lead' staff appointments;
- influencing skills of lead personnel;
- level, timing, and duration of additional funding to support implementation;
- the time involved to develop, win support for, and implement suitable adaptations;

- stability of the local organizational setting and the wider external context;
- policy shifts in the performance objectives the changes were designed to achieve;
- symbolic and financial rewards for adoption and penalties for delay;
- current local issues, problems, and other initiatives demanding attention;
- other local factors focusing attention and resources in particular areas.

From a theoretical point of view, where does this list of additional factors leave us? Can we now argue that an operational innovation possessing most of Rogers' six attributes along with most of those 14 other attributes is more likely to be adopted and spread rapidly? Unfortunately not, for two reasons. First, while we can confidently predict that most of the attributes necessary to encourage adoption and spread appear on this list, we cannot with confidence identify all of the factors that, in a particular setting, could potentially play a vital role in the story. Consequently, that list of factors can never be definitive, and has to rely on local knowledge and judgement. Second, it is difficult to weight those factors in order of potency or influence, as that will also depend on context; what may be overriding factors (e.g. funding, influencing skills) in one setting may be of little consequence in the next (perhaps, where the presence of multiple change agents may be more critical).

We are faced with a more complex, and interesting, form of probabilistic, conjunctural, and interaction-based explanation, which goes something like this. All other things being equal, new working practices will probably be adopted and spread more rapidly where they meet most of the conditions just identified. However, in a given setting, a particular combination of those factors, in interaction with each other, may produce adoption and spread. A different combination of those factors may generate comparable outcomes in another setting. While theoretical narratives are likely to display many similarities across settings, the details of the stories are also likely to contain local variations. This prompts some interesting research questions concerning the relationships between contexts and combinations of factors leading to particular outcomes, and the practical implications are explored in the following chapter.

The 'see and treat' initiative in accident and emergency (Chapter 11) provides an illustration of such a conjunctural causality explanation. In addition to Rogers' six attributes, 'see and treat' in accident and emergency departments was also characterized by:

- appropriate timing;
- considerable media attention, particularly when things went wrong;
- a widely acknowledged national problem and a strong desire to make this work;
- clear and simple targets for waiting times in those departments;

- the link between achieving targets and trust 'star' ratings;
- deep concern to meet those targets;
- simple decision process – only one person's agreement needed to implement;
- non-complex changes required, in terms of substance or process;
- similarity of the current (now 'old') process across adopting departments;
- no additional resources required to implement these changes;
- ability to demonstrate near-instant success with the approach;
- limited 'knock-on' impact on other hospital departments;
- not dependent on the collaboration of other departments or organizations.

This combination of factors appears to explain why over 80 per cent of hospital accident and emergency departments in England and Wales introduced 'see and treat' within one year of its launch. However, anecdotal evidence suggested that, by late 2005, many trusts were reporting difficulties in sustaining this approach. There appear to have been at least two reasons for this. First, although no additional funding was required for implementation, many trusts experienced problems in resourcing this patient management pattern '24/7', given the need for senior medical staff and emergency nurse practitioners. Second, many doctors, while appreciating the benefits to the hospital and patients, did not enjoy the nature of the work, an aspect that was not realized when the approach was first introduced. Perceptions and judgements shifted with experience. Without abandoning the approach altogether, many trusts were reported to have limited the use of 'see and treat' methods to specific times of the week.

The 'see and treat' experience thus appears to confirm our suspicion that the combinations of factors that need to be in place to increase the probability of changes being sustained over the medium to long term may be different from those required to prompt initial development and adoption. The combined conditions necessary to get people to do something in the first place may be quite different from the conditions required to keep them acting in that way.

The extended timescale

We have established that the process of change unfolds through a sequence of events – a narrative – that is iterative, non-linear, politicized, and probabilistic. In addition, it is likely to be affected by organizational context and change substance, and outcomes may be explained through cumulative effects, the conjuncture of particular conditions, and path dependency. It is also apparent that the timescale of these processes varies from setting to setting. With some combinations of change substance, and national and local conditions, the process through which change is implemented, sustained, and spread to other units can unfold rapidly. This happened with the 'see and treat' initiative. However, in other conditions, and with more complex multi-dimensional changes (such as booking), the process can be extended. Observers anticipating rapid results are likely to be disappointed.

There are several plausible reasons for these protracted timescales. First, we might blame the professionalized organization in which perceived threats to the autonomy of professional occupational groups can delay change initiatives that appear to criticize practice. Second, we could refer to the potential risks in breaking with tradition in a risk-averse setting. Third, we can revisit Chapters 2 and 3, and consider the large number of contextual and organizational factors, at different levels of analysis, that can potentially influence sustainability and spread.

The evidence presents another set of explanations, however, which lie primarily with the change substance. First, as discussed earlier, some organizational changes have only one or two elements. To implement 'see and treat' required locating senior doctors and emergency nurse practitioners at the front door of emergency departments. In those circumstances, implementation could be rapid (local conditions permitting). However, initiatives such as patient booking have many interlinked elements. Implementing those kinds of changes simply takes more time. Second, operational innovations invariably require a degree of adaptation to fit local circumstances. The term 'adaptation' implies 'fine tuning'. But in many settings, this involved a major piece of project work, starting perhaps with a set of ideas, concepts, or principles, and then working more or less from scratch through a protracted development and implementation process. As one colleague commented:

> It's not like, 'they've done the big stuff, now we have to fine tune'.
> You've got to go through the big stuff all over again.
>
> (Research associate)

Indeed, there are dangers in trying to accelerate the change process, particularly with regard to the spread of new practices. If those who will be involved in and affected by those changes do not recognize and accept the need for change, efforts to speed up the development and implementation processes are more likely to be wasted. Allowing inadequate time to develop suitable adaptations of an approach may lead to the implementation of inappropriate, incomplete, and ineffective solutions. Staff may require training, and also need time to learn new methods, roles, and relationships, or they may make mistakes. Staff also need experience with new ways of working in order to develop a broad assessment of the benefits, problems, and potential further improvements. Clinicians and managers need time to assess the impact of new ways of working in one area on other related sections and processes, and also to assess the costs and benefits. It may not be possible fully to identify the knock-on implications until new arrangements have been confronted by the range of typical and atypical events.

Temporal factors – the timing, sequencing, and pacing of change initiatives – can thus be critical. This issue reflects a wider debate concerning the pace of change. Some commentators argue that accelerated change is necessary and desirable (Fraser, 2002). Others claim that rapid change is damaging: Abrahamson (2000), for example, argues that change which unfolds in a more measured and controlled manner can bring more benefits. The timing, sequencing, and pacing of change can also have beneficial or fatal consequences for sustainability and spread. Attempts to 'force' the spread of initiatives can damage both sustainability and further adoption, while the period over which it may be desirable to sustain some arrangements may be open to debate. To observe that change is a process that unfolds over time is not controversial. However, most perspectives in this field do not offer analyses sensitive to temporal issues, which are particularly relevant to the issues in focus here.

But there may be a more fundamental reason for resisting the temptation to accelerate the spread of new practices. This concerns the need to adapt new methods to local circumstances. While recognizing the need for, and benefits of, engaging staff in the adaptation process, Plsek (2000) argues that the 'reinvention process' is wasteful. To avoid this, Szulanski and Winter (2002) advocate a 'copy exact' method for spreading best practice. That may be effective where best practice is a simple set of routine and codifiable steps (as in their examples), and where the 'transmitting' and 'receiving' units are broadly comparable. As we have seen, best practice in healthcare often (not always) has multiple dimensions, and organizations, services, and patient populations can differ markedly, in both the same hospital and local health community, and from one region to another, depending on history, demographics, and many other contextual factors. It takes time to adapt working practices to new settings with those characteristics. The rediscovery process can thus be indispensable, to secure an appropriate adaptation or redesign to fit local conditions, to give those involved time to learn how to operate and develop new methods, to allow for complementary changes to develop in related processes, to give individuals time to learn new skills and adjust, and to engage those affected in the design and implementation process, thus securing higher levels of understanding of and commitment to the new methods.

Are these temporal problems unique to healthcare? No. While healthcare settings may illustrate the problems, these are probably generic issues facing any organization seeking to implement changes that are not 'routine and codifiable', but which are more complex and multi-faceted in nature.

Critical debates

1 In what ways can the manner in which new ideas and working practices are spread or disseminated influence whether or not they are subsequently sustained?

2 What are the benefits and drawbacks of attempting to hasten the spread of new ideas and working practices?

3 Why do theoretical narratives based on processual thinking and conjunctural causation offer more appropriate explanations for the sustainability and spread of operational innovations than do conventional variance-based accounts?

13 Sustaining change and avoiding containment: practice and policy

David A. Buchanan, Louise Fitzgerald, and Diane Ketley

Chapter aims

1 To establish practical management guidelines for sustaining organizational changes and avoiding 'initiative decay'.
2 To establish practical management guidelines for encouraging the wider spread and adaptation of new ideas and good working practices, and for avoiding 'containment'.
3 To identify the national policy implications of the findings of this research.

Key point summary

Actions and cautions for managing sustainability and spread

Sustainability actions

Define what 'sustainability' means in your context: a static or a dynamic perspective, and what timescale?

Identify the factors (contextual, temporal, organizational, political) that affect the sustainability of new methods in your context

What combination of factors can you control and adjust in order to increase the probability of sustaining change?

Monitor the support conditions and implement an appropriate mix of preventive and developmental maintenance

Sustainability cautions

Do not defer sustainability planning, as some modes of development and change implementation will damage sustainability

Do not expect changes to survive because they are now working: staff leave, resources are reallocated, novel ideas become familiar

Do not ignore the risk factors: if you are unable to sustain successful changes, that will reduce the probability of other sites adapting the approach, and jeopardize future changes

Sustainability actions

Allow or encourage changes to decay when they no longer fit the context, or when better methods become available

Sustainability cautions

Do not allow efforts to sustain change to block the development of other good ideas

Do not withdraw preventive and developmental maintenance as long as you wish the approach to be sustained

Spread actions

Define what 'spread' means in your context; does this concern meeting targets, using broad principles, changing specific working practices, a combination?

Identify the range of factors (contextual, temporal, organizational, political) that affect the spread of new practices in your context; what combination of issues can you control in order to increase the probability of spreading new methods?

Win the power brokers to your cause; in the professional organization, they will block changes with which they disagree

Encourage other change champions and opinion leaders, but recognize and support change leadership contributions from unexpected sources across the organization

Encourage adaptation (rather than copying) of approaches and practices from elsewhere, to ensure 'fit' with local conditions; 'best practice' is always what's 'best locally'

Adaptation of multi-faceted changes can take as long as initial development; allow this time for learning, as this contributes to effectiveness and sustainability of changes

Spread cautions

Do not expect good ideas to spread 'naturally', even when supported by evidence

Do not always expect spread to take place quickly, as a combination of factors has to be in place for this to happen, and complex organizational changes spread slowly

Do not expect 'evidence' to be the single most important factor in encouraging spread; many other personal, political, professional, organizational factors are influential too

Do not rely on a small number of senior change champions; their voices are important and necessary, but may not be sufficient

Do not rely exclusively on opinion leaders and networks, as they can be just as effective in spreading 'bad' ideas

Do not attempt to spread new approaches too quickly; this short-circuits the learning time, may not allow for adequate customization of the approach, may lead to less effective methods, and could damage sustainability

Do not spread new methods through pilot projects with temporary funding, as this signals transience and damages sustainability

The modernization context

What does this research tell us about how to manage the sustainability and spread of new working practices? To answer this question, it is necessary first to consider the context in which changes were taking place, as context both influences and is in turn affected by management actions. The properties of that context thus have implications for practice. Four aspects appear to be important, concerning the organizational setting, the nature of systemic change, the role of 'best practice', and the professional nature of healthcare organizations.

Public sector service

Given the annual cost of the health service in Britain, it is hardly surprising that public and media expectations were heightened by *The NHS Plan* and the accompanying political rhetoric. With the introduction of performance targets in 2000, and an injection of additional funds, it was anticipated that the pace of reform would be rapid. In some cases it was, but that occurred in pockets, such as the 'see and treat' initiative (Chapter 11). In principle, a large, labour-intensive public sector service provider may be expected to move more slowly than commercial concerns. Change in the private sector is usually driven by economic and technological trends and competitor behaviour, thus generating commercial considerations. Change in the public sector, in contrast, is more often driven by government policy, which stimulates ideological conflicts.

Systemic change

The modernization agenda was ambitious, target driven, and systemic, with changes making a significant impact on the ways in which services were organized and delivered. Those operational innovations, rather than involving a single, easily specified change, often included multi-faceted combinations of new policies, goals, job specifications, roles, role relationships, organization structures, procedures, working methods, inter-organizational collaborations, and in some cases physical facilities. While it may be possible to define such changes for a single site (e.g. Chapter 9), they typically resist codification in a way that allows them simply to be copied elsewhere, without major adaptations to local conditions. Unlike, say, new products, they are only visible when they are working, and they often evolve as those applying new methods learn from the experience. In other words, operational innovations are not always codifiable, universal, visible, or static. Consequently, the sustainability and spread of such changes generate more complex issues.

What price 'best practice'?

The concept of best practice is thus problematic, and may no longer be helpful, for at least two reasons. First, there is often no such thing as 'one best way' to achieve a set of outcomes or to meet specific performance goals, if 'one best way' implies a carefully defined and detailed set of working practices. Attempts simply to impose and to sustain in one setting a solution that has been demonstrably effective elsewhere can be damaging; some local adaptation is almost always necessary, and the adaptation process itself, while potentially time consuming, can contribute to both the effective implementation and sustainability of those changes. Second, the expression can generate resentment. Those being advised to adopt best practice are, by implication, also being advised that their current efforts are 'less than best' in some respect, and can thus be expected to react accordingly.

Professional organization

Healthcare organizations, in common with those in accountancy and law, for example, are professional organizations (Mintzberg, 1979; 2003), characterized by high levels of professional autonomy. In this context, management cannot simply dictate changes, and must first persuade, and if necessary negotiate with, professional staff, without whose consent no change will happen (Powell *et al.*, 1999). The professional organization does not sound like a receptive context for government-inspired redesign initiatives (Pollitt, 1996). Clinically trained professionals may be more likely to resist government and management ideas that appear to challenge their value systems and threaten their autonomy.

The practical management implications of these context features, taking into consideration the process perspective developed in Chapter 12, are as follows:

- Our understanding of key terms, desired outcomes, and appropriate management will always be *contextual*. There are no useful, precise, universal definitions of the concepts of sustainability or spread, terms which are more appropriately viewed as labels for broad categories of problems which share common properties and concerns.
- We are able to indicate, with a high degree of confidence, the kinds of factors most likely to influence sustainability and spread processes. However, we cannot confidently predict the precise combination of issues influencing sustainability or spread in a particular setting. Explanations of these processes rely on *conjunctural causation*; event sequences and outcomes are influenced by *combinations* of factors, at different levels of analysis, interacting over time. Identifying the issues and events which are significant in a given context, therefore, relies on local judgement,

Features of the professional organization

- Professionals have considerable autonomy and discretion, as their work involves the application of knowledge and expertise to complex problems;
- professionals are loyal to their profession and committed to their clients rather than to their employing organization;
- professionals work independently, without reference to each other or to management;
- managers cannot develop strategy independently, but must persuade professionals to support and champion initiatives;
- high-quality work is based on internalized values, beliefs and aspirations, developed through training, rather than on formal bureaucratic controls;
- professional organizations are intensely political, with competition for resources.

Source: Based on Powell *et al.* (1999)

informed by an understanding of what to look for. However, while sustainability and spread are likely to be influenced by similar sets of factors, the configurations that encourage the development and adoption of new working practices may not be the same as the combinations of factors that contribute to sustainability. In addition, the combination of factors necessary to sustain one initiative in one context may be different from the configuration required to sustain the same new working practices in another context.

- Advice will always be *probabilistic*. Prescribed actions will never guarantee desired outcomes, but may increase, or decrease, the probability of outcomes occurring.
- The processes of sustainability and spread unfold over time and are linked in ways that reflect *path dependency*; this means that interventions to drive change trigger a sequence of events in which subsequent steps in the process are influenced by earlier actions. This does not mean that an event sequence is 'locked in' by initial decisions, but that the probability of some sequences and events subsequently taking place, and of particular outcomes being achieved, is influenced by previous steps. Issues that could influence sustainability thus need to be considered when planning implementation and not left until later.
- Sustainability and spread are not always beneficial, although in the programmes studied in this research these were sought-after outcomes. To maintain working practices when they no longer fit the context, or where better approaches are available, can be damaging at all levels, individual, clinical service, corporate. Attempts to spread 'best practice' to contexts where the relevance is poor are also damaging.
- Temporal issues play a significant role; there are no quick fixes. One reason for this concerns the substance of the service improvements with

which we are concerned. As with 'rapid access assessment' (Chapter 10) and 'see and treat' (Chapter 11), the time at which an initiative is launched may stimulate adoption. It is also important to recognize that, while targets may be simple to articulate ('two-week wait'), the changes required to meet those targets can be complex to implement. Multi-dimensional changes take time to develop. The process of adapting an approach to another context is often more than a matter of simply 'copying' an approach with 'fine tuning'. On the contrary, this often involves taking basic principles and starting the local design and implementation process from the beginning, which again takes time.

- Another recurring theme concerns the role of networks of interpersonal influence, exercised by change agents, project leads, and opinion leaders, persuading others to change and to maintain working practices. As several commentators have observed (e.g. Dopson and Fitzgerald, 2005a), 'evidence' is rarely adequate on its own to influence others to adopt new ideas. While evidence clearly plays a role, this is only one element in a more complex social process. We have also seen that evidence may be available in different forms, including quantitative performance measures, the results of small-scale 'plan–do–study–act' cycles, and visual evidence such as the absence of queues in emergency departments. Evidence has to be collated, communicated, absorbed, understood, and linked with other evidence and experience before it may be acted upon. Once again, this can be a prolonged process.

To manage sustainability and spread, we need to think differently about their explanations, moving away from static notions of cause and effect, and working with processes, event sequences, and narratives. This means focusing on the context, and on the combinations of factors over time, that affect the probability of desired outcomes being achieved. Managing sustainability and spread by working with theoretical narratives means abandoning traditional models of causality which rely on associations between independent and dependent variables. This is much more than a theoretical twist, as these perspectives have quite different practical implications. But as traditional causal models do not help us to understand these dynamic and interlinked processes very well, they are not adequate for informing practice.

Managing sustainability

The management of sustainability depends on how this concept is understood in a given organizational context. It could mean managing stability, adopting a static view, with the intent to 'keep things as they are' for a time. Or it could involve the management of a continuous trajectory, adopting a dynamic view, developing an approach that will accommodate changing conditions while retaining basic principles. Indeed, the sustainability of a particular approach may often depend on such adaptability. Whichever perspective applies, managing sustainability can be regarded as maintaining the narrative, keeping the storyline going, preventing sub-plots and diversions from taking over.

We used in Chapter 12 the story of the Rapid Bay Jetty to develop a process narrative to predict either sustainability or decay. The 'decay' narrative predicts that a robust structure in a hostile environment will eventually fail in the absence of attention and maintenance. The environment does not have to be intentionally hostile; in most organizations, there are always other issues and priorities calling for resources and diverting attention. Nevertheless, without surveillance and maintenance, we can predict that the structure will probably fold. There are two things that we cannot predict. The first is the precise timing of events. Second, we cannot predict the actual combination of factors that will lead the structure to collapse. However, this research has identified the kinds of factors likely to support or to jeopardize sustainability.

Change substance

> **Support conditions:** the changes 'fit' the organization, they contribute to strategy, they are perceived as central to effectiveness and survival.

> **Risk conditions:** the changes sit uncomfortably with the organization, the contribution to strategy is unclear, they are seen as marginal to effectiveness and survival.

Context

> **Support conditions:** change is seen as an appropriate response to the environment, meets customer/client needs, external stability does not challenge the status quo, no external threats and distractions, new practices remain relevant, able to recruit, develop, and retain high-calibre staff, change is consistent with social norms, with the tide of popular opinion, 'the right thing to do'.

> **Risk conditions:** change is seen as an inadequate response to the environment, unable to meet customer/client needs, external turbulence challenges the status quo, disruptive external threats and distractions, new practices becoming obsolete, trade union resistance, unable to recruit, develop and retain high-calibre staff, change is inconsistent with social norms, against popular opinion, 'the wrong thing to do'.

Process

Support conditions: clear responsibility for change, strong improvement infrastructure, steering committee and facilitators, dedicated change champions with internal support, implementation with high levels of communication and involvement, diffusion beyond initial setting, sustainability seen as stage in an extended process involving further development, a period of relative calm has allowed stabilization.

Risk conditions: ambiguous responsibility for change, weak improvement infrastructure, no steering committee or facilitators, no (or only temporary) change champions, implementation with little communication or involvement, no further diffusion beyond first implementation, sustainability seen as discrete stage amenable to separate analysis, continuing turbulence is inhibiting stabilization.

Temporal factors

Support conditions: pace and sequence of changes carefully phased, 'winning the time' to demonstrate benefits through the period when gains from 'easy' changes start to slow, allowing time for change to become part of the corporate culture, adequate time allowed for development work to adapt ideas from elsewhere.

Risk conditions: no attention to pace and sequence of changes, the argument that change is too slow is lost when gains from 'easy' changes are complete and development then fades, momentum killed with premature declaration of success, expectation of rapid adaptation with no time allowance for tailored development work.

Organizational factors

Support conditions: decision processes are rapid and flexible, there are procedures to monitor problems, finance policies favour innovation and long-term goals, there are no structural barriers inhibiting cross-functional collaboration, operating policies encourage problem prevention and quality and customer satisfaction, human resource policies encourage teamwork, initiative, and commitment, reward and appraisal systems are consistent and transparent, there are mechanisms for recognizing achievements, training meets both individual and organizational needs, skilled and flexible staff increase responsiveness to changing pressures.

Risk conditions: decision processes are slow and bureaucratic, procedures to monitor problems are lacking, finance policies favour traditional initiatives and short-term payback, structural barriers inhibit cross-functional collaboration, operating policies encourage cost reduction and the pursuit of measurable targets, human resource policies discourage teamwork, initiative, and commitment, reward and appraisal systems are inconsistent and complex, there are no mechanisms for recognizing achievements, training does not meet individual and organizational needs, high dependency on inflexible staff decreases responsiveness to changing pressures.

Finance

Support conditions: the change is contributing to key performance measures, the perceived benefits over time are greater than perceived costs.

Risk conditions: the change is not contributing to key performance measures, the perceived costs are greater than perceived benefits.

Culture

Support conditions: there is a sense of urgency, climate and values are receptive to change, the link between new behaviours and performance is clearly understood, continuous improvement is a priority, change has 'mainstream' status and is integrated, new behaviours 'rooted' in shared norms, teamwork encouraged, belief that change is effective for several stakeholders, goals are shared by staff.

Risk conditions: there is a lack of urgency, climate and values are not receptive to change, the link between new behaviours and performance is poorly understood, continuous improvement is not a priority, change has 'cult' status and is isolated from the organization, new behaviours not 'anchored', teamwork discouraged, change believed to be ineffective because there are no measures, goals are disputed.

Political factors

Support conditions: challenges to change initiatives are defeated as lacking credibility, powerful guiding coalition has support of external networks, management and staff are involved in decision making, powerful stakeholders see themselves as winners.

Risk conditions: credible challenges to change initiatives remain in circulation, weak guiding coalition lacks support of external networks, management and staff excluded from decision making, resistance from powerful stakeholders who see themselves as losers.

Leadership

Support conditions: vision, purpose, priorities, and goals are clear, consistent, and challenging, leadership is strong, persistent, successful and stable, is committed to change, and has staff confidence.

Risk conditions: vision, purpose, priorities and goals are vague, inconsistent, and unchallenging, leadership is weak, unstable, and unsuccessful, is indifferent or resistant to change, and lacks staff confidence.

Management

Support conditions: plans and ideas are seen as credible and legitimate, causes are addressed systematically, 'difficult' issues are confronted despite a risk of conflict, style is open and facilitative, with high-trust, high-discretion relationships, focus is long term, assessing change on a range of benefits, managers accept change to their own behaviour, new managers champion predecessors' ideas.

Risk conditions: plans and ideas lack credibility and legitimacy, symptoms are tackled unsystematically, with the 'easy' changes over, the difficult issues are avoided, style is closed and autocratic, with low-trust, low-discretion relationships, focus is short term, discouraging change with no instant payback, managers reject change to their own behaviour, new managers champion their own initiatives.

Individual factors

Support conditions: those affected are committed to success, they have the skills and knowledge, reward expectations can be met, there is confidence about the future, innovation is welcome.

Risk conditions: commitment is low, skills and knowledge are lacking, reward expectations cannot be met, there is fear and uncertainty about the future, survival and self-protection are dominant attitudes.

Sustainability thus depends on local judgement, which in turn relies on diagnostic awareness, monitoring the mix of risk factors and supports, taking action as necessary. Maintenance can be either preventive, to sustain the status quo, or developmental, to continue adapting an improvement trajectory to circumstances. This perspective must also allow changes to decay, where appropriate, in order to be replaced by more effective methods.

Initiative decay: possible problems, practical solutions

- **The initiators and drivers move on**
  Solutions: Design career development and rewards policies to motivate and retain key change agents. Choose successors with similar competencies and aspirations.

- **Accountability for development has become diffuse**
  Solutions: Establish clear project management and line management responsibilities, and ensure appropriate and visible rewards for those involved in driving changes.

- **Knowledge and experience of new practice are lost through staff turnover**
  Solutions: Develop retention strategies to minimize such loss; adopt a 'buy-back' policy to involve leavers in induction, training, and 'master class' sessions for new staff.

- **Old habits are imported with recruits from less dynamic organizations**
  Solutions: Strengthen the induction and training regime for new recruits, ensuring high familiarity with the organization's approach to new working practices.

- **The issues and pressures that triggered the initiative are no longer visible**
  Solutions: Launch an ongoing 'public relations' campaign that keeps those pressures in the forefront of staff thinking. Identify new reinforcing issues and pressures.

- **New managers want to drive their own agendas**
  Solutions: Fine, but also ensure that new appointments have explicit remits to develop and not dismantle particular initiatives introduced by their predecessors.

- **Powerful stakeholders are using counter-implementation tactics to block progress**
  Solutions: When reason fails, develop a 'counter-counter-implementation' strategy to reduce their influence, marginalize their positions, and neutralize their tactics.

- **The pump-priming funding runs out**
  Solutions: Start to revise budget allocations well in advance, so that extra costs relating to new working practices can be absorbed gradually in a phased manner.

- **Other priorities come on stream, diverting attention and resources**
  Solutions: Develop a time-phased change implementation strategy, with relative stability between radical shifts; do not divert resources before initiatives are embedded.

- **Staff at all levels suffer initiative fatigue, enthusiasm for change falters**
  Solutions: Beware the 'bicycle effect' where loss of forward movement leads to a crash. Relaunch with new focus, themes, goals; sell benefits, clarify WIIFT (What's In It For Them?).

Managing spread

> It is important to stress that these examples have been arrived at *by going through a redesign process*; lifting the outcome off the shelf to re-use somewhere else without going through the redesign process may or may not work, but would miss the point that redesign is about analysing what is done in each local context now, and how local staff believe it could be done better in the interests of their patients.
>
> *Source*: Locock (2001, p.42)

As with sustainability, the management of spread, and the avoidance of containment, depends on context. While it is possible to offer general guidelines on how the spread narrative can be managed, that advice has to be translated into tailored action informed by local knowledge and judgement. Two of the most significant issues concern the substance of the changes and the time frame over which spread can be expected to happen. In these studies, the substance concerned multi-faceted organizational changes, and the timescales were often protracted.

Most of the commentary on change management deals with 'single hit' implementation, and pays little attention to how changes spread to other parts of the organization. One exception is the work of Beer *et al.* (1990) who, from their 'tracking study' of change in large corporations, are concerned with spreading 'revitalization'. Following standard advice about commitment, vision, and consensus, they argue that it is necessary to spread revitalization by encouraging departments to rethink their own roles, to 'reinvent the wheel', rather than forcing change with directives. The management role is to specify the direction, and not detail the solutions. In other words, the spread of change is a 'unit-by-unit learning process rather than a series of programs, and acknowledges the payoffs that result from persistence over a long period of time as opposed to quick fixes' (p.166).

Adapting again

The research reported here suggests that Beer and colleagues are correct to emphasize 'reinvention' as ideas spread. Szulanski and Winter (2002) advocate a different method for reproducing successful routines in new settings, for 'getting it right the second time'. They argue that most attempts to spread good practice fail due to two 'spread errors'. The first involves 'editing', or implementing with improvements, where units 'try to go one

Three management methods for encouraging spread

1 *Create a market for change*: 'set demanding standards for all operations and then hold managers accountable to them' (p.165). But also hold managers accountable for fundamental change in the way they use human resources, to prevent 'overmanagement' simply to meet increasing demands.
2 *Use successfully revitalized units as organizational models for the entire company*: and use successful divisions as 'developmental laboratories'. There are three 'ground rules' here (p.165). First, 'innovative units need support' in terms of management, skilled personnel, and external consultants. Second, 'it is crucial to identify those units with the likeliest chance of success'. Environmental factors beyond local management control can turn successful innovations into failures. Third, these models need to be publicized: 'In the leading companies, visits, conferences, and educational programs facilitated learning from model units'.
3 *Develop career paths that encourage leadership development*: the most scarce resource is leadership. Make leadership an important criterion for promotion, then manage people's careers to develop it. Assign people to units targeted for change.

Source: Beer *et al*. (1990)

better than an operation that's up and running nearly flawlessly' (p.64). The second involves 'cherry picking', or implementing 'the good bits', where units 'try to piece together the best parts of a number of different practices, in hopes of creating the perfect hybrid' (p.64). They argue that local 'reinvention' is fatal. Their illustrations include opening bank loan accounts, selling colour photocopiers, and semiconductor manufacturing. These are codifiable operations. 'Copy exact' may not work for multi-faceted operational innovations, where the various components may each require adaptation to local conditions.

There is another problem with 'copy exact'. This model short-circuits the implementation process, which is often a valuable learning activity for those involved. Plsek (2000) argues that relearning something that has already been learned elsewhere is a wasteful process. However, as we have seen, relearning may be a key part of the familiarization process for those to whom the ideas and working practices are new. More significantly, relearning often involves significant fresh learning, particularly with regard to the way in which ideas and practices need to be tailored to local conditions, and that is not wasted effort. While 'copy exact' seems to offer a model for rapid and effective spread, that may not be the case for all kinds of change. On the contrary, attempts to accelerate the diffusion process are more likely to lead to changes for which there is little support, with inadequate local adaptation, and with damaging implications for the longer-term sustainability of those changes.

The cause of creative, innovative change and continuous improvement is thus damaged by the assumption that changes can be packaged and copied in any straightforward manner. The term 'adaptation' implies fine tuning, but for multi-faceted changes, this involves a prolonged exercise which can take as long to unfold as the original development and implementation process. To spread operational innovations in healthcare, it appears that, on most occasions, more or less significant adaptations to accommodate local circumstances are required. Not only does this imply a protracted process, but that extended timescale may often have advantages for the approaches that are developed and for their sustainability. While we may want to argue that, as a general rule, rapid is better than delayed when it comes to spreading new ideas and practices, that is not always the case (see Chapter 3). There may be advantage in allowing that process to proceed at a slower pace, allowing time for attitudes to change, and for those involved to learn how to adapt new ways of working to local conditions.

The influence game

Social influence is required, independent of the nature of the substance of the change. It would be wrong always to assume that actions to improve quality of care and clinical outcomes for patients would be welcomed without question. Particularly with regard to target-driven changes, and to circumstances where targets appeared to clinical staff to be unrelated to quality of care, change leaders faced scepticism and resistance. Here, the role of networks, opinion leaders, and interpersonal influence tactics was critical. Those tactics (see Chapter 5) involved personalized and tailored strategies to 'sell the benefits'. Rather than rely on transformational leaders and change agents in formal positions, evidence highlights the role of 'below the radar' leadership, exercised by medical secretaries, clinic clerks, and nurses, in addition to project leads, general managers, and chief executives. These 'unconventional leaders' are not often recognized, supported, or rewarded, but research suggests that change may depend on those dispersed contributions.

Tide and time

One component of influence concerns wider social trends: changes and innovations that are seen to be 'swimming with the tide' (Rimmer et al., 1996) appear to spread more readily than those which are unpopular or unfashionable. Thus, with 'see and treat', the history of a known problem, combined with government priorities, publicized in a television documentary, meant that this initiative became 'the thing to do'. But political and media commentary often implies that extra funding for healthcare should have immediate results. Evidence shows, however, that national policy and local management must operate instead with a more realistic framework of expectations concerning the pace with which improvements can be achieved, and the precision with which those improvements can be measured.

The spread narrative

The evidence consistently suggests that the spread of new ideas beyond the site of first implementation depends on more than good ideas and willing adopters. This is a complex social process that depends on multiple aspects of the surrounding context and on a range of time considerations. In particular, the concept of 'best practice' is misleading, as the precise policies, systems, procedures, and practices that 'work best' in one setting may not work elsewhere. While medical treatments may be standardized, to a degree, the ways in which the health service is organized and delivered depend on aspects of the local context.

As discussed in Chapters 2 and 12, Rogers (1995) argues that the spread of new ideas is promoted when they are shown to be advantageous, compatible, understandable, observable, testable, and adaptable. However, we also know that, while those attributes are desirable, and perhaps necessary, they are not alone sufficient to guarantee the spread of new working practices in healthcare, which can depend on a number of other factors, including:

1 **Contextual issues:**
   - stability of the local organization and the wider external context;
   - policy shifts in the performance objectives the changes were designed to achieve;
   - current local issues, problems, and other initiatives demanding attention;
   - organizational readiness for and receptiveness to change;
   - other local factors focusing attention and resources in particular areas.

2 **Change substance:**
   - attractiveness of the idea, fit with local strategy;
   - adaptability to local needs and circumstances.

3 **Leadership issues:**
   - a driving coalition prepared to use symbolic actions and power plays;
   - the ingredients, resourcing, and sequencing of implementation plans;
   - the influencing skills of lead personnel, and other leaders, at all levels.

4 **Political issues:**
   - perceived impact on professional autonomy;
   - perceived impact on other organizational groups, occupations, and power brokers;
   - the nature, source, and perceived credibility of the evidence circulating in support.

5 **Structural issues:**
   - presence of multiple change agents in appropriate roles;
   - creation of dedicated redesign team;
   - organizational positions of 'lead' staff;
   - formal and informal social and organizational networks.

6 **Temporal issues:**
   - timing and duration of those 'lead' staff appointments;
   - the time involved to develop, win support for, and implement adaptations;
   - may need to try later, when supportive factors have come together.

7 **Financial issues:**
   - level, timing, and duration of funding to support implementation;
   - symbolic and financial rewards for adoption and penalties for delay.

8 **Individual issues:**
   - individual readiness for change;
   - stage in behaviour change process – precontemplation, contemplation, action;
   - individual position – innovator, adopter, or laggard;
   - response to tailored influence and persuasion tactics;
   - perceived benefit and/or threat to autonomy.

The list of factors will again depend on local circumstances. As with sustainability, while we cannot confidently identify all of the factors that, in a given setting, will play a vital role in spreading new ideas and practices, we do know what kinds of factors are likely to be influential, and which ones management would be advised to consider. There is no single factor, or cluster of factors, critical for the spread of organizational changes. We know that the features of new ideas are not enough on their own, and that other factors can be important. We also know that social and organizational networks are, in principle, just as capable of disseminating 'bad practice' and suboptimal solutions (Robertson *et al.*, 1996). The weighting of these factors depends on the setting. It may be that pressure for the spread of an initiative can be generated from any combination of these factors such that, while one or more issues appear to be important in achieving spread in one setting, the same factors may be weak or absent in another setting, where spread was effective but propelled by pressure from a different combination of factors. Nevertheless, attention to those recurring themes in narratives of spread can contribute to the more effective management of the process.

This discussion has been conducted as though spread and sustainability are independent constructs. In practice, they are closely linked. It may be argued that new ideas first have to spread before they can be sustained. However, new ideas and working practices that do not have widespread support, that are unlikely to be sustained, or that are not being sustained by early adopters are unlikely to spread to sites that have still to consider those ideas. These are processes that cannot be managed independently but have to be considered in tandem, if the desired outcomes, over the proposed timescale, are to be achieved.

Policy implications

The evidence does not allow a systematic evaluation of healthcare policy, and that was not the purpose of this research. However, these studies offer a lens through which to examine assumptions concerning the modernization process. In this section, therefore, we consider briefly the wider lessons from these studies, concerning:

- the role of the NHS Modernisation Agency;
- the need for structural stability to allow processes to develop;
- the strategy of implementing national programmes in 'waves';
- the impact of performance targets;
- expectations of timing;
- leadership development.

'The Mod Squad'

What does this research reveal concerning the role of an organization development body like the NHS Modernisation Agency, which a number of staff in local NHS organizations affectionately named 'The Mod Squad'? This was a national agency responsible for leading and supporting systemic changes in a large and complex professional organization. Most change management advice is directed at local management teams and project leads. Here, we can consider the role of a corporate body responsible not only for encouraging and monitoring change, but also for playing an active role in service improvement.

The buffer zone

The Agency occupied a 'buffer zone' between the Department of Health, where government policy was framed, and local NHS organizations. Agency staff found themselves, on occasion, defending and implementing policies in the face of resistance. While the Agency made a point of dispersing staff around the country, their relatively small numbers (800 working with 1.3 million) meant that many staff in provider organizations were only dimly aware of the Agency and its purpose, and many may never have heard of it at all. For Agency staff, being an 'insider' working with the health service, and an 'outsider' employed by a remote national agency, could be an uncomfortable role. However, most experienced significant personal development in that role, through exposure to strategic issues, system-wide changes, service improvement methodologies, and the experiences of local NHS organizations with major changes in different parts of the service. As documented elsewhere (Buchanan, 2003), staff in the 'buffer zone' quickly developed valuable transferable skills.

The evolving role

The Agency's experience shows how the role of a central body is not static, but evolves in response to the context, while recognizing that its actions have contributed to those contextual trends. As the Agency's work increased local capabilities for service improvement, through example, support, training, and publications, its leading position evolved into a facilitative, advisory, support role. This evolution doubtless contributed to personal development, as Agency staff recognized the need for flexibility with regard to the exercise of their own responsibilities. However, as well as accepting that a central agency role is dynamic, shifting in line with the context in which it functions, it is also necessary to accept that this role may always be transient. The Agency survived for four years. Over that period, it grew from around 100 to over 800 staff, was responsible for implementing many national programmes, trained thousands of NHS staff in service improvement methods, and consequently was consuming a much larger budget than when it began. However, the benefits derived from this kind of work are often intangible and difficult to quantify, and this meant that the Agency could not itself readily demonstrate the 'return on investment'.

While failure to make an impact on the wider organization, and not to strengthen its role or to increase its influence, would undoubtedly have led to the Agency's closure, paradoxically its success nevertheless also led to that outcome. In broad outline, this may be a generic narrative that could apply to similar central change or organization development bodies in other large, complex organizations. This is a familiar and potentially predictable narrative:

- a small central body is successful with business improvement initiatives, and grows;
- growth means increased staff numbers, increased influence, and a bigger budget;
- success and further growth, as intended, strengthen local capabilities for change;
- as local capability grows, the central role shifts from leading to supporting;
- but increased power and bigger budget raise questions over return on investment;
- and it is difficult to demonstrate the measurable impact of a supporting role;
- so strategic review recommends replacement with smaller (leaner) advisory body.

While some commercial organizations have run a 'programmes office' since the late 1990s, to monitor and co-ordinate strategic change projects and budgets, the role and experience of the Agency (which was much more than a programmes office) are probably unique in healthcare. Generalizing, either to theory or practice, from this narrative, is consequently dangerous. It will be instructive to observe the narrative of the NHS Institute for Innovation and Improvement, formed in 2005. Can we predict closure and replacement in four years? No, not with any confidence. The Institute's mission was to remain small, so the growth chapter in its narrative should not appear. However, power and influence depend on many other factors, and the political need to demonstrate benefits is likely to persist. The interesting question thus concerns whether the Institute will be able to construct a different narrative, or whether it will follow a variation of the plot which ended with the Agency's closure.

The need for structural stability

As Chapter 1 indicated, attention turned from a somewhat fragmented portfolio to the development of a more integrated approach to service improvement, and to 'whole-systems' thinking. One of the key dimensions of this approach involves collaboration between the various providers, in primary, acute, specialist, ambulance, and tertiary care, and others; establishing 'partnerships across boundaries' became a fashionable concept. However, those partnerships were in 2005 and 2006 being undermined by further structural reforms. In addition, the performance management systems which put primary care trusts in commissioning and monitoring roles in relation to secondary care trusts created ambiguities concerning the position of strategic health authorities, while making 'partnerships' between primary and acute care precarious. Large hospitals often face difficulties in improving co-operation across their own 'whole systems'. Establishing partnerships across health communities presented even more significant challenges.

Following the announcement in 2005 of a further series of structural reforms, reducing the number of primary care trusts and strategic health authorities in England, and redefining their functions, the House of Commons Select Committee on Health severely criticized the lack of consultation with those to be affected by these changes, and challenged the wisdom of introducing further changes to organizations that had only been operating for about three years (House of Commons Health Committee, 2006). The report argued that:

> It is clear that the impact of proposed reconfigurations on primary care trusts' day to day functions, including clinical services, will be substantial – it takes on average eighteen months for organizations to 'recover' after restructuring and to bring their performance back to its previous level. . . . After the immediate disruption of reorganization, it is thought to take a further 18 months for the benefits to emerge – a total of three years from the initial reforms. Thus, just as the benefits of primary care trusts (established in 2002) are about to be realized, the Government has decided to restructure them. The cycle of perpetual change is ill-judged and not conducive to the successful provision and improvement of health services.
>
> (House of Commons Health Committee, 2006, pp.4–5)

That argument reinforces the conclusion from this research that unstable organization structures generate problems for both the sustainability and spread of new working practices. As structures change, and staff move into different roles, their knowledge and experience depart with them, and the methods, approaches, and processes with which they have been working naturally decay. In addition, staff who know that their organization faces structural change in the near future may be unwilling to develop new ways of working which may soon be rendered pointless. The national policy preoccupation with new structures not only overlooks the importance of the underpinning processes, but also significantly impedes the sustainability, spread, and development of process or operational innovations.

Changing by waving

The two initiatives for which the Agency was initially responsible were the National Booking Programme and the Cancer Services Collaborative.

As Chapters 6 and 9 explain, both were 'rolled out' in 'waves'. The concept of piloting change, to learn from the experience before committing the rest of the organization, is widely acknowledged. However, the funding model which accompanied the successive waves jeopardized sustainability by providing local project managers with temporary contracts. When the funding for a wave came to an end, local organizations had to find resources to continue to support those positions, and some did not. Many project managers simply moved on to other roles, and the continuity of their work relied on the enthusiasm and capability of local staff. In other words, where change is seen as 'a project' which terminates in 18 months, then commitment (of energy as well as funds) may also terminate at that time. If large-scale changes are to be implemented like this in future, it may be advisable to develop a funding model which supports the longer-term nature of the initiative, rather than signal that its impact will be transient.

Targets, targets

While most health service staff seem to have welcomed *The NHS Plan* in principle, given the commitment to improving quality of healthcare, the numerous performance targets, many of which were quantified in some way, were controversial. The number of targets was intimidating. Many were regarded as having little or no clinical basis. Concentrating on the measurable can marginalize qualitative aspects of care, which may be just as important to patients. Recognizing this controversy, it was notable that, in reviewing *The NHS Plan*, the Department of Health (2004a) referred instead to 'key commitments'. However, the evidence from this research shows that targets had 'dual effects', combining those drawbacks and criticisms with a number of benefits, and these are summarized in Table 13.1.

On this limited evidence, it may be prudent to advise a policy stance that strikes a balance between identifying numerous measurable targets, on the one hand, and a small number of improvement themes, on the other. This would seek to retain the advantages of goal clarity, while avoiding the drawbacks of specifying an intimidating range of targets, many of which could be regarded as politically inspired, not clinically based, and thus inappropriate.

Timing expectations

We have seen how, although many performance targets were simple to articulate, the combinations of changes that were often required in order

Table 13.1 *Targets: perspectives and implications*

Positive	Negative
Encouraged a rethink of how to improve services	Stifled local initiative and adaptation through homogenization
Focused thinking on (perceived) priority areas and issues	Contentious measures, open to manipulation
	Monitoring was seen as punitive
Some measures were widely adopted by everyone	Targets encouraged a focus on measures and not on process
Potentially measurable	Some targets were seen as having no clinical basis, and were discredited
Targets brought additional funding	
Substantial changes in areas in focus	Unknown impact on areas not in focus

to meet those targets could not always be implemented quickly. We have also seen how, even if one area developed a fresh approach, other units could rarely 'copy exact', and more often had to begin their own development process, working from the same basic principles, but designing a version consistent with local conditions. To be effective and subsequently sustainable, these processes must proceed at an appropriate pace, which for systemic organizational change is typically measured, not in days or weeks, but in months or years (see Chapter 7). Politicians and policy makers anticipating rapid results must also, therefore, anticipate some disappointments.

Leaders at all levels

While the concept of 'dispersed leadership' is now widely recognized (Chapter 8), leadership development programmes in healthcare have tended to focus on those in 'obvious' leadership positions, particularly senior nurses, clinical directors, chief executives, and other board-level and related posts. While the range of leadership programmes has broadened significantly in recent years (the NHS has a £4 billion annual learning and development budget covering all disciplines and topics), the contributions of staff in positions not normally regarded as leadership roles are often unrecognized, unrewarded, and unsupported. However, the scale of the modernization agenda now requires contributions on that scale, from significant numbers of experienced and motivated staff. This is an argument for implementing more broadly applicable change leadership development programmes for all healthcare staff, at all levels, and in all occupational groups, and not only those in formal and senior positions.

Critical debates

1 The sustainability or continuity of working practices has many advantages, but also drawbacks. In healthcare, to what extent are the perspectives of clinical staff and patients on this issue likely to be similar or different, and what are the longer-term implications of those comparisons?

2 We know that compelling evidence in support of 'best practice' is not enough to encourage widespread adoption. Is that conclusion a cause for alarm or for celebration, and why?

3 Is ambitious government policy for healthcare, with regard to performance measures and expectations regarding the speed with which changes can be made, detrimental or beneficial in terms of improving quality of patient care?

The Research into Practice team published a series of reports setting out the findings of the studies in which they were involved, focusing on the practical implications.

In January 2005, the team published *The New Improvement Wheel*, a practical diagnostic tool identifying influences on sustainability and spread. This aimed to provide a simple overview of the complex relationships between factors influencing sustainability and spread, and it proved to be popular and influential. The wheel metaphor was chosen to illustrate three properties. First, it emphasized the many influences (the wheel spokes) on these processes. Second, it also highlighted the close links between these processes, indicating how they can be influenced by many of the same kinds of factors. Third, the wheel metaphor emphasized the 'cumulative effects' argument: the presence of more strong 'spokes' would potentially support the 'rim' of sustainability and spread, the absence of some of the factors (some wheel spokes are missing) weakens the potential, and the absence of too many factors (the wheel buckles and will not turn) prevents sustainability and spread. This tool does not suggest which particular spokes could be significant, as that varies with the change substance and the context. All of these reports can be downloaded from: http://www.institute.nhs.uk

14 Researching major change: issues and dilemmas

Elaine Whitby, Rose Gollop, and
David A. Buchanan

Chapter aims

1 To consider the implications for methods and outputs of a collaborative research design, with an internal team funded by and working closely with the potential end-users of the findings.
2 To explore the balance of benefits and drawbacks of collaborative research designs.
3 To identify the implications of this approach for research teams in similar situations.

Key point summary

- Translating research evidence into practice, especially in medicine and also now in management, is a known problem. The linkages are not direct, and are influenced by many personal and social factors as well as by the nature and source of evidence.
- To support the translation of research evidence into practice, collaborative research designs have become more popular, and the Research into Practice team was formed on this basis, to give national programme leads rapid access to findings that would contribute to the development of their initiatives.
- The model of collaborative research adopted by the team had several advantages: good access to data and to research participants, good understanding of practitioner interests and needs, ability to discuss research aims and methods with participants and end-users, ability to influence practice rapidly and directly.
- The collaborative approach presented challenges about which other teams working in such circumstances may need to be aware. The objectivity (to the extent that this is achievable in any research setting) and independence of the research team were potentially jeopardized by being 'close to the customer'. Pressure for results meant that detailed data analysis took place in parallel with the development of practical guidance, which could reduce complexities

to checklists, and some research methods were dropped as they were too time consuming.

● Collaborative designs have been advocated as a way to 'bridge the gap' in time and relevance between research evidence and the translation of that evidence into practice. This experience suggests that collaborative designs, while addressing those issues in part, generate their own problems, and are not easy solutions.

● Collaborative designs have the potential to be more effective in organizational settings where practitioner needs and interest are stable, where practitioners are not directly funding the research work, and where researchers and practitioners share a common understanding with regard to time frame and epistemology.

> Further details concerning the work of the Research into Practice team can be found in the following paper, which has been used in part as the basis for this chapter: Gollop, R., Ketley, D., Buchanan, D., Whitby, E., Lamont, S., Jones, J., *et al.* (2006). Research into Practice: a model for healthcare management research? *Evidence & Policy, 2(2)*, 257–267.

Collaborative designs

> Preliminary evidence suggests that involving decision-makers in the research process is perceived to be beneficial across all models of involvement (formal supporter, responsive audience and integral partner). These early efforts to support researcher and decision-maker interactions appear to be a step in the right direction. Further promotion of decision-maker involvement in the research process should help researchers and decision-makers identify strategic opportunities best suited to researcher and decision-maker contexts, and should increasingly recognize and support the costs associated with the involvement. . . . In other words, all of us – research funders, researchers, and decision-makers – need to be open to new ways of conducting our activities. The ability to create new types of knowledge out of new types of exchanges will benefit us all.
>
> *Source*: Ross *et al.* (2003, p.34)

This research was conducted during a period of rapid large-scale change in public sector healthcare in Britain. The pace and scale of those changes have continued, affecting the overall organization structure of the service and inter-organizational relationships, as well as working practices on 'the front line'. The team which carried out these studies was employed by the health service, and was based in the Agency, rather than operating as a conventional external university academic research group. Although the intent was to generate conclusions and recommendations that would have wide applicability across the service, the Agency's internal funding model clearly identified 'customers' for the findings of the specific projects which they were each supporting. Initially, those customers were the leads for the National Booking Programme and the Cancer Services Collaborative. As the team's work and output became more widely known, a number of other internal 'customers' also requested services in the form of research and evaluation projects. The style and format of the summary reports produced by the team recognized that front line staff were also one of the key target audiences for the research findings and implications.

The problems of linking evidence with practice have attracted much commentary, especially in the context of evidence-based medicine and evidence-based healthcare policy and management (Tranfield *et al.*, 2003). Evidence of any form often struggles to find application, due to a number of personal and social factors as well as the source and nature of the evidence itself (Fitzgerald *et al.*, 1999; Fitzgerald and Dopson, 2005a). Another explanation for the gap between evidence and practice, in medicine or in management, lies with research method. The traditional approach first involves designing and conducting the research, developing conclusions, and then puzzling over how best to translate into practice theory that was initially developed to address a gap in the literature. That process can take a considerable length of time to unfold, and the practical outcomes are potentially unreliable as the initial research aims were not necessarily informed by practical concerns. For this reason, what are now known as 'collaborative' research designs have become more popular, even fashionable. Denis and Lomas (2003) note that there are a number of models of collaborative research, differentiated by the nature of engagement with end-users, who may be involved in project design or in working through the practical implications of the findings, or who may be involved throughout the process as co-researchers. While involving participants in the research process is one form of development, involving researchers in management decision making and policy formulation processes is a further extension of the collaborative approach.

The rationale for establishing the Research into Practice team, therefore, was to address those issues, by giving programme and project leaders rapid access to 'real-time' research findings and learning, from an internal research group, to inform the development of their initiatives through an ongoing exchange of ideas and objectives. This chapter explores the dimensions and implications of this research model, identifying the drawbacks as well as the benefits, and the wider implication for research methods and for similarly positioned research teams.

Issues arising

The experience of the Research into Practice team with a collaborative approach to research illustrates many advantages of this mode of working, but also identifies the difficulties that are likely to arise. The most significant issues concern the team's location in the organization, relationships with internal customers, time pressures with regard to producing useful lessons, and the extent to which research methods had to be adapted to the pattern of demands.

Team location

The team was employed by the Agency, which was based in Leicester, although most members of the team worked from their own homes, which were located across the country. As 'insiders', they had ready access to health service staff. Most team members had clinical backgrounds, 'spoke the language' of many of the participants in the research, and thus had credibility with clinical staff that external management researchers sometimes lack. In addition, with regard to dissemination, clinical audiences appreciated that team members understood their experiences and the difficulties that they faced in spreading and sustaining new practices. However, national programme leads, some of whom had administrative offices in Leicester, were also home based and worked across the country, making it difficult to arrange informal contacts and regular meetings with them. Nevertheless, team members were able to meet with programme leads and other staff to discuss progress on those programmes, the problems they were facing, and how research could contribute to an understanding of those issues and how they could be addressed.

The formation of an internal team could be interpreted as a desire by the Agency to manage research findings and to minimize potential criticism of politically led initiatives, a point made by Bate and Robert (2002) reflecting on their attempts to bring a more formative, interventionist approach to policy-based evaluation research. However, in establishing the team, leaders were keen to ensure not only that it included experienced researchers, backed by neutral, external academic support, but also that findings would be published externally and subject to academic critique. The internal team thus had relatively good access to key staff and information relevant to the research aims concerning particular service improvement programmes. This location and proximity, however, generated three problems.

First, there was concern that internal research could be seen as biased by the wider academic community. Second, some team members felt that they were so close to the issues that it was difficult to maintain objective distance; participants were often colleagues, with shared pressures, and it was vital to maintain relationships of trust and respect while reporting findings accurately. For some researchers, the transition from conventional to collaborative methods may thus be awkward. Third, many of those colleagues interviewed had a vested interest in making their national 'flagship' programmes successful, or in making them appear to be successful, and did not necessarily want internal colleagues publicizing problems or mistakes. This led in at least one instance to the modification of a passage in an internal report, and on other occasions to awkward discussions concerning whether and how the team could share more widely the findings from a particular piece of work, especially where the conclusions contained implied criticism. On occasions when findings implied criticism of the way in which programmes were implemented, the team had to manage not only political sensitivities at Department of Health level, but also those of the programme leaders who were its sponsors. This was handled by maintaining constant, open, and honest communication with them. While 'censorship' is an exaggerated term, and the instances encountered did not materially affect the overall reporting of findings, this experience does suggest how that could easily happen in this type of research context. In summary, therefore, an internal research team's advantage of proximity to the end-users of its work may carry a price, involving a degree of compromise with regard to academic independence and objectivity.

Customer relations

One fundamental benefit of collaborative research in terms of translating evidence into practice was in being 'close to the customer'. The researchers had a detailed first-hand understanding of the problems and needs of their customers. The team's initial remit, with regard to sustainability and spread issues in two major national programmes, was relatively broad. As relationships with those and other customers developed, the team undertook other more focused projects, where the aims and research methods were discussed and agreed in partnership with sponsors, and were designed to answer specific questions raised by programme leaders at the time. Each project was allocated a named researcher, responsible for maintaining close communication with key programme staff.

However, this major advantage of customer proximity was offset by three other issues. First, the Agency itself was changing and evolving (Chapter 1), creating new structures, roles, and priorities, both internally and with respect to the national service improvement programmes for which it was responsible. In other words, the customer base was not static, neither were the customer needs, to which the research team constantly had to respond. Second, as those customers were funding the work of the research team, their requests were treated with an understandable degree of urgency. The team was thus under pressure to produce conclusions and to develop where possible practical tools, as getting results into practice (locally as well as at national programme level) was a key objective. On more than one occasion, while the team was still refining the analysis relating to a particular issue, its provisional conclusions were acted on as final. While the aims and methods of any research are likely to be influenced by the bodies funding the work, the relationships in this instance were closer, and the pressures perhaps more immediate. Third, in responding to customer requests, the team sometimes reduced complexities to checklists, in which more complex processual and contextual dimensions were obscured, so it was important to ensure that those were not the only outputs. Given the nature of management timescales, research in this context creates tension between the aim of comprehensive data analysis and presentation and the desire to generate results that influence practice.

Time pressures

As indicated, the team's remit was to generate useful knowledge rapidly, without compromising the integrity of the research process. The team's organizational location and proximity to customers supported those aims. But once again, those advantages were diluted by other developments. The research governance framework for healthcare introduced in 2001 (Department of Health, 2001b; revised 2005b) created a research ethics review process, based on the standards applied in biomedical research involving patients, but also extended to cover research in organization and management issues. Before fieldwork could begin, proposals had to be vetted first by a multi-site research ethics committee, and might then have to be presented for a similar degree of scrutiny (often, but not always) to relevant local research ethics committees. It was widely known that the ethical review process could take months to complete, especially where (as in this research) several different organizations were involved. These committees could be difficult to address, as they were populated mainly by members trained in biomedical research methods, with limited understanding of the nature of qualitative organizational research. Consequently, their decisions could appear capricious, and were inconsistent. For example, due to their apparent lack of understanding of action research methodology, one proposed study was rejected out of hand by an ethics review committee, without opportunity for revision and resubmission, thus preventing that study from going ahead, wasting much time and effort in the process. The main implication of ethical review, however, was the extent to which this procedure could dramatically extend the time that would elapse between a decision to pursue a set of research objectives and the eventual development of findings and recommendations.

What difference did the team make?

The Research into Practice team aimed to provide sponsors with information that they could use to shape change implementation processes. This was achieved through:

- providing evidence of issues about which programme leaders were informally aware through their own communication channels;
- providing explanations for variations in the spread and sustainability of improvements;
- highlighting issues of importance to programme leaders;
- making recommendations for action.

One example of providing evidence of an issue about which Agency leaders were already aware concerned scepticism and resistance towards the cancer collaborative and booking programmes. The experience of programme leaders and project managers suggested that resistance was widespread (Locock, 2001; Shekelle, 2002). The team was asked to explore the causes of, and to indicate how best to manage, scepticism and resistance in relation to these programmes. Scepticism and resistance were found among all staff groups, but particularly among medical staff. Reasons related to factors concerning the changes themselves, the way in which they were introduced and promoted, and factors concerning individuals' personal responses to change, including fears of loss of power and influence (Gollop *et al.*, 2004). Formalizing this understanding influenced decisions to increase the numbers of clinical leads appointed in one programme, and highlighted awareness among change leaders of the importance of winning over clinicians to service improvement initiatives.

An example that highlighted and helped to explain variations in practice was provided by the evaluation of a sample of prostate cancer assessment pathways in secondary care in England (Gollop, 2004b). This showed that consultant urologists were interpreting evidence regarding mortality and morbidity in different ways, some to support the development of rapid access assessment pathways, and others to argue against them. Patients were not being consulted formally about their preferences, and there was little evidence of sharing ideas about assessment pathways between consultants, even within the same department. Sharing these findings with the National Cancer Director resulted in our study recommendations being included in the Department of Health's report 'Making Progress on Prostate Cancer' just months after the findings had been reported to programme leaders (Department of Health, 2004b). This also led to renewed talks between national urology leaders and prostate cancer patient groups, in an effort to increase patients' influence on clinical pathway development.

In terms of highlighting significant issues to programme leaders, evaluation of the later phases of the National Booking Programme in 2003–2004 confirmed the important role that administrative and clerical staff, particularly medical secretaries, played in the spread and sustainability of the programme at local levels (Neath, 2004a). It showed their influence in team members' decision making, notably that of consultant colleagues, who were likely to accept or reject booking on the basis of their recommendation. These findings illustrated the role of multiple levels of leadership and influence in clinical teams in terms of the adoption of new practice, building on the findings of an earlier evaluation that had noted the powerful position held by medical secretaries in the introduction of booked appointments (Kipping *et al.*, 2000). This led to booking programme leaders focusing their attention on administrative staff, commissioning the Research into Practice team to conduct a survey of their opinions, and running a series of national conferences exclusively for staff in these roles.

Time pressures also had implications for research methods. One component of the team's approach involved in-depth qualitative case studies, exploring sustainability and spread issues with regard to those two main national programmes, in two acute hospitals. Qualitative case research, however, is time consuming to conduct, and typically generates a volume of data that is difficult to reduce and to analyse quickly. Some team members felt that they did not have enough time to pursue the themes emerging from these studies, and that some of the complexities were potentially being overlooked. And while those case reports were of high interest and relevance to the team's aim of generating a rich theoretical understanding of the underlying processes, the reports themselves were of limited value to the host organizations, because they did not necessarily reflect local priorities. Many of the benefits to participating sites derived from regular interaction with and feedback from team members during and immediately after the study, through briefing sessions, presentations, workshops, and facilitated discussions, which helped to share findings and further inform the work.

With regard to publications, rapid dissemination was the expectation. This meant that the team produced a stream of two dozen corporate-style reports, short and focused, clearly written, and professionally printed on glossy paper with colour and photographs. However, there was little time to generate more traditional academic publications such as refereed journal articles, and no priority was given to that activity by internal customers.

Methodological compromise

The team's original research design, determined after much deliberation and involving a series of comparative case studies, was never completed. Case work proved too time consuming, and did not generate findings quickly enough. Subsequent projects instead relied on interviews with relatively small samples of key informants. Inevitably, choice of methods was driven as much by logistical constraints and pressures as by theoretical considerations. This is common across all forms of organizational research, although much published research does not make this explicit. However, in this particular organizational context, rapidly changing, time pressured, customer funded, there were perhaps even fewer degrees of freedom than usual concerning choice of appropriate research methods.

The researcher role

Through using this collaborative approach, the team was able to demonstrate several achievements. The programmes sponsoring the research were given feedback information that helped them to shape their implementation processes, strategically and operationally. The team was able to give programme leads robust evidence concerning issues of which they were informally aware through their own communication networks, but could not act on confidently without some formal justification. The research evidence helped to explain variations in practice regarding the sustainability and spread of service improvements, and highlighted issues of which programme leaders were not previously aware. This was done not only through internal publications, but also through informal and formal meetings and presentations, briefings, sharing events, and conferences.

If bridging the gap between evidence and practice is the problem, collaborative research designs are only a partial answer. Traditional methods may indeed be too slow in relation to the needs of rapidly changing practice, and research questions and aims may often be framed in ways that are not immediately relevant to the resolution of practitioners' problems. However, collaborative designs, while apparently addressing those criticisms directly, generate problems of their own. To generate the benefits from this kind of approach, it appears to be necessary also to accommodate the problems. In particular, this requires of the researcher degrees of adaptability and opportunism not commonly advocated in research methods textbooks. This implies maintaining a clear sense of the researcher's position and role in, or in relation to, the organization under investigation, and the expectations, demands, and pressures that flow from that position. While this will generate valuable opportunities for data collection, analysis, feedback, and respondent validation, and for translating research findings directly into practice, it will also generate pressures and constraints with regard to timing, and especially with regard to research methods. In particular it may be necessary to accept, on the one hand, the trade-off between access to data and participants, and on the other hand the ability freely to determine optimum research methods for addressing the questions and problems under investigation.

Traditionally, academic research aims are specified at the beginning of a project, and while those may be refined somewhat as understanding develops, they typically do not undergo major transformation during the life of the project. Indeed, contemporary research governance procedures are likely to be critical of research designs and methodological proposals underpinned by fluid and uncertain objectives. In contrast, the collaborative researcher is always going to be working at the pace of participants, being encouraged to alter the research focus, aims, and methods as personal and organizational priorities and agendas evolve. The continuity of the research agenda is thus constantly compromised, and a more flexible approach is required. One of the ironies of this fluid and demanding context for the Research into Practice team was that it proved impossible to sustain in full the original qualitative case-based research design, as the research agenda evolved (still focusing on sustainability and spread) in response to demand. Research teams considering a similar collaborative approach may thus find it helpful to take into account the following conclusions from this experience:

- Collaborative designs may work more effectively where end-user needs and interests are relatively stable; in contrast, where those needs are subject to frequent priority shifts, it can be difficult to maintain a focused research agenda.
- Collaborative designs may work more effectively where end-users are not directly funding the research project; where funding does come direct from end-users, research team independence may be jeopardized.
- Researchers and practitioners must understand each other's time frames; tensions arise between users who want results now and researchers who want first to complete and refine their analysis. The word 'quick' may have a different meaning in each of these communities.
- Researchers and their practitioner audiences must appreciate each other's epistemologies. Healthcare management researchers using qualitative processual perspectives will have problems communicating with healthcare practitioners wedded to double-blind randomized control trial methodology.
- Collaboration and integration can benefit the research process, as well as the phases of dissemination and application. However, it is important to recognize that those benefits are accompanied by costs and tensions, which both parties must appreciate.

Critical debates

1 To what extent should researchers and practitioners remain independent and at a distance, as they have such different interests, aims, timescales, and priorities?

2 In what kinds of organizational settings, in healthcare and in other sectors, would collaborative research methods be appropriate and valuable, and in what kinds of settings would this kind of approach be better avoided?

3 Researchers often complain that practitioners are reluctant to implement their findings, while practitioners complain that research findings arrive too late and are not relevant to their needs (Denis and Lomas, 2003). Other than collaborative research designs, how else can this gap between research and practice be bridged?

Bibliography

Abbott, A. (1990). A primer on sequence methods. *Organization Science, 1*(4), 375–392.

Abrahamson, E. (2000). Change without pain. *Harvard Business Review, 78*(4), 75–79.

Ansoff, I. (1997). Measuring and managing for environmental turbulence: the Ansoff Associates approach. In A. W. Hiam (ed.), *The Portable Conference on Change Management* (pp.67–83). Amherst, MA: HRD Press.

Appleby, J. (2005). *Cutting NHS Waiting Times: Identifying Strategies for Sustainable Reductions*. London: King's Fund.

Audit Commission. (2001). *Acute Hospital Portfolio: Review of National Findings – Accident and Emergency*. London: Audit Commission.

Badaracco, J. L. (2001). We don't need another hero. *Harvard Business Review, 79*(8), 121–126.

Bate, P. and Robert, G. (2002). Studying health care 'quality' qualitatively: the dilemmas and tensions between different forms of evaluation research within the UK National Health Service. *Qualitative Health Research, 12*(7), 966–981.

Bate, P., Robert, G., and Bevan, H. (2004). The next phase of healthcare improvement: what can we learn from social movements? *Quality and Safety in Health Care, 13*, 62–66.

Beer, M., Eisenstat, R. A., and Spector, B. (1990). Why change programs don't produce change. *Harvard Business Review, 68*(6), 158–166.

Bensley, D., Halsall, J., McIlwain, C. and Scott, L. (1997). *Total Booking Systems for Elective Admission: Feedback from Site Visits*. London: Department of Health.

Berwick, D. M. (2003). Disseminating innovations in healthcare. *Journal of the American Medical Association, 289*(15), 1969–1975.

Brooks, I. (1996). Leadership of a cultural change process. *Leadership and Organization Development Journal, 17*(5), 31–37.

Brown, J. S. and Duguid, P. (1998). Organizing knowledge. *California Management Review, 40*(3), 90–111.

Browne, G. J., Lam, L., Giles, H., McCaskill, M., Exley, B., and Fasher, B. (2000). The effects of a seamless model of management on the quality of care for emergency department patients. *Journal of Quality in Clinical Practice, 20*(4), 120–126.

Bryman, A. (1996). Leadership in organizations. In S. R. Clegg, C. Hardy, and W. R. Nord (eds), *Handbook of Organization Studies* (pp.276–292). London: Sage.

Buchanan, D. (2003). Demands, instabilities, manipulations, careers: the lived experience of driving change. *Human Relations, 56*(6), 663–684.

Buchanan, D. and Huczynski, A. (2004). *Organizational Behaviour: An Introductory Text* (fifth edition). Harlow: Financial Times Prentice Hall.

Buchanan, D., Claydon, T., and Doyle, M. (1999). Organization development and change: the legacy of the nineties. *Human Resource Management, 9*(2), 20–37.

Buchanan, D., Ketley, D., Gollop, R., Jones, J. L., Lamont, S. S., Neath, A., *et al.* (2005). No going back: a review of the literature on sustaining organizational change. *International Journal of Management Reviews, 7*(3), 189–205.

Burns, T. and Stalker, G. M. (1961). *The Management of Innovation*. London: Tavistock.

Byrne, G., Richardson, M., Brunsdon, J., and Patel, A. (2000). An evaluation of the care of patients with minor injuries in emergency settings. *Accident and Emergency Nurse, 8*(2), 101–109.

Caldwell, R. (2003). Models of change agency: a fourfold classification. *British Journal of Management, 14*(2), 131–142.

Caldwell, R. (2005). *Agency and Change: Rethinking Change Agency in Organizations*. Abingdon: Routledge.

Calman, K. and Hine, D. (1995). *A Policy Framework for Commissioning Cancer Services*. London: Department of Health.

Castille, K. and Cooke, M. (2003). One size does not fit all. *Emergency Medicine Journal, 20*(2), 120–122.

Christensen, C. M., Bohmer, R., and Kenagy, J. (2000). Will disruptive innovations cure healthcare? *Harvard Business Review, 78*(5), 102–112.

Cohen, W. M. and Levinthal, D. A. (1990). Absorptive capacity: a new perspective on learning and innovation. *Administrative Science Quarterly, 30*, 560–585.

Cooke, M. W., Higgins, J., and Bridge, P. (2000). *Minor Injury Services: The Present State*. Warwick: Emergency Medicine Research Group, Warwick University.

Cooke, M. W., Wilson, S., and Pearson, D. (2002). The effect of a separate stream for minor injuries on accident and emergency department waiting rooms. *Emergency Medicine Journal, 19*(1), 28–30.

Cornford, C. S., Harley, J., and Oswald, N. (2004). The '2-week rule' for suspected breast carcinoma: a qualitative study of the views of patients and professionals. *British Journal of General Practice, 54*(505), 584–588.

Czarniawska, B. (1999). *Writing Management: Organization Theory as a Literary Genre*. Oxford: Oxford University Press.

Dale, B., Boaden, R. J., Wilcox, M., and McQuater, R. E. (1997a). Sustaining total quality management: what are the key issues? *The TQM Magazine, 9*(5), 372–380.

Dale, B., Boaden, R. J., Wilcox, M., and McQuater, R. E. (1997b). Total quality management sustaining audit tool: description and use. *Total Quality Management, 8*(6), 395–408.

Dale, B., Boaden, R. J., Wilcox, M., and McQuater, R. E. (1999). Sustaining continuous improvement: what are the key issues? *Quality Engineering, 11*(3), 369–377.

Dash, P., Gowman, N., and Traynor, M. (2003). Increasing the impact of health services research. *British Medical Journal, 327*, 1339–1341.

Davenport, T. H., Prusak, L., and Wilson, H. J. (2003). Who's bringing you hot ideas and how are you responding? *Harvard Business Review, 81*(2), 58–64.

Dawson, P. (1994). *Organizational Change: A Processual Approach*. London: Paul Chapman.

Dawson, P. (1996). *Technology and Quality: Change in the Workplace*. London: International Thomson.

Dawson, P. (2003a). *Reshaping Change: A Processual Approach*. London: Routledge.

Dawson, P. (2003b). *Understanding Organizational Change: The Contemporary Experience of People at Work*. London: Sage.

Degeling, P., Maxwell, S., Kennedy, J., and Coyle, B. (2003). Medicine, management and modernization: a dance macabre? *British Medical Journal, 326*, 649–652.

Denis, J.-L. and Lomas, J. (2003). Convergent evolution: the academic and policy roots of collaborative research. *Journal of Health Services Research and Policy, 8*(2), 1–5.

Denis, J.-L., Lamothe, L., and Langley, A. (2001). The dynamics of collective leadership and strategic change in pluralistic organizations. *Academy of Management Journal, 44*(4), 809–837.

Department of Health. (1997). *The New NHS, Modern, Dependable*. London: Department of Health.

Department of Health. (1998). *A First Class Service: Quality in the New NHS*. London: Department of Health.

Department of Health. (2000a). *The NHS Plan: A Plan for Investment, a Plan for Reform*. London: Department of Health.

Department of Health. (2000b). *The NHS Cancer Plan: A Plan for Investment, a Plan for Reform*. London: Department of Health.

Department of Health. (2001a). *Governance Arrangements for NHS Research Ethics Committees*. London: Central Office for Research Ethics Committees (COREC).

Department of Health. (2001b). *Research Governance Framework for Health and Social Care*. London: Department of Health.

Department of Health. (2001c). *Reforming Emergency Care*. London: Department of Health.

Department of Health. (2002a). *NHS Leadership Qualities Framework*. London: NHS Modernization Agency Leadership Centre.

Department of Health. (2002b). *Raising Standards Across the NHS: A Programme of Rewards and Support for all NHS Trusts*. London: Department of Health.

Department of Health. (2004a). *The NHS Improvement Plan: Putting People at the Heart of Public Services*. London: HMSO.

Department of Health. (2004b). *Making Progress on Prostate Cancer*. London: Department of Health.

Department of Health. (2005a). *Staff in the NHS 2004*. London: Department of Health.

Department of Health. (2005b). *Research Governance Framework for Health and Social Care* (second edition). London: Department of Health.

Department of Health. (2005c). *Commissioning a Patient-Led NHS*. London: Department of Health.

Department of Health. (2005d). *The NHS Cancer Plan: A Progress Report*. London: Department of Health.

Derlet, R. W. and Richards, J. R. (2000). Overcrowding in the nation's emergency departments: complex causes and disturbing effects. *Annals of Emergency Medicine, 35*(1), 63–68.

Dopson, S. and Fitzgerald, L. (eds). (2005a). *Knowledge to Action? Evidence-Based Health Care in Context*. Oxford: Oxford University Press.

Dopson, S. and Fitzgerald, L. (2005b). The active role of context. In S. Dopson and L. Fitzgerald (eds), *Knowledge to Action? Evidence-Based Health Care in Context* (pp.79–103). Oxford: Oxford University Press.

Dopson, S., Fitzgerald, L., Ferlie, E., Gabbay, J., and Locock, L. (2002). No magic targets! Changing clinical practice to become more evidence based. *Health Care Management Review, 27*(3), 35–47.

Dopson, S., Locock, L., Gabbay, J., Ferlie, E., and Fitzgerald, L. (2003). Evidence based medicine and the implementation gap. *Health: An Interdisciplinary Journal for the Social Study of Health, Illness and Medicine, 7*, 311–330.

Dougherty, D. (1996). Organizing for innovation. In S. R. Clegg, C. Hardy, and W. R. Nord (eds), *Handbook of Organization Studies* (pp.424–439). London: Sage.

Dunphy, D. C. and Stace, D. A. (1990). *Under New Management: Australian Organizations in Transition*. Sydney: McGraw-Hill.

Eaton, L. (2004). Emergency service is closer to four hour target but still lacks consultants. *British Medical Journal, 329*(7471), 877.

Edwards, N. and Marshall, M. (2003). Doctors and managers. *British Medical Journal, 326*, 116–117.

Ekvall, G. (1996). Organizational climate for creativity and innovation. *European Journal of Work and Organizational Psychology, 5*(1), 105–123.

Ellis, D. (2003). See and treat is great – if you're a general practitioner. *Emergency Medicine Journal, 20*(2), 120.

Evans, S., Tritter, J., Barley, V., Daykin, N., McNeill, J., Palmer, N., *et al.* (2003). User involvement in UK cancer services: bridging the policy gap. *European Journal of Cancer Care, 12*(4), 331–338.

Ferlie, E. (2005). Conclusion: from evidence to actionable knowledge? In S. Dopson and L. Fitzgerald (eds), *Knowledge to Action? Evidence-Based Health Care in Context* (pp.182–197). Oxford: Oxford University Press.

Ferlie, E. and Addicott, R. (2004). *The introduction, impact and performance of cancer networks: a process evaluation*. London: Tanaka Business School, Imperial College London.

Ferlie, E. B. and Shortell, S. M. (2001). Improving quality of health care in the United Kingdom and the United States: a framework for change. *The Milbank Quarterly, 79*(2), 281–315.

Ferlie, E. and Wood, M. (2003). Novel modes of knowledge production? Producers and consumers in health services research. *Journal of Health Services Research and Policy, 8*(2), 51–57.

Ferlie, E., Fitzgerald, L., Wood, M., and Hawkins, C. (2005). The (non) spread of innovations: the mediating role of professionals. *Academy of Management Journal, 48*(1), 117–134.

Fitzgerald, L. and Dopson, S. (2005a). Professional boundaries and the diffusion of innovation. In S. Dopson and L. Fitzgerald (eds), *Knowledge to Action? Evidence-Based Health Care in Context* (pp.104–131). Oxford: Oxford University Press.

Fitzgerald, L. and Dopson, S. (2005b). Knowledge, credible evidence, and utilization. In S. Dopson and L. Fitzgerald (eds), *Knowledge to Action? Evidence-Based Health Care in Context* (pp.132–154). Oxford: Oxford University Press.

Fitzgerald, L., Ferlie, E., Wood, M., and Hawkins, C. (1999). Evidence into practice? An exploratory analysis of the interpretation of evidence. In A. Mark and S. Dopson (eds), *Organizational Behaviour in Health Care: The Research Agenda* (pp.189–206). London: Macmillan.

Fitzgerald, L., Ferlie, E., Wood, M., and Hawkins, C. (2002). Interlocking interactions, the diffusion of innovations in healthcare. *Human Relations, 55*(12), 1429–1449.

Fleck, J., Webster, J., and Williams, R. (1990). Dynamics of information technology implementation: a reassessment of paradigms and trajectories of development. *Futures* (July/August), 618–640.

Fox-Wolfgramm, S. J. and Boal, K. B. (1998). Organizational adaptation to institutional change: a comparative study of first-order change in prospector and defender banks. *Administrative Science Quarterly, 43*(1), 87–126.

Fraser, S. W. (2002). *Accelerating the Spread of Good Practice: A Workbook for Health Care*. Chichester: Kingsham Press.

Garside, P. (1999). Evidence based mergers? Two things are important in mergers: clear goals, clearly communicated. *British Medical Journal, 318*, 345–347.

Goldstone, J. A. (2003). Comparative historical analysis and knowledge accumulation in the study of revolutions. In J. Mahoney and D. Rueschemeyer (eds), *Comparative Historical Analysis in the Social Sciences* (pp.41–90). Cambridge: Cambridge University Press.

Gollop, R. (2002). *Sustainability and Spread in the National Booking Programme: Research into Practice Summary Report No.2*. Leicester: The NHS Modernisation Agency.

Gollop, R. (2003). *Teamworking for Improvement: Planning for Spread and Sustainability*. Leicester: NHS Modernisation Agency.

Gollop, R. (2004a). *Helping staff to accept change*, bmjlearning.com.

Gollop, R. (2004b). *Rapid Access Prostate Assessment. Report of a Study*

Commissioned by the Cancer Services Collaborative 'Improvement Partnership'. Leicester: NHS Modernisation Agency.

Gollop, R., Whitby, E., Buchanan, D., and Ketley, D. (2004). Influencing sceptical staff to become supporters of service improvement: a qualitative study of doctors' and managers' views. *Quality and Safety in Healthcare, 13*(2), 108–114.

Gollop, R., Ketley, D., Buchanan, D., Whitby, E., Lamont, S., Jones, J., *et al.* (2006). Research into Practice: a model for healthcare management research? *Evidence & Policy, 2*(2), 257–267.

Granovetter, M. S. (1973). The strength of weak ties. *American Journal of Sociology, 78*, 1360–1380.

Greenhalgh, T., Robert, G., Bate, P., Kyriakidou, O., Macfarlane, F., and Peacock, R. (2004). *How to Spread Good Ideas: A Systematic Review of the Literature on Diffusion, Dissemination and Sustainability of Innovations in Health Service Delivery and Organization*. London: University College London, and NHS Service Delivery and Organization Research Programme.

Grouse, A. and Bishop, R. (2001). Non-medical technicians reduce emergency department waiting times. *Emergency Medicine Journal, 13*(1), 66–69.

Hackett, M. and Spurgeon, P. (1998). Developing our leaders in the future. *Health Manpower Management, 24*(5), 170.

Hall, G. E. and Hord, S. M. (1987). *Change in Schools*. New York: Albany.

Ham, C. (2004). *Health Policy in Britain* (fifth edition). Basingstoke: Palgrave Macmillan.

Ham, C., Kipping, R., and McLeod, H. (2003). Redesigning work processes in health care: lessons from the National Health Service. *The Milbank Quarterly, 81*(3), 415–439.

Ham, C., Kipping, R., McLeod, H., and Meredith, P. (2002). *Capacity, Culture and Leadership: Lessons from Experience of Improving Access to Hospital Services*. Birmingham: The University of Birmingham Health Services Management Centre.

Hammer, M. (2004). Deep change: how operational innovation can transform your company. *Harvard Business Review, 82*(4), 84–93.

Hawkes, N. (2004, Saturday 26 June). Public depressed by state of the health service. *The Times*, p.14.

Holloway, I. (1997). *Basic Concepts for Qualitative Research*. Oxford: Blackwell Science.

Horton, R. (2000). Doctors in the NHS: the restless many and the squabbling few. *The Lancet, 355*(9220), 2010–2012.

House of Commons Health Committee. (2006). *Changes to Primary Care Trusts*. London: The Stationery Office.

Huy, Q. N. (1999). Emotional capability, emotional intelligence, and radical change. *Academy of Management Review, 24*, 325–345.

Iles, V. and Sutherland, K. (2001). *Organizational Change: A Review for Health Care Managers, Professionals and Researchers*. London: National Co-ordinating Centre for NHS Service Delivery and Organization Research and Development.

Ingersoll, G. L., Kirsch, J. C., Merk, S. E., and Lightfoot, L. (2000). Relationship of organizational culture and readiness for change to employee commitment to the organization. *Journal of Nursing Administration, 30*(1), 11–20.

Issel, L. M., Anderson, R. A., and Kane, D. J. (2003). Administrative characteristics of comprehensive prenatal case management programs. *Public Health Nursing, 20*, 349–360.

Jacobs, R. L. (2002). Institutionalizing organizational change through cascade training. *Journal of European Industrial Training, 26*(2–4), 177–182.

Jones, J. L. (2003). *Spread and Sustainability of Service Improvement: Research into Practice Summary Report No.4.* Leicester: NHS Modernisation Agency.

Kanter, R. M. (1983). *The Change Masters: Corporate Entrepreneurs at Work.* London: George Allen & Unwin.

Kanter, R. M. (2002). Creating the culture for innovation. In F. Hesselbein, M. Goldsmith, and I. Somerville (eds), *Leading for Innovation and Organizing for Results* (pp.73–85). San Francisco: Jossey-Bass.

Kemp, A., Pryor, S., and Dale, B. (1997). Sustaining TQM: a case study at Aeroquip Iberica. *The TQM Magazine, 9*(1), 21–28.

Kerr, D., Bevan, H., Gowland, B., Penny, J., and Berwick, D. (2002). Redesigning cancer care. *British Medical Journal, 324*, 164–166.

Ketley, D. and Woods, K. (1993). Impact of clinical trials on clinical practice: example of thrombolysis for acute myocardial infarction. *The Lancet, 342*, 891–894.

Kilo, C. M. (1998). A framework for collaborative improvement: lessons from the Institute for Healthcare Improvement's breakthrough series. *Quality Management in Health Care, 6*(4), 1–13.

Kipping, R., Meredith, P., and Ham, C. (2001). Briefing paper: progress of the first wave National Booked Admissions Programme. Paper presented at the NHS Modernisation Agency, Moving to Mainstream Booked Admissions Programme, London.

Kipping, R., Meredith, P., McLeod, H., and Ham, C. (2000). *Booking Patients for Hospital Care: Second Interim Report from the Evaluation of the National Booked Admissions Programme.* Birmingham: The University of Birmingham Health Services Management Centre.

Kneebone, R. and Darzi, A. (2005). New professional roles in surgery. *British Medical Journal, 330*, 803–804.

Kotter, J. P. (1995). Leading change: why transformation efforts fail. *Harvard Business Review, 73*(2), 59–67.

Kotter, J. P. (1996). *Leading Change.* Boston, MA: Harvard University Press.

Laennec, R. T. H. (1821). *A Treatise on Diseases of the Chest and on Mediate Auscultation*, trans. and Preface by John Forbes (London: T. & G. Underwood) (Original title *De l'Auscultation Médiate ou Traité du Diagnostic des Maladies des Poumons et du coeur*).

Lamont, S. S. (2004). *The Spread of See and Treat.* Leicester: Research into Practice, NHS Modernisation Agency.

Lamont, S. S. (2005). See and treat: spreading like wildfire? A qualitative study into factors affecting its introduction and spread. *Emergency Medicine Journal, 22,* 548–552.

Langley, A. (1999). Strategies for theorizing from process data. *Academy of Management Review, 24*(4), 691–710.

Langley, G., Nolan, K., and Nolan, T. (1996). *The Improvement Guide: A Practical Approach to Enhancing Organizational Performance.* San Francisco: Jossey-Bass.

Leaman, A. M. (2003). See and treat: a management-driven method of achieving targets or a tool for better patient care? *Emergency Medicine Journal, 20*(2), 118.

Leatherman, S. and Sutherland, K. (2003). *The Quest for Quality in the NHS: A Mid-Term Evaluation of the Ten-Year Quality Agenda.* London: Nuffield Trust.

Lewin, K. (ed.) (1951). *Field Theory in Social Science: Selected Theoretical Papers by Kurt Lewin* (UK edition published 1952, ed. Dorwin Cartwright). London: Tavistock.

Lindley-Jones, M. and Finlayson, B. J. (2000). Triage nurse-requested X rays: are they worthwhile? *Emergency Medicine Journal, 17*(2), 103–107.

Locock, L. (2001). *Maps and Journeys: Redesign in the NHS.* Birmingham: The University of Birmingham Health Services Management Centre.

Locock, L. (2003). Redesigning health care: new wine from old bottles? *Journal of Health Services Research and Policy, 8*(2), 120–122.

Locock, L., Dopson, S., Chambers, D., and Gabbay, J. (2000). Understanding opinion leaders' roles. *Social Science and Medicine, 49,* 1–11.

Mabin, V. J., Forgeson, S., and Green, L. (2001). Harnessing resistance: using the theory of constraints to assist change management. *Journal of European Industrial Training, 25*(2), 168–191.

McNulty, T. and Ferlie, E. (2002). *Re-engineering Health Care: The Complexities of Organizational Transformation.* Oxford: Oxford University Press.

Mahoney, J. (2001). Path-dependent explanations of regime-change: Central America in comparative perspective. *Studies in Comparative International Development, 36*(1), 111–141.

Mannion, R., Davies, H. T. O., and Marshall, M. N. (2003). *Cultures for Performance in Health Care: Evidence on the Relationship between Organizational Culture and Organizational Performance in the NHS.* York: Universities of York, St Andrews, and Manchester.

Meredith, P., Ham, C., and Kipping, R. (1999). *Modernizing the NHS: Booking Patients for Hospital Care: First Interim Report from the Evaluation of the National Booked Admissions Programme.* Birmingham: The University of Birmingham Health Services Management Centre.

Meyerson, D. E. (2001). Radical change, the quiet way. *Harvard Business Review, 79*(9), 92–100.

Miller, D. (1982). Evolution and revolution: a quantum view of structural change in organizations. *Journal of Management Studies, 19*(2), 131–151.

Mintzberg, H. (1979). *The Structuring of Organizations: A Synthesis of the Research.* Englewood Cliffs, NJ: Prentice Hall.

Mintzberg, H. (2003). The professional organization. In H. Mintzberg, J. Lampel,

J. B. Quinn, and S. Ghoshal (eds), *Strategy Process: Concepts, Contexts, Cases*. Harlow: Pearson Education.

Mohr, L. B. (1982). *Explaining Organizational Behaviour: The Limits and Possibilities of Theory and Research*. San Francisco: Jossey-Bass.

Morgan, N. (2001). How to overcome 'change fatigue'. *Harvard Management Update*, 1–3.

Murphy, E., Dingwall, R., Greatbatch, D., Parker, S., and Watson, P. (1998). Qualitative research methods in health technology assessment: a review of the literature. *Health Technology Assessment, 2*(16) (whole issue).

Narine, L. and Persaud, D. D. (2003). Gaining and maintaining commitment to large-scale change in health care organizations. *Health Services Management Research, 16*(3), 179–193.

National Patients Access Team. (1998). *The National Booked Admissions Programme*. Leicester: NHS Modernisation Agency.

Neath, A. (2004a). *Layers of Leadership: Hidden Influencers of Healthcare Improvement*. Leicester: NHS Modernisation Agency.

Neath, A. (2004b). *The National Booking Team – Full Evaluation of 4th Wave 'Moving to Mainstream'*. Leicester: NHS Modernisation Agency.

Newell, S., Edelman, L., Scarborough, H., Swan, J., and Bresnen, M. (2003). Best practice development and transfer in the NHS: the importance of process as well as process knowledge. *Health Services Management Research, 16*, 1–12.

NHS Modernisation Agency. (2001a). *Supporting Delivery: NHS Modernisation Agency Work Programme 2001/2002*. Leicester: NHS Modernisation Agency.

NHS Modernisation Agency. (2001). *Cancer Services Collaborative: Service Improvement Guide – Prostate Cancer*. London: Hayward Medical Communications.

NHS Modernisation Agency. (2002). *See and Treat*. Leicester: NHS Modernisation Agency.

NHS Modernisation Agency. (2002b). *Improvement Leaders' Guide to Sustainability and Spread*. Ipswich: Ancient House Printing Group.

NHS Modernisation Agency. (2002c). *Improvement Leaders' Guide to Setting up a Collaborative Programme*. Leicester: NHS Modernisation Agency.

NHS Modernisation Agency. (2004a). *Making See and Treat Work for Patients and Staff*. Leicester: Emergency Services Collaborative, NHS Modernisation Agency.

NHS Modernisation Agency. (2004b). *10 High Impact Changes for Service Improvement and Delivery*. Leicester: NHS Modernisation Agency.

NHS Modernisation Agency. (2005). *Applying High Impact Changes to Cancer Care*. Leicester: NHS Modernisation Agency.

Osborne, S. P. (1998). Naming the beast: delivering and classifying service innovations in social policy. *Human Relations, 51*, 1133–1154.

Øvretveit, J. (2000). Total quality management in European healthcare. *International Journal of Healthcare Quality Assurance, 13*(2), 74–79.

Øvretveit, J., Bate, P., Cleary, P., Cretin, S., Gustafson, D., McInnes, K., *et al.* (2002). Quality collaboratives: lessons from research. *Quality and Safety in Health Care, 11*(4), 345–351.

Parker, H., Meredith, P., Kipping, R., McLeod, H., and Ham, C. (2001). *Improving Patient Experience and Outcomes in Cancer: The Early Phase of the NHS Cancer Services Collaborative: First Interim Report from the CSC External Evaluation*. Birmingham: The University of Birmingham Health Services Management Centre.

Pettigrew, A. M. (1985). *The Awakening Giant: Continuity and Change in ICI*. Oxford: Basil Blackwell.

Pettigrew, A. M. and Fenton, E. M. (eds). (2000). *The Innovating Organization*. London: Sage.

Pettigrew, A. M., Ferlie, E., and McKee, L. (1992). *Shaping Strategic Change: Making Change in Large Organizations – The Case of the National Health Service*. London: Sage.

Pettigrew, A. M., Woodman, R. W., and Cameron, K. S. (2001). Studying organizational change and development: challenges for future research. *Academy of Management Journal, 44*(4), 697–713.

Pierson, P. (2003). Big, slow-moving, and . . . invisible. In J. Mahoney and D. Rueschemeyer (eds), *Comparative Historical Analysis in the Social Sciences*. Cambridge: Cambridge University Press.

Plsek, P. (2000). *Spreading Good Ideas for Better Health Care: Perspectives and Information for Healthcare Leaders, Research Series*, Volume 2, Dallas, TX: Veterans Hospitals Administration.

Plsek, P. and Kilo, C. M. (1999). From resistance to attraction: a different approach to change. *Physician Exec, 25*(6), 40–42.

Pollitt, C. (1996). Business approaches to quality improvement: why they are hard for the NHS to swallow. *Quality in Health Care, 5*, 104–110.

Poole, M. S., Van de Ven, A. H., Dooley, K., and Holmes, M. E. (2000). *Organizational Change and Innovation Processes: Theory and Methods for Research*. Oxford and New York: Oxford University Press.

Powell, M. J., Brock, D. M., and Hinings, C. R. (1999). The changing professional organization. In D. M. Brock, M. J. Powell, and C. R. Hinings (eds), *Restructuring the Professional Organization: Accounting, Health Care and Law* (pp.1–19). London and New York: Routledge.

Prochaska, J. M. (2000). A transtheoretical model approach to organizational change. *Families in Society, 81*, 76–84.

Prochaska, J. and DiClemente, C. (1984). *The Transtheoretical Approach: Crossing Traditional Boundaries of Therapy*. New York: Dow-Jones Irwin.

Prochaska, J. M., Prochaska, J. O., and Levesque, D. A. (2001). A transtheoretical approach to changing organizations. *Administration and Policy in Mental Health, 28*(4), 247–261.

Quinn, J. B., Anderson, P., and Finkelstein, S. (2003). Managing intellect. In H. Mintzberg, J. Lampel, J. B. Quinn, and S. Ghoshal (eds), *The Strategy Process: Concepts, Contexts*. Harlow: Pearson Education.

Reisner, R. A. F. (2002). When a turnaround stalls. *Harvard Business Review, 80*(2), 45–52.

Research into Practice. (2004). *Engaging Individual Staff in Service Improvement*. Leicester: NHS Modernisation Agency.

Rimmer, M., Macneil, J., Chenhall, R., Langfield-Smith, K., and Watts, L. (1996). *Reinventing Competitiveness: Achieving Best Practice in Australia*. South Melbourne: Pitman.

Robertson, M., Swan, J., and Newell, S. (1996). The role of networks in the diffusion of technological innovation. *Journal of Management Studies, 33*(3), 333–359.

Rogers, E. (1995). *The Diffusion of Innovation* (fourth edition). New York: Free Press.

Ross, S., Lavis, J., Rodriguez, C., Woodside, J., and Denis, J.-L. (2003). Partnership experiences: involving decision-makers in the research process. *Journal of Health Services Research and Policy, 8*(2), 26–34.

Schaffer, R. H. and Thomson, H. A. (1992). Successful change programs begin with results. *Harvard Business Review, 70*(1), 80–89.

Schön, D. A. (1963). Champions for radical new inventions. *Harvard Business Review, 41*(2), 77–86.

Senge, P. M. and Kaeufer, K. H. (2000). Creating change. *Executive Focus, 17*(10), 4–5.

Senge, P., Kleiner, A., Roberts, C., Ross, R., Roth, G., and Smith, B. (1999). *The Dance of Change: The Challenges of Sustaining Momentum in Learning Organizations*. London: Nicholas Brealey.

Sharpe, A. (2002). *Evaluation of 3rd Wave of the National Booking Programme*. Leicester: NHS Modernisation Agency.

Sheaff, R., Schofield, J., Mannion, R., Dowling, B., Marshall, M. N., and McNally, R. (2003). *Organizational Factors and Performance: A Review of the Literature*. London: National Co-ordinating Centre for NHS Service Delivery and Organization Research and Development Programme.

Shekelle, P. G. (2002). Why don't physicians enthusiastically support quality improvement programmes? *Quality and Safety in Health Care, 11*(1), 6.

Sherman, J. (2004, Friday 18 June). Labour promises to cut waiting time for hospital to 18 weeks. *The Times*, p. 1.

Shortell, S. (2002). Developing individual leaders is not enough. *Journal of Health Services Research and Policy, 7*(4), 193–194.

Shortell, S., Bennet, C., and Byck, G. (1998). Assessing the impact of continuous quality improvement on clinical practice: what will it take to accelerate progress? *Milbank Quarterly, 76*(4), 593–624.

Spurgeon, P., Barwell, F., and Kerr, D. (2000). Waiting times for cancer patients in England after general practitioners' referrals: retrospective national survey. *British Medical Journal, 320*, 838–839.

Stake, R. E. (1994). Case studies. In N. K. Denzin and Y. S. Lincoln (eds), *Handbook of Qualitative Research* (pp.236–247). Thousand Oaks, CA: Sage.

Stake, R. E. (1995). *The Art of Case Study Research*. Thousand Oaks, CA: Sage.

Stake, R. E. (2000). Case studies. In N. K. Denzin and Y. S. Lincoln (eds), *Handbook of Qualitative Research* (second edition, pp.435–454). Thousand Oaks, CA: Sage.

Stogdill, R. M. (1950). Leadership, membership and organization. *Psychological Bulletin, 47*, 1–14.

Szulanski, G. (2003). *Sticky Knowledge: Barriers to Knowing in the Firm*. London: Sage.

Szulanski, G. and Winter, S. (2002). Getting it right the second time. *Harvard Business Review, 80*(1), 62–69.

Thelen, K. (2003). How institutions evolve: insights from comparative historical analysis. In J. Mahoney and D. Rueschemeyer (eds), *Comparative Historical Analysis in the Social Sciences* (pp.208–240). Cambridge: Cambridge University Press.

Tranfield, D., Denyer, D., and Smart, P. (2003). Towards a methodology for developing evidence-informed management knowledge by means of systematic review. *British Journal of Management, 14*(3), 207–222.

Trout, A., Magnusson, A. R., and Hedges, J. R. (2000). Patient satisfaction investigations and the emergency department: what does the literature say? *Academic Emergency Medicine, 7*(6), 695–709.

Tsoukas, H. (1989). The validity of idiographic research explanations. *Academy of Management Review, 14*, 551–561.

Tushman, M. L. and Romanelli, E. (1985). Organizational revolution: a metamorphosis model of convergence and reorientation. *Research in Organizational Behaviour, 7*, 171–222.

Valente, T. W. (1995). *Network Models of the Diffusion of Innovations*. Cresskill, NJ: Hampton Press.

Van de Ven, A. H. and Poole, M. S. (1995). Explaining development and change in organizations. *Academy of Management Review, 20*(3), 510–540.

Van de Ven, A. H. and Poole, M. S. (2002). Field research methods. In J. A. C. Baum (ed.), *The Blackwell Companion to Organizations* (pp.867–888). Malden, MA, and Oxford: Blackwell.

Van de Ven, A. H., Polley, D. E., Garud, R., and Venkataraman, S. (1999). *The Innovation Journey*. New York and Oxford: Oxford University Press.

Wadell, D. and Sohal, A. S. (2001). Resistance: a constructive tool for change management. *Management Decision, 36*(8), 168–191.

Walshe, K. (1995). *Public Services and Market Mechanisms: Competition, Contracting and the New Public Management*. London: Macmillan.

Walton, R. E. (1975). The diffusion of new work structures: explaining why success didn't take. *Organizational Dynamics, 3*(3), 3–22.

Wardrope, J. and Driscoll, P. (2003). Turbulent times. *Emergency Medicine Journal, 20*(2), 116.

Weick, K. E. and Quinn, R. E. (1999). Organizational change and development. *Annual Review of Psychology, 50*, 361–386.

West, M. and Johnson, R. (2002). A matter of life and death. *People Management, 8*(4), 30–36.

West, M. A., Barron, D. N., Dowsett, J., and Newton, J. N. (1999). Hierarchies and cliques in the social networks of health professionals: implications for the design of dissemination strategies. *Social Science and Medicine, 48*(5), 633–646.

West, M. A., Borrill, C., Dawson, J., Brodbeck, F., Shapiro, D. A., and Haward, B. (2003). Leadership clarity and team innovation in health care. *The Leadership Quarterly, 14*, 393–410.

West, M. A., Borrill, C., Dawson, J., Scully, J., Carter, M., Anelay, S., *et al.* (2002). The link between the management of employees and patient mortality in acute hospitals. *International Journal of Human Resource Management, 13*, 1299–1310.

Whitby, E. (2002). *Spreading and Sustaining New Practices: Sharing the Learning from the Cancer Services Collaborative: Research into Practice Summary Report No.3*. Leicester: NHS Modernisation Agency.

Windle, J. and Mackway-Jones, K. (2003). Don't throw triage out with the bathwater. *Emergency Medicine Journal, 20*(2), 119–120.

Winyard, G. (2003). Doctors, managers and politicians. *Clinical Medicine, 3*(5), 465–469.

Woodward, V. and Webb, C. (2001). Women's anxieties surrounding breast disorders: a systematic review of the literature. *Journal of Advanced Nursing, 33*(1), 29–41.

Index

DATE DUE

Demco, Inc. 38-293